Refactoring SQL Applications

Other resources from O'Reilly

Refactoring
SQL Applications

Stéphane Faroult with Pascal L'Hermite

O'REILLY®

Beijing • Cambridge • Farnham • Köln • Sebastopol • Taipei • Tokyo

Refactoring SQL Applications
by Stéphane Faroult with Pascal L'Hermite

Published by O'Reilly Media, Inc. 1005 Gravenstein Highway North, Sebastopol, CA 95472

O'Reilly books may be purchased for educational, business, or sales promotional use. Online editions are also available for most titles (*safari.oreilly.com*). For more information, contact our corporate/institutional sales department: (800) 998-9938 or *corporate@oreilly.com*.

Editor: Mary Treseler	**Cover Designer:** Mark Paglietti
Production Editor: Rachel Monaghan	**Interior Designer:** Marcia Friedman
Copyeditor: Audrey Doyle	**Illustrator:** Robert Romano
Indexer: Lucie Haskins	

Printing History:

August 2008:   First Edition.

 This book uses RepKover™, a durable and flexible lay-flat binding.

ISBN: 978-0-596-51497-6
[M]

CONTENTS

Preface

Ma, sendo l'intento mio scrivere cosa utile a chi la intende, mi è parso più conveniente andare drieto alla verità effettuale della cosa, che alla immaginazione di essa.

But, it being my intention to write a thing which shall be useful to him who apprehends it, it appears to me more appropriate to follow up the real truth of a matter than the imagination of it.

—Niccolò Machiavelli

Il Principe, XV

THERE IS A STORY BEHIND THIS BOOK. I HAD HARDLY FINISHED THE ART OF SQL, WHICH WASN'T ON sale yet, when my then editor, Jonathan Gennick, raised the idea of writing a book about SQL refactoring. SQL, I knew. But I had never heard about refactoring. I Googled the word. In a famous play by Molière, a wealthy but little-educated man who takes lessons in his mature years marvels when he discovers that he has been speaking "prose" for all his life. Like Monsieur Jourdain, I discovered that I had been refactoring SQL code for years without even knowing it—performance analysis for my customers led quite naturally to improving code through small, incremental changes that didn't alter program behavior. It is one thing to try to design a database as best as you can, and to lay out an architecture and programs that access this database efficiently. It is another matter to try to get the best performance from systems that were not necessarily well designed from the start, or which have grown out of control over the years but that you have to live with. And there was something appealing in the idea of presenting SQL from a point of view that is so often mine in my professional life.

The last thing you want to do when you are done with a book is to start writing another one. But the idea had caught my fancy. I discussed it with a number of friends, one of whom is one of the most redoubtable SQL specialists I know. This friend burst into righteous indignation against buzzwords. For once, I begged to differ with him. It is true that the idea first popularized by Martin Fowler* of improving code by small, almost insignificant, localized changes may look like a fad—the stuff that fills reports by corporate consultants who have just graduated from university. But for me, the true significance of refactoring lies in the fact that code that has made it to production is no longer considered sacred, and in the recognition that a lot of mediocre systems could, with a little effort, do much better. Refactoring is also the acknowledgment that the fault for unsatisfactory performance is in ourselves, not in our stars—and this is quite a revelation in the corporate world.

I have seen too many sites where IT managers had an almost tragic attitude toward performance, people who felt crushed by fate and were putting their last hope into "tuning." If the efforts of database and system administrators failed, the only remaining option in their view was to sign and send the purchase order for more powerful machines. I have read too many audit reports by self-styled database experts who, after reformatting the output of system utilities, concluded that a few parameters should be bumped up and that more memory should be added. To be fair, some of these reports mentioned that a couple of terrible queries "should be tuned," without being much more explicit than pasting execution plans as appendixes.

I haven't touched database parameters for years (the technical teams of my customers are usually competent). But I have improved many programs, fearlessly digging into them, and I have tried as much as I could to work with developers, rather than stay in my ivory tower and prescribe from far above. I have mostly met people who were eager to learn and understand, who needed little encouragement when put on the right tracks, who enjoyed developing their SQL skills, and who soon began to set performance targets for themselves.

When the passing of time wiped from my memory the pains of book writing, I took the plunge and began to write again, with the intent to expand the ideas I usually try to transmit when I work with developers. Database accesses are probably one of the areas where there is the most to gain by improving the code. My purpose in writing this book has been to give not recipes, but a framework to try to improve the less-than-ideal SQL applications that surround us without rewriting them from scratch (in spite of a very strong temptation sometimes).

Why Refactor?

Most applications bump, sooner or later, into performance issues. In the best of cases, the success of some old and venerable application has led it to handle, over time, volumes of data for which it had never been designed, and the old programs need to be given a new lease on life until a replacement application is rolled out in production. In the worst of cases, performance tests conducted before switching to production may reveal a dismal failure to meet service-level requirements. Somewhere in between, data volume

---

* Fowler, M. et al. *Refactoring: Improving the Design of Existing Code*. Boston: Addison-Wesley Professional.

increases, new functionalities, software upgrades, or configuration changes sometimes reveal flaws that had so far remained hidden, and backtracking isn't always an option. All of those cases share extremely tight deadlines to improve performance, and high pressure levels.

The first rescue expedition is usually mounted by system engineers and database administrators who are asked to perform the magical parameter dance. Unless some very big mistake has been overlooked (it happens), database and system tuning often improves performance only marginally.

At this point, the traditional next step has long been to throw more hardware at the application. This is a very costly option, because the price of hardware will probably be compounded by the higher cost of software licenses. It will interrupt business operations. It requires planning. Worryingly, there is no real guarantee of return on investment. More than one massive hardware upgrade has failed to live up to expectations. It may seem counterintuitive, but there are horror stories of massive hardware upgrades that actually led to performance *degradation*. There are cases when adding more processors to a machine simply increased contention among competing processes.

The concept of *refactoring* introduces a much-needed intermediate stage between tuning and massive hardware injection. Martin Fowler's seminal book on the topic focuses on object technologies. But the context of databases is significantly different from the context of application programs written in an object or procedural language, and the differences bring some particular twists to refactoring efforts. For instance:

Small changes are not always what they appear to be
> Due to the declarative nature of SQL, a small change to the code often brings a massive upheaval in what the SQL engine executes, which leads to massive performance changes—for better or for worse.

Testing the validity of a change may be difficult
> If it is reasonably easy to check that a value returned by a function is the same in all cases before and after a code change, it is a different matter to check that the contents of a large table are still the same after a major update statement rewrite.

The context is often critical
> Database applications may work satisfactorily for years before problems emerge; it's often when volumes or loads cross some thresholds, or when a software upgrade changes the behavior of the optimizer, that performance suddenly becomes unacceptable. Performance improvement work on database applications usually takes place in a crisis.

Database applications are therefore a difficult ground for refactoring, but at the same time the endeavor can also be, and often is, highly rewarding.

Refactoring Database Accesses

Database specialists have long known that the most effective way to improve performance is, once indexing has been checked, to review and tweak the database access patterns. In spite of the ostensibly declarative nature of SQL, this language is infamous for the sometimes amazing difference in execution time between alternative writings of functionally identical statements.

There is, however, more to database access refactoring than the unitary rewriting of problem queries, which is where most people stop. For instance, the slow but continuous enrichment of the SQL language over the years sometimes enables developers to write efficient statements that replace in a single stroke what could formerly be performed only by a complex procedure with multiple statements. New mechanisms built into the database engine may allow you to do things differently and more efficiently than in the past. Reviewing old programs in the light of new features can often lead to substantial performance improvements.

It would really be a brave new world if the only reason behind refactoring was the desire to rejuvenate old applications by taking advantage of new features. A sound approach to database applications can also work wonders on what I'll tactfully call less-than-optimal code.

Changing part of the logic of an application may seem contradictory to the stated goal of keeping changes small. In fact, your understanding of what *small* and *incremental* mean depends a lot on your mileage; when you go to an unknown place for the very first time, the road always seems much longer than when you return to this place, now familiar, for the umpteenth time.

What Can We Expect from Refactoring?

It is important to understand that two factors broadly control the possible benefits of refactoring (this being the real world, they are conflicting factors):

- First, the benefits of refactoring are directly linked to the original application: if the quality of the code is poor, there are great odds that spectacular improvement is within reach. If the code were optimal, there would be—barring the introduction of new features—no opportunity for refactoring, and that would be the end of the story. It's exactly like with companies: only the badly managed ones can be spectacularly turned around.

- Second, when the database design is really bad, refactoring cannot do much. Making things slightly less bad has never led to satisfactory results. Refactoring is an evolutionary process. In the particular case of databases, if there is no trace of initial intelligent design, even an intelligent evolution will not manage to make the application fit for survival. It will collapse and become extinct.

It is unlikely that the great Latin poet, Horace, had refactoring in mind when he wrote about *aurea mediocritas*, the golden mediocrity, but it truly is mediocre applications for which we can have the best hopes. They are in ample supply, because much too often "the first way that everyone agrees will functionally work becomes the design," as wrote a reviewer for this book, Roy Owens.

How This Book Is Organized

This book tries to take a realistic and honest view of the improvement of applications with a strong SQL component, and to define a rational framework for tactical maneuvers. The exercise of refactoring is often performed as a frantic quest for quick wins and spectacular improvements that will prevent budget cuts and keep heads firmly attached to shoulders. It's precisely in times of general panic that keeping a cool head and taking a methodical approach matter most. Let's state upfront that miracles, by definition, are the preserve of a few very gifted individuals, and they usually apply to worthier causes than your application (whatever you may think of it). But the reasoned and systematic application of sound principles may nevertheless have impressive results. This book tries to help you define different tactics, as well as assess the feasibility of different solutions and the risks attached to different interpretations of the word *incremental*.

Very often, refactoring an SQL application follows the reverse order of development: you start with easy things and slowly walk back, cutting deeper and deeper, until you reach the point where it hurts or you have attained a self-imposed limit. I have tried to follow the same order in this book, which is organized as follows:

Chapter 1, *Assessment*
> Can be considered as the prologue and is concerned with assessing the situation. Refactoring is usually associated with times when resources are scarce and need to be allocated carefully. There is no margin for error or for improving the wrong target. This chapter will guide you in trying to assess first whether there is any hope in refactoring, and second what kind of hope you can reasonably have.

The next two chapters deal with the dream of every manager: quick wins. I discuss in these chapters the changes that take place primarily on the database side, as opposed to the application program. Sometimes you can even apply some of those changes to "canned applications" for which you don't have access to the code.

Chapter 2, *Sanity Checks*
> Deals with points that must be controlled by priority—in particular, indexing review.

Chapter 3, *User Functions and Views*
> Explains how user-written functions and an exuberant use of views can sometimes bring an application to its knees, and how you can try to minimize their impact on performance.

In the next three chapters, I deal with changes that you can make to the application proper.

Chapter 4, *Testing Framework*

Shows how to set up a proper testing framework. When modifying code it is critical to ensure that we still get the same results, as any modification—however small—can introduce bugs; there is no such thing as a totally risk-free change. I'll discuss tactics for comparing before and after versions of a program.

Chapter 5, *Statement Refactoring*

Discusses in depth the proper approach to writing different SQL statements. Optimizers rewrite suboptimal statements. That is, this is what they are supposed to do. But the cleverest optimizer can only try to make the best out of an existing situation. I'll show you how to analyze and rewrite SQL statements so as to turn the optimizer into your friend, not your foe.

Chapter 6, *Task Refactoring*

Goes further in Chapter 5's discussion, explaining how changing the operational mode—and in particular, getting rid of row-based processing—can take us to the next level. Most often, rewriting individual statements results in only a small fraction of potential improvements. Bolder moves, such as coalescing several statements or replacing iterative, procedural statements with sweeping SQL statements, often lead to awe-inspiring gains. These gains demand good SQL skills, and an SQL mindset that is very different from both the traditional procedural mindset and the object-oriented mindset. I'll go through a number of examples.

If you are still unsatisfied with performance at this stage, your last hope is in the next chapter.

Chapter 7, *Refactoring Flows and Databases*

Returns to the database and discusses changes that are more fundamental. First I'll discuss how you can improve performance by altering flows and introducing parallelism, and I'll show the new issues—such as data consistency, contention, and locking—that you have to take into account when parallelizing processes. Then I'll discuss changes that you sometimes can bring, physically and logically, to the database structure as a last resort, to try to gain extra performance points.

And to conclude the book:

Chapter 8, *How It Works: Refactoring in Practice*

Provides a kind of summary of the whole book as an extended checklist. In this chapter I describe, with references to previous chapters, what goes through my mind and what I do whenever I have to deal with the performance issues of a database application. This was a difficult exercise for me, because sometimes experience (and gut instinct acquired through that experience) suggests shortcuts that are not really the conscious product of a clear, logical analysis. But I hope it will serve as a useful reference.

Appendix A, *Scripts and Sample Programs*, and Appendix B, *Tools*

Describe scripts, sample programs, and tools that are available for download from O'Reilly's website for this book, *http://www.oreilly.com/catalog/9780596514976*.

Audience

This book is written for IT professionals, developers, project managers, maintenance teams, database administrators, and tuning specialists who may be involved in the rescue operation of an application with a strong database component.

Assumptions This Book Makes

This book assumes a good working knowledge of SQL, and of course, some comfort with at least one programming language.

Conventions Used in This Book

The following typographical conventions are used in this book:

Italic

> Indicates emphasis, new terms, URLs, filenames, and file extensions.

`Constant width`

> Indicates computer coding in a broad sense. This includes commands, options, variables, attributes, keys, requests, functions, methods, types, classes, modules, properties, parameters, values, objects, events, event handlers, XML and XHTML tags, macros, and keywords. It also indicates identifiers such as table and column names, and is used for code samples and command output.

`Constant width bold`

> Indicates emphasis in code samples.

`Constant width italic`

> Shows text that should be replaced with user-supplied values.

Using Code Examples

This book is here to help you get your job done. In general, you may use the code in this book in your programs and documentation. You do not need to contact us for permission unless you're reproducing a significant portion of the code. For example, writing a program that uses several chunks of code from this book does not require permission. Selling or distributing a CD-ROM of examples from O'Reilly books does require permission. Answering a question by citing this book and quoting example code does not require permission. Incorporating a significant amount of example code from this book into your product's documentation does require permission.

We appreciate, but do not require, attribution. An attribution usually includes the title, author, publisher, and ISBN. For example: "*Refactoring SQL Applications* by Stéphane Faroult with Pascal L'Hermite. Copyright 2008 Stéphane Faroult and Pascal L'Hermite, 978-0-596-51497-6."

If you feel your use of code examples falls outside fair use or the permission given here, feel free to contact us at *permissions@oreilly.com*.

Comments and Questions

Please address comments and questions concerning this book to the publisher:

> O'Reilly Media, Inc.
> 1005 Gravenstein Highway North
> Sebastopol, CA 95472
> 800-998-9938 (in the United States or Canada)
> 707-829-0515 (international or local)
> 707-829-0104 (fax)

We have a web page for this book, where we list errata, examples, and any additional information. You can access this page at:

> *http://www.oreilly.com/catalog/9780596514976*

To comment or ask technical questions about this book, send email to:

> *bookquestions@oreilly.com*

For more information about our books, conferences, Resource Centers, and the O'Reilly Network, see our web site at:

> *http://www.oreilly.com*

Safari® Books Online

 When you see a Safari® Books Online icon on the cover of your favorite technology book, that means the book is available online through the O'Reilly Network Safari Bookshelf.

Safari offers a solution that's better than e-books. It's a virtual library that lets you easily search thousands of top tech books, cut and paste code samples, download chapters, and find quick answers when you need the most accurate, current information. Try it for free at *http://safari.oreilly.com.*

Acknowledgments

A book is always the result of the work of far more people than those who have their names on the cover. First I want to thank Pascal L'Hermite whose Oracle and SQL Server knowledge was extremely valuable as I wrote this book. In a technical book, writing is only the visible part of the endeavor. Setting up test environments, devising example programs, porting them to various products, and sometimes trying ideas that in the end will lead nowhere are all tasks that take a lot of time. There is much paddling below the float line, and there are many efforts that appear only as casual references and faint shadows in the finished book. Without Pascal's help, this book would have taken even longer to write.

Every project needs a coordinator, and Mary Treseler, my editor, played this role on the O'Reilly side. Mary selected a very fine team of reviewers, several of them authors. First among them was Brand Hunt, who was the development editor for this book. My hearty thanks go to Brand, who helped me give this book its final shape, but also to Dwayne King, particularly for his attention both to prose and to code samples. David Noor, Roy Owens, and Michael Blaha were also very helpful. I also want to thank two expert long-time friends, Philippe Bertolino and Cyril Thankappan, who carefully reviewed my first drafts as well.

Besides correcting some mistakes, all of these reviewers contributed remarks or clarifications that found their way into the final product, and made it better.

When the work is over for the author and the reviewers, it just starts for many O'Reilly people: under the leadership of the production editor, copyediting, book designing, cover designing, turning my lousy figures into something more compatible with the O'Reilly standards, indexing—all of these tasks helped to give this book its final appearance. All of my most sincere thanks to Rachel Monaghan, Audrey Doyle, Mark Paglietti, Karen Montgomery, Marcia Friedman, Rob Romano, and Lucie Haskins.

Assessment

From the ashes of disaster grow the roses of success!
—*Richard M. Sherman (b. 1928) and Robert B. Sherman (b. 1925),*

Lyrics of "Chitty Chitty Bang Bang," after Ian Fleming (1908–1964)

WHENEVER THE QUESTION OF REFACTORING CODE IS RAISED, YOU CAN BE CERTAIN THAT EITHER THERE IS a glaring problem or a problem is expected to show its ugly head before long. You know what you functionally have to improve, but you must be careful about the precise nature of the problem.

Whichever way you look at it, any computer application ultimately boils down to CPU consumption, memory usage, and input/output (I/O) operations from a disk, a network, or another I/O device. When you have performance issues, the first point to diagnose is whether any one of these three resources has reached problematic levels, because that will guide you in your search of what needs to be improved, and how to improve it.

The exciting thing about database applications is the fact that you can try to improve resource usage at various levels. If you really want to improve the performance of an SQL application, you can stop at what looks like the obvious bottleneck and try to alleviate pain at that point (e.g., "let's give more memory to the DBMS," or "let's use faster disks").

Such behavior was the conventional wisdom for most of the 1980s, when SQL became accepted as the language of choice for accessing corporate data. You can still find many people who seem to think that the best, if not the only, way to improve database performance is either to tweak a number of preferably obscure database parameters or to upgrade the hardware. At a more advanced level, you can track full scans of big tables, and add indexes so as to eliminate them. At an even more advanced level, you can try to tune SQL statements and rewrite them so as to optimize their execution plan. Or you can reconsider the whole process.

This book focuses on the last three options, and explores various ways to achieve performance improvements that are sometimes spectacular, independent of database parameter tuning or hardware upgrades.

Before trying to define how you can confidently assess whether a particular piece of code would benefit from refactoring, let's take a simple but not too trivial example to illustrate the difference between refactoring and tuning. The following example is artificial, but inspired by some real-life cases.

WARNING
The tests in this book were carried out on different machines, usually with out-of-the-box installations, and although the same program was used to generate data in the three databases used—MySQL, Oracle, and SQL Server—which was more convenient than transferring the data, the use of random numbers resulted in identical global volumes but different data sets with very different numbers of rows to process. Time comparisons are therefore meaningless among the different products. What *is* meaningful, however, is the relative difference between the programs for one product, as well as the overall patterns.

A Simple Example

Suppose you have a number of "areas," whatever that means, to which are attached "accounts," and suppose amounts in various currencies are associated with these accounts. Each amount corresponds to a transaction. You want to check for one area whether any amounts are above a given threshold for transactions that occurred in the 30 days preceding a given date. This threshold depends on the currency, and it isn't defined for all currencies. If the threshold is defined, and if the amount is above the threshold for the given currency, you must log the transaction ID as well as the amount, converted to the local currency as of a particular valuation date.

I generated a two-million-row transaction table for the purpose of this example, and I used some Java™/JDBC code to show how different ways of coding can impact performance. The Java code is simplistic so that anyone who knows a programming or scripting language can understand its main line.

Let's say the core of the application is as follows (date arithmetic in the following code uses MySQL syntax), a program that I called *FirstExample.java*:

```
1   try {
2       long    txid;
3       long    accountid;
4       float   amount;
5       String  curr;
6       float   conv_amount;
7
8       PreparedStatement st1 = con.prepareStatement("select accountid"
9                               + " from area_accounts"
10                              + " where areaid = ?");
11      ResultSet           rs1;
12      PreparedStatement st2 = con.prepareStatement("select txid,amount,curr"
13                              + " from transactions"
14                              + " where accountid=?"
15                              + " and txdate >= date_sub(?, interval 30 day)"
16                              + " order by txdate");
17      ResultSet           rs2 = null;
18      PreparedStatement st3 = con.prepareStatement("insert into check_log(txid,"
19                              + " conv_amount)"
20                              + " values(?,?)");
21
22      st1.setInt(1, areaid);
23      rs1 = st1.executeQuery();
24      while (rs1.next()) {
25          accountid = rs1.getLong(1);
26          st2.setLong(1, accountid);
27          st2.setDate(2, somedate);
28          rs2 = st2.executeQuery();
29          while (rs2.next()) {
30              txid = rs2.getLong(1);
31              amount = rs2.getFloat(2);
32              curr = rs2.getString(3);
33              if (AboveThreshold(amount, curr)) {
34                  // Convert
35                  conv_amount = Convert(amount, curr, valuationdate);
36                  st3.setLong(1, txid);
37                  st3.setFloat(2, conv_amount);
38                  dummy = st3.executeUpdate();
39              }
40          }
41      }
42      rs1.close();
43      st1.close();
44      if (rs2 != null) {
45          rs2.close();
46      }
47      st2.close();
48      st3.close();
49  } catch(SQLException ex){
50          System.err.println("==> SQLException: ");
51          while (ex != null) {
52              System.out.println("Message:   " + ex.getMessage ());
53              System.out.println("SQLState:  " + ex.getSQLState ());
54              System.out.println("ErrorCode: " + ex.getErrorCode ());
55              ex = ex.getNextException();
56              System.out.println("");
57          }
58  }
```

This code snippet is not particularly atrocious and resembles many pieces of code that run in real-world applications. A few words of explanation for the JDBC-challenged follow:

- We have three SQL statements (lines 8, 12, and 18) that are prepared statements. Prepared statements are the proper way to code with JDBC when we repeatedly execute statements that are identical except for a few values that change with each call (I will talk more about prepared statements in Chapter 2). Those values are represented by question marks that act as place markers, and we associate an actual value to each marker with calls such as the setInt( ) on line 22, or the setLong( ) and setDate( ) on lines 26 and 27.

- On line 22, I set a value (areaid) that I defined and initialized in a part of the program that isn't shown here.

- Once actual values are bound to the place markers, I can call executeQuery( ) as in line 23 if the SQL statement is a select, or executeUpdate( ) as in line 38 if the statement is anything else. For select statements, I get a result set on which I can loop to get all the values in turn, as you can see on lines 30, 31, and 32, for example.

Two utility functions are called: AboveThreshold( ) on line 33, which checks whether an amount is above the threshold for a given currency, and Convert( ) on line 35, which converts an amount that is above the threshold into the reference currency for reporting purposes. Here is the code for these two functions:

```
private static boolean AboveThreshold(float  amount,
                                      String iso) throws Exception {
   PreparedStatement thresholdstmt = con.prepareStatement("select threshold"
                                       + " from thresholds"
                                       + " where iso=?");
   ResultSet        rs;
   boolean          returnval = false;

   thresholdstmt.setString(1, iso);
   rs = thresholdstmt.executeQuery( );
   if (rs.next( )) {
      if (amount >= rs.getFloat(1)){
         returnval = true;
      } else {
         returnval = false;
      }
   } else {    // not found - assume no problem
     returnval = false;
   }
   if (rs != null) {
      rs.close( );
   }
   thresholdstmt.close( );
   return returnval;
}

private static float Convert(float  amount,
                             String iso,
                             Date   valuationdate) throws Exception {
```

```
PreparedStatement conversionstmt = con.prepareStatement("select ? * rate"
                                        + " from currency_rates"
                                        + " where iso = ?"
                                        + " and rate_date = ?");
ResultSet        rs;
float            val = (float)0.0;

conversionstmt.setFloat(1, amount);
conversionstmt.setString(2, iso);
conversionstmt.setDate(3, valuationdate);
rs = conversionstmt.executeQuery( );
if (rs.next( )) {
   val = rs.getFloat(1);
}
if (rs != null) {
   rs.close( );
}
conversionstmt.close( );
return val;
}
```

All tables have primary keys defined. When I ran this program over the sample data, checking about one-seventh of the two million rows and ultimately logging very few rows, the program took around 11 minutes to run against MySQL* on my test machine.

After slightly modifying the SQL code to accommodate the different ways in which the various dialects express the month preceding a given date, I ran the same program against the same volume of data on SQL Server and Oracle.[†]

The program took about five and a half minutes with SQL Server and slightly less than three minutes with Oracle. For comparison purposes, Table 1-1 lists the amount of time it took to run the program for each database management system (DBMS); as you can see, in all three cases it took much too long. Before rushing out to buy faster hardware, what can we do?

TABLE 1-1. Baseline for SimpleExample.Java

DBMS	Baseline result
MySQL	11 minutes
Oracle	3 minutes
SQL Server	5.5 minutes

SQL Tuning, the Traditional Way

The usual approach at this stage is to forward the program to the in-house tuning specialist (usually a database administrator [DBA]). Very conscientiously, the MySQL DBA will

---

* MySQL 5.1.

† SQL Server 2005 and Oracle 11.

probably run the program again in a test environment after confirming that the test database has been started with the following two options:

```
--log-slow-queries
--log-queries-not-using-indexes
```

The resultant logfile shows many repeated calls, all taking three to four seconds each, to the main culprit, which is the following query:

```
select txid,amount,curr
from transactions
where accountid=?
 and txdate >= date_sub(?, interval 30 day)
order by txdate
```

Inspecting the information_schema database (or using a tool such as phpMyAdmin) quickly shows that the transactions table has a single index—the primary key index on txid, which is unusable in this case because we have no condition on that column. As a result, the database server can do nothing else but scan the big table from beginning to end—and it does so in a loop. The solution is obvious: create an additional index on accountid and run the process again. The result? Now it executes in a little less than four minutes, a performance improvement by a factor of 3.1. Once again, the mild-mannered DBA has saved the day, and he announces the result to the awe-struck developers who have come to regard him as the last hope before pilgrimage.

For our MySQL DBA, this is likely to be the end of the story. However, his Oracle and SQL Server colleagues haven't got it so easy. No less wise than the MySQL DBA, the Oracle DBA activated the magic weapon of Oracle tuning, known among the initiated as *event 10046 level 8* (or used, to the same effect, an "advisor"), and he got a trace file showing clearly where time was spent. In such a trace file, you can determine how many times statements were executed, the CPU time they used, the elapsed time, and other key information such as the number of logical reads (which appear as query and current in the trace file)—that is, the number of data blocks that were accessed to process the query, and waits that explain at least part of the difference between CPU and elapsed times:

```
****************************************************************************

SQL ID : 1nup7kcbvt072
select txid,amount,curr
from
 transactions where accountid=:1 and txdate >= to_date(:2, 'DD-MON-YYYY') -
  30 order by txdate
```

call	count	cpu	elapsed	disk	query	current	rows
Parse	1	0.00	0.00	0	0	0	0
Execute	252	0.00	0.01	0	0	0	0
Fetch	11903	32.21	32.16	0	2163420	0	117676
total	12156	32.22	32.18	0	2163420	0	117676

```
Misses in library cache during parse: 1
Misses in library cache during execute: 1
Optimizer mode: ALL_ROWS
Parsing user id: 88


Rows     Row Source Operation
-------  ----------------------------------------------------
    495  SORT ORDER BY (cr=8585 [...] card=466)
    495  TABLE ACCESS FULL TRANSACTIONS (cr=8585 [...] card=466)



Elapsed times include waiting on following events:
  Event waited on                        Times    Max. Wait  Total Waited
  -------------------------------------  Waited   ---------- ------------
  SQL*Net message to client              11903      0.00          0.02
  SQL*Net message from client            11903      0.00          2.30
  *****************************************************************************

SQL ID : gx2cn564cdsds
select threshold
from
 thresholds where iso=:1


call      count      cpu   elapsed      disk      query    current       rows
-------  ------  -------- ---------- ---------- ---------- ---------- ----------
Parse    117674     2.68      2.63         0          0          0          0
Execute  117674     5.13      5.10         0          0          0          0
Fetch    117674     4.00      3.87         0     232504          0     114830
-------  ------  -------- ---------- ---------- ---------- ---------- ----------
total    353022    11.82     11.61         0     232504          0     114830

Misses in library cache during parse: 1
Misses in library cache during execute: 1
Optimizer mode: ALL_ROWS
Parsing user id: 88

Rows     Row Source Operation
-------  ----------------------------------------------------
      1  TABLE ACCESS BY INDEX ROWID THRESHOLDS (cr=2 [...] card=1)
      1  INDEX UNIQUE SCAN SYS_C009785 (cr=1 [...] card=1)(object id 71355)



Elapsed times include waiting on following events:
  Event waited on                        Times    Max. Wait  Total Waited
  -------------------------------------  Waited   ---------- ------------
  SQL*Net message to client             117675      0.00          0.30
  SQL*Net message from client           117675      0.14         25.04
  *****************************************************************************
```

Seeing TABLE ACCESS FULL TRANSACTION in the execution plan of the slowest query (particularly when it is executed 252 times) triggers the same reaction with an Oracle administrator as with a MySQL administrator. With Oracle, the same index on accountid improved performance by a factor of 1.2, bringing the runtime to about two minutes and 20 seconds.

The SQL Server DBA isn't any luckier. After using SQL Profiler, or running:

```
select a.*
from (select execution_count,
             total_elapsed_time,
             total_logical_reads,
             substring(st.text, (qs.statement_start_offset/2) + 1,
                       ((case statement_end_offset
                           when -1 then datalength(st.text)
                           else qs.statement_end_offset
                         end
                         - qs.statement_start_offset)/2) + 1) as statement_text
      from sys.dm_exec_query_stats as qs
           cross apply sys.dm_exec_sql_text(qs.sql_handle) as st) a
where a. statement_text not like '%select a.*%'
order by a.creation_time
```

which results in:

execution_count	total_elapsed_time	total_logical_reads	statement_text
228	98590420	3062040	select txid,amount, ...
212270	22156494	849080	select threshold from ...
1	2135214	13430	...
...			

the SQL Server DBA, noticing that the costliest query by far is the select on transactions, reaches the same conclusion as the other DBAs: the transactions table misses an index. Unfortunately, the corrective action leads once again to disappointment. Creating an index on accountid improves performance by a very modest 1:3 ratio, down to a little over four minutes, which is not really enough to trigger managerial enthusiasm and achieve hero status. Table 1-2 shows by DBMS the speed improvement that the new index achieved.

TABLE 1-2. Speed improvement factor after adding an index on transactions

DBMS	Speed improvement
MySQL	x3.1
Oracle	x1.2
SQL Server	x1.3

Tuning by indexing is very popular with developers because no change is required to their code; it is equally popular with DBAs, who don't often see the code and know that proper indexing is much more likely to bring noticeable results than the tweaking of obscure parameters. But I'd like to take you farther down the road and show you what is within reach with little effort.

Code Dusting

Before anything else, I modified the code of *FirstExample.java* to create *SecondExample.java*. I made two improvements to the original code. When you think about it, you can but wonder what the purpose of the order by clause is in the main query:

```
select txid,amount,curr
from transactions
where accountid=?
  and txdate >= date_sub(?, interval 30 day)
order by txdate
```

We are merely taking data out of a table to feed another table. If we want a sorted result, we will add an order by clause to the query that gets data out of the result table when we present it to the end-user. At the present, intermediary stage, an order by is merely pointless; this is a very common mistake and you really have a sharp eye if you noticed it.

The second improvement is linked to my repeatedly inserting data, at a moderate rate (I get a few hundred rows in my logging table in the end). By default, a JDBC connection is in autocommit mode. In this case, it means that each insert will be implicitly followed by a commit statement and each change will be synchronously flushed to disk. The flush to persistent storage ensures that my change isn't lost even if the system crashes in the millisecond that follows; without a commit, the change takes place in memory and may be lost. Do I really need to ensure that every row I insert is securely written to disk before inserting the next row? I guess that if the system crashes, I'll just run the process again, especially if I succeed in making it fast—I don't expect a crash to happen that often. Therefore, I have inserted one statement at the beginning to disable the default behavior, and another one at the end to explicitly commit changes when I'm done:

```
// Turn autocommit off
con.setAutoCommit(false);
```

and:

```
con.commit();
```

These two very small changes result in a very small improvement: their cumulative effect makes the MySQL version about 10% faster. However, we receive hardly any measurable gain with Oracle and SQL Server (see Table 1-3).

TABLE 1-3. Speed improvement factor after index, code cleanup, and no auto-commit

DBMS	Speed improvement
MySQL	x3.2
Oracle	x1.2
SQL Server	x1.3

SQL Tuning, Revisited

When one index fails to achieve the result we aim for, sometimes a better index can provide better performance. For one thing, why create an index on accountid alone? Basically, an index is a sorted list (sorted in a tree) of key values associated with the physical addresses of the rows that match these key values, in the same way the index of this book is a sorted list of keywords associated with page numbers. If we search on the values of two columns and index only one of them, we'll have to fetch all the rows that correspond to the key we search, and discard the subset of these rows that doesn't match the other column. If we index both columns, we go straight for what we really want.

We can create an index on (accountid, txdate) because the transaction date is another criterion in the query. By creating a composite index on both columns, we ensure that the SQL engine can perform an efficient bounded search (known as a *range scan*) on the index. With my test data, if the single-column index improved MySQL performance by a factor of 3.1, I achieved a speed increase of more than 3.4 times with the two-column index, so now it takes about three and a half minutes to run the program. The bad news is that with Oracle and SQL Server, even with a two-column index, I achieved no improvement relative to the previous case of the single-column index (see Table 1-4).

TABLE 1-4. Speed improvement factor after index change

DBMS	Speed
MySQL	x3.4
Oracle	x1.2
SQL Server	x1.3

So far, I have taken what I'd call the "traditional approach" of tuning, a combination of some minimal improvement to SQL statements, common-sense use of features such as transaction management, and a sound indexing strategy. I will now be more radical, and take two different standpoints in succession. Let's first consider how the program is organized.

Refactoring, First Standpoint

As in many real-life processes I encounter, a striking feature of my example is the nesting of loops. And deep inside the loops, we find a call to the AboveThreshold( ) utility function that is fired for every row that is returned. I already mentioned that the transactions table contains two million rows, and that about one-seventh of the rows refer to the "area" under scrutiny. We therefore call the AboveThreshold( ) function many, many times. Whenever a function is called a high number of times, any very small unitary gain benefits from a tremendous leverage effect. For example, suppose we take the duration of a call from 0.005 seconds down to 0.004 seconds; when the function is called 200,000 times it amounts to 200 seconds overall, or more than three minutes. If we expect a 20-fold volume increase in the next few months, that time may increase to a full hour before long.

A good way to shave off time is to decrease the number of accesses to the database. Although many developers consider the database to be an immediately available resource, querying the database is not free. Actually, querying the database is a costly operation. You must communicate with the server, which entails some network latency, especially when your program isn't running on the server. In addition, what you send to the server is not immediately executable machine code, but an SQL statement. The server must analyze it and translate it to actual machine code. It may have executed a similar statement already, in which case computing the "signature" of the statement may be enough to allow the server to reuse a cached statement. Or it may be the first time we encounter the statement, and the server may have to determine the proper execution plan and run recursive queries against the data dictionary. Or the statement may have been executed, but it may have been flushed out of the statement cache since then to make room for another statement, in which case it is as though we're encountering it for the first time. Then the SQL command must be executed, and will return, via the network, data that may be held in the database server cache or fetched from disk. In other words, a database call translates into a succession of operations that are not necessarily very long but imply the consumption of resources—network bandwidth, memory, CPU, and I/O operations. Concurrency between sessions may add waits for nonsharable resources that are simultaneously requested.

Let's return to the AboveThreshold( ) function. In this function, we are checking thresholds associated with currencies. There is a peculiarity with currencies; although there are about 170 currencies in the world, even a big financial institution will deal in few currencies—the local currency, the currencies of the main trading partners of the country, and a few unavoidable major currencies that weigh heavily in world trade: the U.S. dollar, the euro, and probably the Japanese yen and British pound, among a few others.

When I prepared the data, I based the distribution of currencies on a sample taken from an application at a big bank in the euro zone, and here is the (realistic) distribution I applied when generating data for my sample table:

Currency Code	Currency Name	Percentage
EUR	Euro	41.3
USD	US Dollar	24.3
JPY	Japanese Yen	13.6
GBP	British Pound	11.1
CHF	Swiss Franc	2.6
HKD	Hong Kong Dollar	2.1
SEK	Swedish Krona	1.1
AUD	Australian Dollar	0.7
SGD	Singapore Dollar	0.5

The total percentage of the main currencies amounts to 97.3%. I completed the remaining 2.7% by randomly picking currencies among the 170 currencies (including the major currencies for this particular bank) that are recorded.

As a result, not only are we calling AboveThreshold( ) hundreds of thousands of times, but also the function repeatedly calls the same rows from the threshold table. You might think that because those few rows will probably be held in the database server cache it will not matter much. But it does matter, and next I will show the full extent of the damage caused by wasteful calls by rewriting the function in a more efficient way.

I called the new version of the program *ThirdExample.java*, and I used some specific Java collections, or HashMaps, to store the data; these collections store key/value pairs by hashing the key to get an array index that tells where the pair should go. I could have used arrays with another language. But the idea is to avoid querying the database by using the memory space of the process as a cache. When I request some data for the first time, I get it from the database and store it in my collection before returning the value to the caller.

The next time I request the same data, I find it in my small local cache and return almost immediately. Two circumstances allow me to cache the data:

- I am not in a real-time context, and I know that if I repeatedly ask for the threshold associated with a given currency, I'll repeatedly get the same value: there will be no change between calls.

- I am operating against a small amount of data. What I'll hold in my cache will not be gigabytes of data. Memory requirements are an important point to consider when there is or can be a large number of concurrent sessions.

I have therefore rewritten the two functions (the most critical is AboveThreshold( ), but applying the same logic to Convert( ) can also be beneficial):

```java
// Use hashmaps for thresholds and exchange rates
private static HashMap  thresholds = new HashMap( );
private static HashMap  rates = new HashMap( );
private static Date     previousdate = 0;

...

private static boolean AboveThreshold(float  amount,
                                      String iso) throws Exception {
  float threshold;

  if (!thresholds.containsKey(iso)){

      PreparedStatement thresholdstmt = con.prepareStatement("select threshold"
                                            + " from thresholds"
                                            + " where iso=?");
      ResultSet          rs;

      thresholdstmt.setString(1, iso);
      rs = thresholdstmt.executeQuery( );
      if (rs.next( )) {
         threshold = rs.getFloat(1);
         rs.close( );
      } else {
         threshold = (float)-1;
      }
      thresholds.put(iso, new Float(threshold));
      thresholdstmt.close( );
  } else {
     threshold = ((Float)thresholds.get(iso)).floatValue( );
  }
  if (threshold == -1){
     return false;
  } else {
     return(amount >= threshold);
  }
}

private static float Convert(float  amount,
                             String iso,
                             Date   valuationdate) throws Exception {
  float rate;
```

```
if ((valuationdate != previousdate)
    || (!rates.containsKey(iso))){
    PreparedStatement conversionstmt = con.prepareStatement("select rate"
                                               + " from currency_rates"
                                               + " where iso = ?"
                                               + " and rate_date = ?");

    ResultSet        rs;

    conversionstmt.setString(1, iso);
    conversionstmt.setDate(2, valuationdate);
    rs = conversionstmt.executeQuery();
    if (rs.next()) {
        rate = rs.getFloat(1);
        previousdate = valuationdate;
        rs.close();
    } else {    // not found - There should be an issue!
        rate = (float)1.0;
    }
    rates.put(iso, rate);
    conversionstmt.close();
} else {
    rate = ((Float)rates.get(iso)).floatValue();
}
return(rate * amount);
}
```

With this rewriting plus the composite index on the two columns (accountid, txdate), the execution time falls dramatically: 30 seconds with MySQL, 10 seconds with Oracle, and a little under 9 seconds with SQL Server, improvements by respective factors of 24, 16, and 38 compared to the initial situation (see Table 1-5).

TABLE 1-5. Speed improvement factor with a two-column index and function rewriting

DBMS	Speed improvement
MySQL	x24
Oracle	x16
SQL Server	x38

Another possible improvement is hinted at in the MySQL log (as well as the Oracle trace and the sys.dm_exec_query_stats dynamic SQL Server table), which is that the main query:

```
select txid,amount,curr
from transactions
where accountid=?
  and txdate >= [date expression]
```

is executed several hundred times. Needless to say, it is much less painful when the table is properly indexed. But the value that is provided for accountid is nothing but the result of another query. There is no need to query the server, get an accountid value, feed it into the main query, and finally execute the main query. We can have a single query, with a subquery "piping in" the accountid values:

```
select txid,amount,curr
from transactions
where accountid in (select accountid
                     from area_accounts
                     where areaid = ?)
  and txdate >= date_sub(?, interval 30 day)
```

This is the only other improvement I made to generate *FourthExample.java*. I obtained a rather disappointing result with Oracle (as it is hardly more efficient than *ThirdExample.java*), but the program now runs against SQL Server in 7.5 seconds and against MySQL in 20.5 seconds, respectively 44 and 34 times faster than the initial version (see Table 1-6). However, there is something both new and interesting with *FourthExample.java*: with all products, the speed remains about the same whether there is or isn't an index on the accountid column in transactions, and whether it is an index on accountid alone or on accountid and txdate.

TABLE 1-6. Speed improvement factor with SQL rewriting and function rewriting

DBMS	Speed improvement
MySQL	x34
Oracle	x16
SQL Server	x44

Refactoring, Second Standpoint

The preceding change is already a change of perspective: instead of only modifying the code so as to execute fewer SQL statements, I have begun to replace two SQL statements with one. I already pointed out that loops are a remarkable feature (and not an uncommon one) of my sample program. Moreover, most program variables are used to store data that is fetched by a query before being fed into another one: once again a regular feature of numerous production-grade programs. Does fetching data from one table to compare it to data from another table before inserting it into a third table require passing through our code? In theory, all operations could take place on the server only, without any need for multiple exchanges between the application and the database server. We can write a stored procedure to perform most of the work on the server, and only on the server, or simply write a single, admittedly moderately complex, statement to perform the task. Moreover, a single statement will be less DBMS-dependent than a stored procedure:

```
try {
    PreparedStatement st = con.prepareStatement("insert into check_log(txid,"
                 + "conv_amount)"
                 + "select x.txid,x.amount*y.rate"
                 + " from(select a.txid,"
                 + "             a.amount,"
                 + "             a.curr"
                 + "      from transactions a"
```

```
          + "      where a.accountid in"
          + "              (select accountid"
          + "                 from area_accounts"
          + "                  where areaid = ?)"
          + "        and a.txdate >= date_sub(?, interval 30 day)"
          + "        and exists (select 1"
          + "                     from thresholds c"
          + "                     where c.iso = a.curr"
          + "                       and a.amount >= c.threshold)) x,"
          + "      currency_rates y"
          + "  where y.iso = x.curr"
          + "  and y.rate_date=?");
    ...
        st.setInt(1, areaid);
        st.setDate(2, somedate);
        st.setDate(3, valuationdate);
        // Wham bam
        st.executeUpdate( );
    ...
```

Interestingly, my single query gets rid of the two utility functions, which means that I am going down a totally different, and incompatible, refactoring path compared to the previous case when I refactored the lookup functions. I check thresholds by joining transactions to thresholds, and I convert by joining the resultant transactions that are above the threshold to the currency_rates table. On the one hand, we get one more complex (but still legible) query instead of several very simple ones. On the other hand, the calling program, *FifthExample.java*, is much simplified overall.

Before I show you the result, I want to present a variant of the preceding program, named *SixthExample.java*, in which I have simply written the SQL statement in a different way, using more joins and fewer subqueries:

```
PreparedStatement st = con.prepareStatement("insert into check_log(txid,"
                      + "conv_amount)"
                      + "select x.txid,x.amount*y.rate"
                      + " from(select a.txid,"
                      + "              a.amount,"
                      + "              a.curr"
                      + "        from transactions a"
                      + "             inner join area_accounts b"
                      + "                    on b.accountid = a.accountid"
                      + "             inner join thresholds c"
                      + "                    on c.iso = a.curr"
                      + "        where b.areaid = ?"
                      + "          and a.txdate >= date_sub(?, interval 30 day)"
                      + "          and a.amount >= c.threshold) x"
                      + "        inner join currency_rates y"
                      + "                on y.iso = x.curr"
                      + "  where y.rate_date=?");
```

Comparison and Comments

I ran the five improved versions, first without any additional index and then with an index on accountid, and finally with a composite index on (accountid, txdate), against MySQL, Oracle, and SQL Server, and measured the performance ratio compared to the initial version. The results for *FirstExample.java* don't appear explicitly in the figures that follow (Figures 1-1, 1-2, and 1-3), but the "floor" represents the initial run of *FirstExample*.

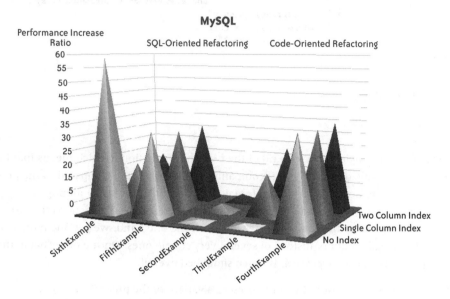

FIGURE 1-1. *Refactoring gains with MySQL*

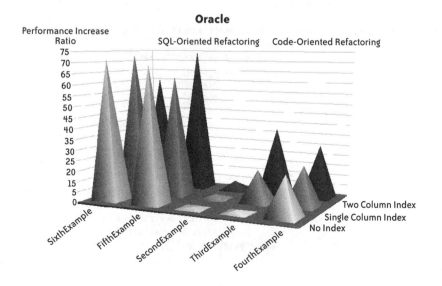

FIGURE 1-2. *Refactoring gains with Oracle*

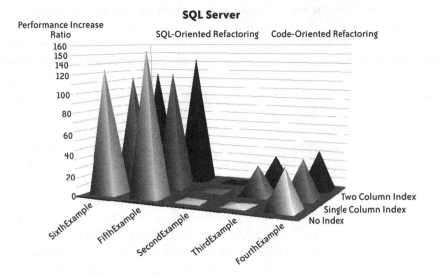

FIGURE 1-3. Refactoring gains with SQL Server

I plotted the following:

On one axis

The version of the program that has the minimally improved code in the middle (*SecondExample.java*). On one side we have code-oriented refactoring: *ThirdExample.java*, which minimizes the calls in lookup functions, and *FourthExample.java*, which is identical except for a query with a subquery replacing two queries. On the other side we have SQL-oriented refactoring, in which the lookup functions have vanished, but with two variants of the main SQL statement.

On the other axis

The different additional indexes (no index, single-column index, and two-column index).

Two characteristics are immediately striking:

- The similarity of performance improvement patterns, particularly in the case of Oracle and SQL Server.

- The fact that the "indexing-only" approach, which is represented in the figures by *SecondExample* with a single-column index or a two-column index, leads to a performance improvement that varies between nonexistent and extremely shy. The true gains are obtained elsewhere, although with MySQL there is an interesting case when the presence of an index severely cripples performance (compared to what it ought to be), as you can see with *SixthExample*.

The best result by far with MySQL is obtained, as with all other products, with a single query and no additional index. However, it must be noted not only that in this version the optimizer may sometimes try to use indexes even when they are harmful, but also that it is quite sensitive to the way queries are written. The comparison between *FifthExample* and *SixthExample* denotes a preference for joins over (logically equivalent) subqueries.

By contrast, Oracle and SQL Server appear in this example like the tweedledum and tweedle-dee of the database world. Both demonstrate that their optimizer is fairly insensitive to syntactical variations (even if SQL Server denotes, contrary to MySQL, a slight preference for subqueries over joins), and is smart enough in this case to not use indexes when they don't speed up the query (the optimizers may unfortunately behave less ideally when statements are much more complicated than in this simple example, which is why I'll devote Chapter 5 to statement refactoring). Both Oracle and SQL Server are the reliable workhorses of the corporate world, where many IT processes consist of batch processes and massive table scans. When you consider the performance of Oracle with the initial query, three minutes is a very decent time to perform several hundred full scans of a two-million-row table (on a modest machine). But you mustn't forget that a little reworking brought down the time required to perform the same process (as in "business require-ment") to a little less than two seconds. Sometimes superior performance when perform-ing full scans just means that response times will be mediocre but not terrible, and that serious code defects will go undetected. Only one full scan of the transaction table is required by this process. Perhaps nothing would have raised an alarm if the program had performed 10 full scans instead of 252, but it wouldn't have been any less faulty.

Choosing Among Various Approaches

As I have pointed out, the two different approaches I took to refactoring my sample code are incompatible: in one case, I concentrated my efforts on improving functions that the other case eliminated. It seems pretty evident from Figures 1-1, 1-2, and 1-3 that the best approach with all products is the "single query" approach, which makes creating a new index unnecessary. The fact that any additional index is unnecessary makes sense when you consider that one areaid value defines a perimeter that represents a significant subset in the table. Fetching many rows with an index is costlier than scanning them (more on this topic in the next chapter). An index is necessary only when we have one query to return accountid values and one query to get transaction data, because the date range is selective for *one* accountid value—but not for the whole set of accounts. Using indexes (including the creation of appropriate additional indexes), which is often associated in people's minds with the traditional approach to SQL tuning, may become less important when you take a refactoring approach.

I certainly am not stating that indexes are unimportant; they are *highly* important, particu-larly in online transaction processing (OLTP) environments. But contrary to popular belief, they are not all-important; they are just one factor among several others, and in many cases they are not the most important element to consider when you are trying to deliver better performance.

Most significantly, adding a new index risks wreaking havoc elsewhere. Besides additional storage requirements, which can be quite high sometimes, an index adds overhead to all insertions into and deletions from the table, as well as to updates to the indexed columns; all indexes have to be maintained alongside the table. It may be a minor concern if the big issue is the performance of queries, and if we have plenty of time for data loads.

There is, however, an even more worrying fact. Just consider, in Figure 1-1, the effect of the index on the performance of *SixthExample.java*: it turned a very fast query into a comparatively slow one. What if we already have queries written on the same pattern as the query in *SixthExample.java*? I may fix one issue but create problem queries where there were none. Indexing is very important, and I'll discuss the matter in the next chapter, but when something is already in production, touching indexes is always a risk.* The same is true of every change that affects the database globally, particularly parameter changes that impact even more queries than an index.

There may be other considerations to take into account, though. Depending on the development team's strengths and weaknesses, to say nothing of the skittishness of management, optimizing lookup functions and adding an index may be *perceived* as a lesser risk than rethinking the process's core query. The preceding example is a simple one, and the core query, without being absolutely trivial, is of very moderate complexity. There may be cases in which writing a satisfactory query may either exceed the skills of developers on the team, or be impossible because of a bad database design that cannot be changed.

In spite of the lesser performance improvement and the thorough nonregression tests required by such a change to the database structure as an additional index, separately improving functions and the main query may sometimes be a more palatable solution to your boss than what I might call *grand refactoring*. After all, adequate indexing brought performance improvement factors of 16 to 35 with *ThirdExample.java*, which isn't negligible.

It is sometimes wise to stick to "acceptable" even when "excellent" is within reach—you can always mention the excellent solution as the last option.

Whichever solution you finally settle for, and whatever the reason, you must understand that the same idea drives both refactoring approaches: minimizing the number of calls to the database server, and in particular, decreasing the shockingly high number of queries issued by the AboveThreshold( ) function that we got in the initial version of the code.

Assessing Possible Gains

The greatest difficulty when undertaking a refactoring assignment is, without a shadow of a doubt, assessing how much improvement is within your grasp.

When you consider the alternative option of "throwing more hardware to the performance problem," you swim in an ocean of figures: number of processors, CPU frequency, memory, disk transfer rates…and of course, hardware price. Never mind the fact that more hardware sometimes means a ridiculous improvement and, in some cases, worse performance† (this is when a whole range of improvement possibilities can be welcome).

---

* Even if, in the worst case, dropping an index (or making it invisible with Oracle 11 and later) is an operation that can be performed relatively quickly.

† Through aggrieved contention. It isn't as frequent as pathetic improvement, but it happens.

It is a deeply ingrained belief in the subconscious minds of chief information officers (CIOs) that twice the computing power will mean better performance—if not twice as fast, at least pretty close. If you confront the hardware option by suggesting refactoring, you are fighting an uphill battle and you must come out with figures that are at least as plausible as the ones pinned on hardware, and are hopefully truer. As Mark Twain once famously remarked to a visiting fellow journalist[*]:

> Get your facts first, and then you can distort 'em as much as you please.

Using a system of trial and error for an undefined number of days, trying random changes and hoping to hit the nail on the head, is neither efficient nor guarantees success. If, after assessing what needs to be done, you cannot offer credible figures for the time required to implement the changes and the expected benefits, you simply stand no chance of proving yourself right unless the hardware vendor is temporarily out of stock.

Assessing by how much you can improve a given program is a very difficult exercise. First, you must define in which unit you are going to express "how much." Needless to say, what users (or CIOs) would probably love to hear is "we can reduce the time this process needs by 50%" or something similar. But reasoning in terms of response time is very dangerous and leads you down the road to failure. When you consider the hardware option, what you take into account is additional computing power. If you want to compete on a level field with more powerful hardware, the safest strategy is to try to estimate how much power you can spare by processing data more efficiently, and how much time you can save by eliminating some processes, such as repeating thousands or millions of times queries that need to run just once. The key point, therefore, is not to boast about a hypothetical performance gain that is very difficult to predict, but to prove that first there are some gross inefficiencies in the current code, and second that these inefficiencies are easy to remedy.

The best way to prove that a refactoring exercise will pay off is probably to delve a little deeper into the trace file obtained with Oracle for the initial program (needless to say, analysis of SQL Server runtime statistics would give a similar result).

The Oracle trace file gives detailed figures about the CPU and elapsed times used by the various phases (parsing, execution, and, for select statements, data fetching) of each statement execution, as well as the various "wait events" and time spent by the DBMS engine waiting for the availability of a resource. I plotted the numbers in Figure 1-4 to show how Oracle spent its time executing the SQL statements in the initial version of this chapter's example.

You can see that the 128 seconds the trace file recorded can roughly be divided into three parts:

- CPU time consumed by Oracle to process the queries, which you can subdivide into time required by the parsing of statements, time required by the execution of statements, and time required for fetching rows. *Parsing* refers to the analysis of statements and the choice of an execution path. *Execution* is the time required to locate the first

---

[*] No less than Rudyard Kipling, who told of his interview of Twain in *From Sea to Sea*.

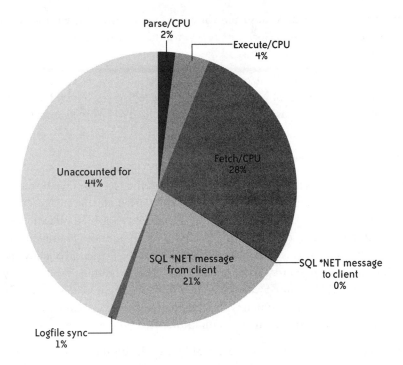

Parse/CPU
2%

Execute/CPU
4%

Fetch/CPU
28%

Unaccounted for
44%

SQL *NET message
from client
21%

SQL *NET message
to client
0%

Logfile sync
1%

FIGURE 1-4. How time was spent in Oracle with the first version

row in the result set for a select statement (it may include the time needed to sort this result set prior to identifying the first row), and actual table modification for statements that change the data. You might also see *recursive statements*, which are statements against the data dictionary that result from the program statements, either during the parsing phase or, for instance, to handle space allocation when inserting data. Thanks to my using prepared statements and the absence of any massive sort, the bulk of this section is occupied by the fetching of rows. With hardcoded statements, each statement appears as a brand-new query to the SQL engine, which means getting information from the data dictionary for analysis and identification of the best execution plan; likewise, sorts usually require dynamic allocation of temporary storage, which also means recording allocation data to the data dictionary.

- Wait time, during which the DBMS engine is either idle (such as SQL*Net message from client, which is the time when Oracle is merely waiting for an SQL statement to process), or waiting for a resource or the completion of an operation, such as I/O operations denoted by the two db file events (db file sequential read primarily refers to index accesses, and db file scattered read to table scans, which is hard to guess when one doesn't know Oracle), both of which are totally absent here. (All the data was loaded in memory by prior statistical computations on tables and indexes.) Actually, the only I/O operation we see is the writing to logfiles, owing to the auto-commit mode of JDBC. You now understand why switching auto-commit off changed very little in that case, because it accounted for only 1% of the database time.

- Unaccounted time, which results from various systemic errors such as the fact that precision cannot be better than clock frequency, rounding errors, uninstrumented Oracle operations, and so on.

If I had based my analysis on the percentages in Figure 1-4 to try to predict by how much the process could be improved, I would have been unable to come out with any reliable improvement ratio. This is a case when you can be tempted to follow Samuel Goldwyn's advice:

> Never make forecasts, especially about the future.

For one thing, most waits are waits for work (although the fact that the DBMS is waiting for work should immediately ring a bell with an experienced practitioner). I/O operations are not a problem, in spite of the missing index. You could expect an index to speed up fetch time, but the previous experiments proved that index-induced improvement was far from massive. If you naively assume that it would be possible to get rid of all waits, including time that is unaccounted for, you would no less naively assume that the best you can achieve is to divide the runtime by about 3—or 4 with a little bit of luck—when by energetic refactoring I divided it by 100. It is certainly better to predict 3 and achieve 100 than the reverse, but it still doesn't sound like you know what you are doing.

How I obtained a factor of 100 is easy to explain (after the deed is done): I no longer fetched the rows, and by reducing the process to basically a single statement I also removed the waits for input from the application (in the guise of multiple SQL statements to execute). But waits by themselves gave me no useful information about where to strike; the best I can get from trace files and wait analysis is the assurance that some of the most popular recipes for tuning a database will have no or very little effect.

Wait times are really useful when your changes are narrowly circumscribed, which is what happens when you tune a system: they tell you where time is wasted and where you should try to increase throughput, by whatever means are at your disposal. Somehow wait times also fix an upper bound on the improvement you can expect. They can still be useful when you want to refactor the code, as an indicator of the weaknesses of the current version (although there are several ways to spot weaknesses). Unfortunately, they will be of little use when trying to forecast performance after code overhaul. Waiting for input for the application and much-unaccounted-for time (when the sum of rounding errors is big, it means you have many basic operations) are both symptoms of a very "chatty" application. However, to understand why the application is so chatty and to ascertain whether it can be made less chatty and more efficient (other than by tuning low-level TCP parameters) I need to know not what the DBMS is waiting for, but what keeps it busy. In determining what keeps a DBMS busy, you usually find a lot of operations that, when you think hard about them, can be dispensed with, rather than done faster. As Abraham Maslow put it:

> What is not worth doing is not worth doing well.

Tuning is about trying to do the same thing faster; refactoring is about achieving the same result faster. If you compare what the database is doing to what it should or could be doing, you can issue some reliable and credible figures, wrapped in suitable oratorical precautions. As I have pointed out, what was really interesting in the Oracle trace wasn't the full scan of the two-million-row table. If I analyze the same trace file in a different way, I can create Table 1-7. (Note that the elapsed time is smaller than the CPU time for the third and fourth statements; it isn't a typo, but what the trace file indicates—just the result of rounding errors.)

TABLE 1-7. What the Oracle trace file says the DBMS was doing

Statement	Executions	CPU	Elapsed	Rows
select accountid from area_accounts where areaid=:1	1	0.01	0.04	270
select txid, amount, curr from transactions ...	270	38.14	39.67	31,029
select threshold from thresholds where iso=:1	31,029	3.51	3.38	30,301
select :1 * rate from currency_rates ...	61	0.02	0.01	61
insert into check_log(...)	61	0.01	0.01	61

When looking at Table 1-7, you may have noticed the following:

- The first striking feature in Table 1-7 is that the number of rows returned by one statement is most often the number of executions of the next statement: an obvious sign that we are just feeding the result of one query into the next query instead of performing joins.

- The second striking feature is that all the elapsed time, on the DBMS side, is CPU time. The two-million-row table is mostly cached in memory, and scanned in memory. A full table scan doesn't necessarily mean I/O operations.

- We query the thresholds table more than 30,000 times, returning one row in most cases. This table contains 20 rows. It means that each single value is fetched 1,500 times on average.

- Oracle gives an elapsed time of about 43 seconds. The measured elapsed time for this run was 128 seconds. Because there are no I/O operations worth talking about, the difference can come only from the Java code runtime and from the "dialogue" between the Java program and the DBMS server. If we decrease the number of executions, we can expect the time spent waiting for the DBMS to return from our JDBC calls to decrease in proportion.

We are already getting a fairly good idea of what is going wrong: we are spending a lot of time fetching data from transactions, we are querying thresholds of 1,500 more times than needed, and we are not using joins, thus multiplying exchanges between the application and the server.

But the question is, what can we hope for? It's quite obvious from the figures that if we fetch only 20 times (or even 100 times) from the thresholds table, the time globally taken by the query will dwindle to next to nothing. More difficult to estimate is the amount of time we need to spend querying the transactions table, and we can do that by imagining the worst case. There is no need to return a single transaction several times; therefore, the worst case I can imagine is to fully scan the table and return about one sixty-fourth (2,000,000 divided by 31,000) of its rows. I can easily write a query that, thanks to the Oracle pseudocolumn that numbers rows as they are returned (I could have used a session variable with another DBMS), returns one row every 65 rows, and run this query under SQL*Plus as follows:

```
SQL> set timing on
SQL> set autotrace traceonly
SQL> select *
  2  from (select rownum rn, t.*
  3          from transactions t)
  4  where mod(rn, 65) = 0
  5  /

30769 rows selected.

Elapsed: 00:00:03.67

Execution Plan
-----------------------------------------------------------
Plan hash value: 3537505522
```

Id	Operation	Name	Rows	Bytes	Cost (%CPU)	Time
0	SELECT STATEMENT		2000K	125M	2495 (2)	00:00:30
* 1	VIEW		2000K	125M	2495 (2)	00:00:30
2	COUNT					
3	TABLE ACCESS FULL	TRANSACTIONS	2000K	47M	2495 (2)	00:00:30

```
Predicate Information (identified by operation id):
---------------------------------------------------

   1 - filter(MOD("RN",65)=0)

Statistics
-----------------------------------------------------------
          1  recursive calls
          0  db block gets
      10622  consistent gets
       8572  physical reads
```

```
        0  redo size
  1246889  bytes sent via SQL*Net to client
    22980  bytes received via SQL*Net from client
     2053  SQL*Net roundtrips to/from client
        0  sorts (memory)
        0  sorts (disk)
    30769  rows processed
```

I have my full scan and about the same number of rows returned as in my program—and it took less than four seconds, in spite of not having found data in memory 8 times out of 10 (the ratio of *physical reads* to *consistent gets + db block gets* that is the count of logical references to the Oracle blocks that contain data). This simple test is the proof that there is no need to spend almost 40 seconds fetching information from transactions.

Short of rewriting the initial program, there isn't much more that we can do at this stage. But we have a good proof of concept that is convincing enough to demonstrate that properly rewriting the program could make it use less than 5 seconds of *CPU time* instead of 40; I emphasize CPU time here, not elapsed time, because elapsed time includes wait times that I know will vanish but on which I cannot honestly pin any figure. By talking CPU time, I can compare the result of code rewriting to buying a machine eight times faster than the current one, which has a price. From here you can estimate how much time it will take to refactor the program, how much time will be required for testing, whether you need external help in the guise of consulting—all things that depend on your environment, the amount of code that has to be revised, and the strengths of the development team. Compute how much it will cost you, and compare this to the cost of a server that is eight times more powerful (as in this example) than your current server, if such a beast exists. You are likely to find yourself in a very convincing position—and then it will be your mission to deliver and meet (or exceed) expectations.

Assessing whether you can pin any hope on refactoring, therefore, demands two steps:

1. Find out what the database is doing. Only when you know what your server is doing can you notice the queries that take the whole edifice down. It's then that you discover that several costly operations can be grouped and performed as a single pass, and that therefore, this particular query has no reason to be executed as many times as it is executed, or that a loop over the result of a query to execute another query could be replaced by a more efficient join.

2. Analyze current activity with a critical eye, and create simple, reasonable proofs of concept that demonstrate convincingly that the code could be much more efficient.

Most of this book is devoted to describing patterns that are likely to be a fertile ground for refactoring and, as a consequence, to give you ideas about what the proof of concept might be. But before we discuss those patterns, let's review how you can identify SQL statements that are executed.

Finding Out What the Database Is Doing

You have different ways to monitor SQL activity on your database. Every option isn't available with every DBMS, and some methods are more appropriate for test databases than for production databases. Furthermore, some methods allow you to monitor everything that is happening, whereas others let you focus on particular sessions. All of them have their use.

Querying dynamic views

Oracle started with version 6 what is now a popular trend: *dynamic views*, relational (tabular) representations of memory structures that the system updates in real time and that you can query using SQL. Some views, such as v$session with Oracle, sys.dm_exec_requests with SQL Server, and information_schema.processlist with MySQL, let you view what is currently executing (or has just been executed). However, sampling these views will not yield anything conclusive unless you also know either the rate at which queries are executed or their duration. The dynamic views that are truly interesting are those that map the statement cache, complete with counters regarding the number of executions of each statement, the CPU time used by each statement, the number of basic data units (called *blocks* with Oracle and *pages* elsewhere) referenced by the statement, and so on. The number of data pages accessed to execute the query is usually called the *logical read* and is a good indicator of the amount of work required by a statement. The relevant dynamic views are v$sqlstats* with Oracle and sys.dm_exec_query_stats with SQL Server. As you can infer from their names, these views cannot be queried by every Tom, Dick, or Harry, and you may need to charm your DBA to get the license to drill. They are also the basis for built-in (but sometimes separately licensed) monitoring utilities such as Oracle's Automatic Workload Repository (AWR) and companion products.

Dynamic views are a wonderful source of information, but they have three issues:

- They give instant snapshots, even if the counters are cumulative. If you want to have a clear picture of what happens during the day, or simply for a few hours, you must take regular snapshots and store them somewhere. Otherwise, you risk focusing on a big costly query that took place at 2 a.m. when no one cared, and you may miss the real issues. Taking regular snapshots is what Oracle's Statspack utility does, as well as Oracle's ASH (which stands for Active Session History) product, which is subject to particular licensing conditions (in plain English, you have to pay a lot more if you want it).

- Querying memory structures that display vital and highly volatile information takes time that may be modest compared to many of the queries on the database, but may harm the whole system. This is not equally true of all dynamic views (some are more sensitive than others), but to return consistent information, the process that returns data from the innermost parts of the DBMS must somehow lock the structures while it reads them: in other words, while you read the information stating that one particular

---

* Available since Oracle 10, but the information was available in v$sql in previous versions.

statement has been executed 1,768,934 times, the process that has just executed it again and wants to record the deed must wait to update the counter. It will not take long, but on a system with a very big cache and many statements, it is likely that your select on the view, which, behind the scenes, is a traversal of some complicated memory structure, will hamper more than one process. You mustn't forget that you'll have to store what is returned to record the snapshot, necessarily slowing down your query. In other words, you don't want to poll dynamic views at a frantic rate, because if you do, hardly anybody else will be able to work properly.

- As a result, there is a definite risk of missing something. The problem is that counters are associated with a cached statement. Whatever way you look at the problem, the cache has a finite size, and if you execute a very high number of different statements, at some point the DBMS will have to reuse the cache that was previously holding an aged-out statement. If you execute a very, very big number of different statements, rotation can be quick, and pop goes the SQL, taking counters with it. It's easy to execute a lot of different statements; you just have to hardcode everything and shun prepared statements and stored procedures.

Acknowledging the last two issues, some third-party tool suppliers provide programs that attach to the DBMS memory structures and read them directly, without incurring the overhead of the SQL layer. This allows them to scan memory at a much higher rate with a minimized impact over regular DBMS activity. Their ability to scan memory several times per second may make particularly surprising the fact that, for instance, many successful Oracle DBAs routinely take snapshots of activity at intervals of 30 minutes.

Actually, missing a statement isn't something that is, in itself, very important when you try to assess what the database server is busy doing. You just need to catch *important* statements, statements that massively contribute to the load of the machine and/or to unsatisfactory response times. If I grossly simplify, I can say that there are two big categories of statements worth tuning:

- The big, ugly, and slow SQL statements that everyone wants to tune (and that are hard to miss)

- Statements which are not, by themselves, costly, but which are executed so many times that the cumulative effect *is* very costly

In the sample program at the beginning of this chapter, we encountered examples of both categories: the full scan on a two-million-row table, which can qualify as a slow query, and the super-fast, frequently used lookup functions.

If we check the contents of the statement cache at regular intervals, we will miss statements that were first executed *and* that aged out of the cache between two inspections. I have never met an application that was executing an enormous quantity of different statement patterns. But the worry is that a DBMS will recognize two statements to be identical only when the text is identical, byte for byte:

- If statements are prepared and use variables, or if we call stored procedures, even if we poll at a low rate, we will get a picture that may not be absolutely complete but which is a fair representation of what is going on, because statements will be executed over and over again and will stay in the cache.

- If, instead of using prepared statements, you build them dynamically, concatenating constant values that are never the same, then your statements may be identical in practice, but the SQL engine will only see and report myriad different statements—all very fast, all executed once—which will move in and out of the cache at lightning speed to make room for other similar statements. If you casually check the cache contents, you will catch only a small fraction of what really was executed, and you will get an inaccurate idea of what is going on, because the few statements that may correctly use parameters will take a disproportionate "weight" compared to the hardcoded statements that may be (and probably are) the real problem. In the case of SQL Server, for which stored procedures get preferential treatment as far as cache residency is concerned, SQL statements executed outside stored procedures, because they are more volatile, may look less harmful than they really are.

To picture exactly how this might work in practice, suppose we have a query (or stored procedure) that uses parameters and has a cost of 200 units, and a short, hardcoded query that has a cost of 3 units. Figure that, between 2 times when we query the statement cache, the costlier query is executed 5 times and the short query 4,000 times—looking like 4,000 distinct statements. Furthermore, let's say that our statement cache can hold only 100 queries (something much lower than typical real values). If you check the top five queries, the costlier query will appear with a cumulated cost of 1,000 (5×200), and will be followed by four queries with a comparatively ridiculous cost of 3 (1×3 each time). Moreover, if you try to express the relative importance of each query by comparing the cost of each to the cumulated cost of cached statements, you may wrongly compute the full value for the cache as $1 \times 1,000 + 99 \times 3 = 1,297$ (based on current cache values), of which the costly query represents 77%. Using the current cache values alone grossly underreports the total cost of the fast query. Applying the cost units from the current cache to the total number of statements executed during this period, the actual full cost for the period was $5 \times 200 + 4,000 \times 3 = 13,000$, which means that the "costly" query represents only 7% of the real cost—and the "fast" query 93%.

You must therefore collect not only statements, but also global figures that will tell you which proportion of the real load is explained by the statements you have collected. Therefore, if you choose to query v$sqlstats with Oracle (or sys.dm_exec_query_stats with SQL Server), you must also find global counters. With Oracle, you can find them easily within v$sysstat: you'll find there the total number of statements that were executed, the CPU time that has been consumed, the number of logical reads, and the number of physical I/O operations since database startup. With SQL Server, you will find many key figures as variables, such as @@CPU_BUSY, @@TIMETICKS, @@TOTAL_READ, and @@TOTAL_WRITE. However, the figure that probably represents the best measure of work performed by any DBMS is the number of logical reads, and it is available from `sys.dm_os_performance_counters` as the value associated with the rather misleadingly named counter, `Page lookups/sec` (it's a cumulative value and not a rate).

Now, what do you do if you realize that by probing the statement cache, say, every 10 minutes, you miss a lot of statements? For instance, with my previous example, I would explain a cost of 1,297 out of 13,000. This is, in itself, a rather bad sign, and as we'll see in the next chapter, there are probably significant gains to expect from merely using prepared statements. A solution might be to increase the frequency that is used for polling, but as I explained, probing may be costly. Polling too often can deliver a fatal blow to a system that is already likely to be in rather bad health.

When you are missing a lot of statements, there are two solutions for getting a less distorted view of what the database is doing: one is to switch to logfile-based analysis (my next topic), and the other is to base analysis on execution plans instead of statement texts.

The slot in the statement cache associated with each statement also contains a reference to the execution plan associated with that statement (`plan_hash_value` in Oracle's `v$sqlstats`, `plan_handle` in SQL Server's `sys.dm_exec_query_stats`; note that in Oracle, each plan points to the address of a "parent cursor" instead of having statements pointing to a plan, as with SQL Server). Associated plan statistics can respectively be found in `v$sql_plan_statistics` (which is extremely detailed and, when statistics collection is set at a high level for the database, provides almost as much information as trace files) and `sys.dm_exec_cached_plans`.

Execution plans are not what we are interested in; after all, if we run *FirstExample.java* with an additional index, we get very nice execution plans but still pathetic performance. However, hardcoded statements that differ only in terms of constant values will, for the most part, use the same execution plan. Therefore, aggregating statement statistics by the associated execution plan instead of doing it by text alone will give a much truer vision of what the database is really doing. Needless to say, execution plans are not a perfect indicator. Some changes at the session level can lead to different execution plans with the same statement text for two sessions (we can also have synonyms resolving to totally different objects); and, any simple query on an unindexed table will result in the same table scan, whichever column(s) you use for filtering rows. But even if there isn't a one-to-one correspondence between a statement pattern and an execution plan, execution plans (with an associated sample query) will definitely give you a much better idea of what type of statement really matters than statement text alone when numbers don't add up with statements.

Dumping statements to a trace file

It is possible to make all DBMS products log SQL statements that are executed. Logging is based on intercepting the statement before (or after) it is executed and writing it to a file. Interception can take place in several locations: where the statement is executed (on the database server), or where it is issued (on the application side)—or somewhere in between.

Server-side logging. Server-side logging is the type of logging most people think of. The scope can be either the whole system or the current session. For instance, when you log slow queries with MySQL by starting the server with the `--log-slow-queries` option, it affects every session. The snag is that if you want to collect interesting information, the amount of data you need to log is often rather high. For instance, if we run *FirstExample.java* against a MySQL server that was started with `--log-slow-queries`, we find nothing in the logfile when we have the additional index on `transactions`: there is no slow query (it's the whole process that is slow), and I have made the point that it can nevertheless be made 15 to 20 times faster. Logging these slow queries can be useful to administrators for identifying big mistakes and horrid queries that have managed to slip into production, but it will tell you nothing about what the database is truly doing as long as each unit of work is fast enough.

If you really want to see what matters, therefore, you must log every statement the DBMS executes (by starting the MySQL server with `--log`, setting the global `general_log` variable to `ON`, and by setting the Oracle `sql_trace` parameter to true or activating event 10046; if you are using SQL Server, call `sp_trace_create` to define your trace file, then `sp_trace_setevent` multiple times to define what you want to trace, and then `sp_trace_setstatus` to start tracing). In practice, this means you will get gigantic logfiles if you want to put a busy server in trace mode. (Sometimes you will get many gigantic logfiles. Oracle will create one trace file per server process, and it isn't unusual to have hundreds of them. For SQL Server, it may create a new trace file each time the current file becomes too big.) This is something you will definitely want to avoid on a production server, particularly if it is already showing some signs of running out of breath. In addition to the overhead incurred by timing, catching, and writing statements, you incur the risk of filling up disks, a situation that a DBMS often finds uncomfortable. However, it may be the smart thing to do within a good-quality assurance environment and if you are able to generate a load that simulates production.

When you want to collect data on a production system, though, it is usually safer to trace a single session, which you will do with MySQL by setting the `sql_log_off` session variable to `ON` and with Oracle by executing:

```
alter session set timed_statistics=true,
alter session set max_dump_file_size=unlimited;
alter session se tracefile_identifier='something meaningful';
alter session set events '10046 trace name context forever, level 8';
```

The `level` parameter for the event specifies how much information to collect. Possible values are:

- 1 (displays basic trace information)

- .4 (displays bind variables, values that are passed)

- 8 (displays wait statistics)

- 12 (displays wait statistics and bind variables)

With SQL Server, you need to call sp_trace_filter to specify the Service Profile Identifier (SPID) or login name (depending on which is more convenient) that you want to trace before turning tracing on.

Because it isn't always convenient to modify an existing program to add this type of statement, you can ask a DBA either to trace your session when it is started (DBAs sometimes can do that) or, better perhaps, to create a special user account on which a login trigger turns tracing on whenever you connect to the database through this account.

Client-side logging. Unfortunately, there are some downsides to server-side logging:

- Because logging takes place on the server, it consumes resources that may be in short supply and that may impact global performance even when you are tracing a single session.

- Tracing a single session may prove difficult when you are using an application server that pools database connections: there is no longer a one-to-one link between the end-user session and a database session. As a result, you may trace more or less than you initially intended and find it difficult to get a clear picture of activity out of trace files without the proper tools.

When you are a developer, the production database server is often off-limits. Trace files will be created under accounts you have no access to, and you will depend on administrators to obtain and process the trace files you generate. Depending on people who are often extremely busy may not be very convenient, particularly if you want to repeat tracing operations a number of times.

An alternative possibility is to trace SQL statements where they are issued: on the application server side. The ideal case is, of course, when the application itself is properly instrumented. But there may be other possibilities:

- If you are using an application server such as JBoss, WebLogic, or WebSphere—or simple JDBC—you can use the free p6spy tracer, which will time each statement that is executed.

- With JDBC, you can sometimes enable logging in the JDBC driver. (For instance, you can do this with the MySQL JDBC driver.)

In-between logging. Also available are hybrid solutions. An example is SQL Server's SQL Profiler, which activates server-side traces but is a client tool that receives trace data from the server. Although SQL Profiler is much more pleasant to use than the T-SQL system procedures, the data traffic that flows toward the tool somewhat counterbalances the creation of a trace file on the server, and it is often frowned upon as not being as efficient as "pure" server-side logging.

I must mention that you can trap and time SQL statements in other ways, even if they require a fair amount of programming; you may encounter these techniques in some third-party products. When you "talk" to a DBMS you actually send your SQL statements to a TCP/IP port on the server. It is sometimes possible to have a program that listens on a port other than the port on which the true DBMS listener program is listening; that program will trap and log whatever you send it before forwarding it to the DBMS. Sometimes the DBMS vendor officially acknowledges this method and provides a true proxy (such as MySQL Proxy, or the pioneering Sybase Open Server). The technique of using a proxy is similar to the implementation of web filtering through a proxy server.

Exploiting trace files

With trace files, you will not miss any statements, which means you may get a lot of data. I already explained that if statements are hardcoded, you will miss many of them, and you will, generally speaking, get a biased view of what is going on if you poll the statement cache. With trace files, the problem is slightly different: you will get so many statements in your file that it may well be unusable, even after processing raw logfiles with a tool such as tkprof for Oracle or mysqlsla* for MySQL.

One good way to handle data afterward is to load it into a database and query it! Oracle's tkprof has long been able to generate insert statements instead of a text report, and SQL Server's tools and the fn_trace_gettable( ) function make loading a trace file into a table a very easy operation. There is only one snag: you need a database to load into. If you have no development database at your disposal, or if you are a consultant who is eager to keep your work separate from your customers', think of SQLite:† you can use it to create a file in which data is stored in tables and queried with SQL, even if loading the trace file may require a little coding.

The problem is that even with a database at your disposal, the volume of data to analyze may be daunting. I once traced with Oracle (knowing that querying v$sqlstats would give me nothing because most statements were hardcoded) a program, supplied by a third-party editor, that was taking around 80 minutes to generate a 70-page report. That was on a corporate-grade Sun server running Solaris; the text report resulting from the output of tkprof was so big that I couldn't open it with vi and carried out my analysis using commands such as grep, sed, awk, and wc (if you are not conversant in Unix-based operating systems, these are powerful but rather low-level command-line utilities). The purpose wasn't to refactor the code (there was no source code to modify, only binary programs were available), but to audit the client/server application and understand why it was taking so long to run on a powerful server while the same report, with the same data, was taking much less time on the laptop of the vendor's technical consultant (who was all the same advising to buy a more powerful server). The trace file nevertheless gave me the answer: there were 600,000 statements in the file; average execution time was 80 minutes / 600,000 = 8 milliseconds. Oracle was idle 90% of the time, actually, and most of the elapsed time was local area network (LAN) latency. I would have loved to have been given the opportunity to refactor this program. It would have been easy to slash execution time by several orders of magnitude.

* *http://hackmysql.com*
† *http://www.sqlite.org*

You must process trace files (or trace data) if you want to get anything out of them. If statements are hardcoded, it's better to be a regular expression fiend and replace all constant strings with something fixed (say, 'constant') and all number constants with something such as 0. This will be your only chance to be able to aggregate statements that are identical from the standpoint of the application but not from that of the DBMS. You may have to massage the trace file so as to assign one timestamp to every line (the only way to know exactly when each statement was executed). After that's done, you must aggregate any timing information you have and count how many identical patterns you have. You will then get solid material that you analyze to see what you can do to improve performance.

Analyzing Collected Material

Let's now see how we can analyze data we have collected either through cache probing or through logging and what it tells us about performance improvement possibilities.

In all the cases I have experienced, most of the database load for considerable parts of the day (or night) was the result of fewer than 10 queries or query patterns, and you can usually narrow the "queries that count" down to 4 or 5.

Most of these queries will be very big queries, or fast queries that are executed too often. As we saw previously, even if we cannot ignore big queries, focusing on single queries may make us miss big performance gains. We must step back and relate SQL activity to business activity and check whether what is done often can be done less frequently or not at all. If we succeed in identifying queries that we could run less often, we must determine how much CPU time they currently use and compute how much we can save. This is easier and safer to do than trying to predict response times. When you buy a more powerful server, all you really know is that you are in fact buying CPU time, and the vendor's own benchmark lets you know the power ratio between your current server and the projected one. If you can plausibly demonstrate that refactoring the code would decrease CPU consumption by 20% at peak time, for all practical purposes that means the proposed refactoring effort would have the same result as buying a new server that is 20% more powerful, minus migration costs.

Actually, there is more to refactoring than the reduction of CPU consumption on the server, and I hope that Figure 1-5 will give you a good understanding of the real benefits to expect. In many poorly written applications, you have an incessant chat between the application side and the server side. Suppose we have a cursor loop—some select statement that returns a number of rows and performs, say, an update in the loop. The application will issue a number of database calls:

- First it will issue an execute call that will analyze the select statement, parse it, determine an execution plan if necessary, and do whatever is required (including sorts) to locate the first row to return.

- Then it will iterate on fetch calls that will return rows, either one by one or, sometimes, in batches.

- While still in the loop, another execute call will perform an update. Because this operation changes the database, no other call follows the execute for this statement.

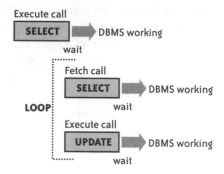

FIGURE 1-5. A chatty SQL application

Basic database calls are synchronous, which means that most applications are suspended and they wait until the DBMS is done with its side of the job. This wait time is actually the assembly of several components:

- The communication time it takes for your statement to reach the server

- The time it takes the server to compute a checksum on your statement and check whether it already has a matching execution plan in its cache

- Optionally, the time it takes to actually parse the statement and determine an execution plan

- The actual execution time for your statement, a "service time" that includes CPU time and, possibly, I/O wait time or wait time for a resource that cannot be shared

- The time it takes to receive data from the server or obtain execution information such as a return code and the number of rows processed

By tuning statements on a unitary basis, you improve only the fourth component. If we manage to get rid of unnecessary calls, as we did in the earlier example by improving lookup functions, we can remove in a loop the execution of the five components a significant number of times. If we get rid of the loop, we get rid of all the overhead at once.

Now that we know the top statements that keep our DBMS busy, we should look for the following several patterns:

- If the statements that are (globally) the most costly are fast statements that are executed a large number of times, you stand a high chance of success with refactoring, and giving an estimate is reasonably easy. If you have a static table, such as a reference lookup table, for which the average number of queries per active session is greater than the number of rows in the table, on average each row is called several times. Very often, "several" doesn't mean two or three times, but thousands of times or more. You can be sure that you can reduce this number of calls and therefore spare the CPU consumption attached with each execution. You usually find this type of call when you are performing transcoding, currency conversion, or calendar computations, among other operations. I will discuss in more detail how to minimize the number of calls in Chapter 3.

- If you have some very costly statements, predicting how much you can save by rewriting statements in a better way is much more difficult; if the indexing strategy, which I'll discuss in Chapter 2, is sound, and if, as you'll see in Chapter 3, there is no complicated view that can be simplified, your success here strongly depends on your SQL skills. I hope that after you read Chapter 5 your chances of significantly improving a badly written statement will be in the 40% to 60% range.

- When you see several similar updates applied to the same tables, and if your SQL skills are not too rusty, you also stand a very good chance of merging some of them, as I'll discuss in Chapter 6. Doing in one statement what two statements were previously doing routinely improves (surprise!) performance by a factor of two; unfortunately, sometimes you can't do this. A relatively safe assumption is to bet on a possible improvement in 20% to 25% of cases.

When you can describe which statements load the server and can assign to each of them a probability of improving them in terms of CPU consumption, you'll have figures that you can compare to faster hardware, but never talk response times. CPU time is just one component of response time, and you can improve response times a lot by getting rid of all the time wasted in communication between the application and the DBMS. Now, the difficulty for you will be to estimate at what cost you can obtain these gains. The following chapters will help you to refine estimates of what you can get, and at what price.

## CHAPTER TWO

Sanity Checks

And can you, by no drift of circumstance,
Get from him why he puts on this confusion,
Grating so harshly all his days of quiet
With turbulent and dangerous lunacy?

—*William Shakespeare (1564–1616)*

Hamlet, III, 1

BEFORE ENGAGING IN SERIOUS REFACTORING WORK, YOU SHOULD CHECK SEVERAL POINTS, PARTICULARLY if there are a significant number of big, costly queries. Sometimes gross mistakes that are easy to fix have slipped in because of time pressures, ignorance, or a simple misunderstanding about how a DBMS works. In this chapter, I will discuss a number of points that you should control and, if necessary, correct, before you take reference performance measurements for a refactoring campaign. With any luck (I am lazy), refactoring may seem less urgent afterward.

One of the most critical aspects of DBMS performance with regard to unitary queries is the efficiency of the query optimizer (unfortunately, the optimizer cannot do much for poor algorithms). The optimizer bases its search for the best execution plan on a number of clues: typically, what the data dictionary says about existing indexes. But it also derives its choice of plan from what it knows about the data—that is, statistics that are stored in the data dictionary, the collection of which is usually a routine part of database administration. Or should be.

There are two things to check before anything else when you encounter performance issues on particular queries: whether statistics are reasonably up-to-date and detailed enough, and whether indexing is appropriate. Those are the two prerequisites for the optimizer to perform its job properly (whether the optimizer actually performs its job properly when indexing and statistics are beyond reproach is another question). First I will review the topic of statistics, including index statistics, before briefly discussing indexing. This order may surprise you, because so many people equate good SQL performance with proper use of indexes. But in fact, good performance has as much to do with using the appropriate index as it does with not using a poor index, which only statistics can help the optimizer to decide. In some way, statistics are the flip side of indexes—or vice versa.

Statistics and Data Skewness

Statistics is a generic term that covers a lot of data that a DBMS accumulates regarding what it stores. The space required for storing the statistics is negligible, but the time that is required to collect them isn't; statistics gathering can be either automated or triggered by administrators. Because collecting detailed statistics can be a very heavy operation (at worst, you can end up scanning all the data in your database), you can ask for more or less refined statistics, computed or estimated; different DBMS products collect slightly different information.

Available Statistics

It would be rather tedious to review in detail all the statistics that the various products collect, which can be extensive in the case of Oracle and SQL Server. Let's just consider what might be useful information for the optimizer to ponder when contemplating alternative execution paths.

First, you must understand that when you scan a table or access it through an index, there are differences other than brute force versus targeted strikes. The way the SQL engine reads rows is also different, and that has a lot to do with the physical storage of data. When a DBMS stores data, it allocates storage for a table, and storage allocation isn't something continuous, but discrete: a big chunk is reserved in a file for a particular table, and when this chunk is full another one is reserved. You don't allocate space with each new row you insert. As a consequence, the data that belongs to a table is physically clustered, to an extent that depends on your storage medium (if you are using disk arrays, the table will not be as clustered as it might be in a single partition of a single disk). But when the DBMS scans a table, it reads a lot of data at once, because what follows that particular piece of storage where one row is stored stands a very high chance of holding the rows that will be required next.

By contrast, an index associates to the same index key rows that are not necessarily close to one another (unless it is an SQL Server clustered index, an Oracle index-organized table, or a similar type of storage that the DBMS will know how to handle). When a DBMS retrieves data, the addressable unit is a *page* (called a *block* with Oracle) of a few kilobytes. One index entry associated with a key value will tell us that there is a row that matches the key in one page, but quite possibly no other row in the page will match the same key. Fetches will operate on a row-by-row basis much more than in the case of full scans. The spoon of indexes will be excellent for a relatively small number of rows, but not necessarily as good as the shovel of full scans with a large number of rows.

As a result, when filtering rows and applying a where clause, the optimizer's chief concern in deciding whether an index can be beneficial is selectivity—in other words, which percentage of rows satisfies a given criterion. This requires the knowledge of two quantities: the number of rows in the table and the number of rows that pass the search criterion.

For example, a condition such as the following can be more or less easy to estimate:

```
where my_column = some_value
```

When my_column is indexed, and if the index has been created as unique, we need no statistics: the condition will be satisfied by either one row or no rows. It gets a little more interesting when the column is indexed by a nonunique index. To estimate selectivity, we must rely on information such as the number of different keys in the index; this is how you can compute, for example, that if you are a Han Chinese, your family name is one out of about three thousand, and because Han Chinese compose 92% of the population in China, one family name is shared, on average, by 400,000 people. If you think that 1:3,000 is a selective ratio, you can contrast Chinese names to French names, of which there are about 1.3 million (including names of foreign origin) for a population of about sixty million, or 46 people per family name on average.

Selectivity is a serious topic, and the advantages of index accesses over plain table scans are sometimes dubious when selectivity is low. To illustrate this point, I created a five-million-row table with five columns—C0, C1, C2, C3, and C4—and populated the columns respectively with a random value between 1 and 5, a random value between 1 and 10, a random value between 1 and 100, a random value between 1 and 1,000, and a random value between 1 and 5,000. Then, I issued queries against one specific value for each column, queries that return between 1,000,000 and 1,000 rows depending on the column that is used as the search criterion. I issued those queries several times, first on the unindexed table and then after having indexed each column.* Furthermore, I never asked for any statistics to be computed.

Table 2-1 summarizes the performance improvement I obtained with indexes. The value is the ratio of the time it took to run a query when the column wasn't indexed over the time it took when the column was indexed; a value less than 1 indicates that it actually took *longer* to fetch the rows when there was an index than when there was none.

TABLE 2-1. Performance gain due to indexing

Rows returned	MySQL	Oracle	SQL Server
~ 1,000,000	x0.6	x1.1	x1.7
~ 500,000	x0.8	x1.0	x1.5
~ 50,000	x4.3	x1.0	x2.1
~ 5,000	x39.2	x1.1	x20.1
~ 1,000	x222.3	x20.8	x257.2

---

* Only regular indexes, not clustered indexes.

The only product for which, in this example, index searches are consistently better than full scans is SQL Server. In the case of MySQL, in this example it's only when 1% of the rows are returned that the positive effect of an index can be felt; when 10% or more of the rows are returned, the effect of the index is very damaging. In the case of Oracle, whether there is an index or not is fairly inconsequential, until we return 0.02% of rows. Even with SQL Server, we don't gain an order-of-magnitude improvement (a factor of 10) until the number of rows returned dwindles to a very modest fraction of the table size.

There is no magical percentage that lends itself to a comfortable hard-and-fast rule, such as "with Oracle, if you return less than *magical percentage* of rows, you should have an index." Many factors may intervene, such as the relative ordering of rows in the table (an index on a column containing values that increase as rows are inserted is, for instance, more efficient for querying than an index of similar selectivity on a column whose values are random). My point is merely that it's not because a column is used as a search criterion that it should be indexed, and sometimes it shouldn't.

Selectivity is important, but unfortunately, selectivity isn't everything. I populated my five-million-row table with randomly generated values, and random generators produce uniformly distributed numbers. In real life, distributions are most often anything but uniform. The previous comparison between family names in China and in France may have brought the following issue to your mind: even in France, the average hides striking disparities. If you are French and your name is Martin, you are sharing your family name with more than 200,000 other French people (not to mention Anglo-Saxons); even if your name is Mercier, more than 50,000 French people answer to the same name. Of course, those are still pretty tame numbers, compared to the names Li, Wang, and Zhang, which together represent around 250 million people in China. But for many people the family name isn't in the same league as a Social Security number, even in France.

The fact that you cannot assume a uniform distribution of data values means that when you search for some values an index will take you directly to the result set you want, and when you search for other values it isn't that efficient. Rating the efficiency of an index in relation to a certain value is particularly important when you have several criteria and several usable indexes, of which not one emerges as the clear winner in terms of average selectivity. To help the optimizer make an informed choice, you may need to collect *histograms*. To compute histograms, the DBMS divides the range of values for each column into a number of categories (one category per value if you have less than a couple hundred distinct values, a fixed number otherwise) and counts how many values fall into each category. That way, the optimizer knows that when you search for people who bear a particular name and who were born between two dates, it would rather use the index on the name because it is a rare name, and when you search another name for the same range of dates it will use the index on the date because the name is very common. This is basically the idea of histograms, although you will see later in this chapter that histograms may indirectly bring performance issues of their own.

Values other than the number of rows in a table, the average selectivity of indexes, and (optionally) how values are distributed may be very useful. I already alluded to the relationship between the order of index keys and the order of table rows (which couldn't be stronger when you have a clustered index with SQL Server or MySQL); if this relationship is strong, the index will be effective when searching on a range of keys, because the matching rows will be clustered. Many other values of a statistical nature can be useful to an optimizer to appraise alternative execution paths and to estimate the number of rows (or *cardinality*) remaining after each successive layer of screening conditions. Here is a list of some of these values:

Number of null values

When null values aren't stored in an index (as is the case with Oracle), knowing that most values are null in a column* tells the optimizer that when the column is mentioned as having to take a given value, the condition is probably very selective, even if there are few distinct key values in the index.

Range of values

Knowing in which range the values in a column are located is very helpful when trying to estimate how many rows may be returned by a condition such as >=, <=, or between, particularly when no histogram is available. Also, an equality condition on a value that falls outside the known range is likely to be highly selective. When columns are indexed, though, minimum and maximum values can easily be derived from the index.

Checking for the presence of statistics is easy. For instance, with Oracle you can run under SQL*Plus a script such as the following:

```
col "TABLE" format A18
col "INDEX" like "TABLE"
col "COLUMN" like "TABLE"
col "BUCKETS" format 999990
break on "TABLE" on "ANALYZED" on sample_size on "ROWS" on "INDEX" on "KEYS"
select t.table_name    "TABLE",
       to_char(t.last_analyzed, 'DD-MON') "ANALYZED",
       t.sample_size,
       t.num_rows      "ROWS",
       i.index_name    "INDEX",
       i.distinct_keys "KEYS",
       i.column_name   "COLUMN",
       i.num_distinct  "VALUES",
       i.num_nulls     "NULLS",
       i.num_buckets   "BUCKETS"
from user_tables t
     left outer join (select i.table_name,
                             i.index_name,
                             i.distinct_keys,
                             substr(ic.column_name, 1, 30) column_name,
                             ic.column_position pos,
                             c.num_distinct,
```

---

* Which may hint at an uncertain table design.

```
                        c.num_nulls,
                        c.num_buckets
                 from user_indexes i
                        inner join user_ind_columns ic
                               on ic.table_name = i.table_name
                               and ic.index_name = i.index_name
                        inner join user_tab_columns c
                               on c.table_name = ic.table_name
                               and c.column_name = ic.column_name) i
                    on i.table_name = t.table_name
     order by t.table_name,
              i.index_name,
              i.pos
     /
```

Or, with MySQL (where there is much less to check), you can run the following:

```
select t.table_name,
       t.table_rows,
       s.index_name,
       s.column_name,
       s.cardinality
from information_schema.tables t
     left outer join information_schema.statistics s
                  on s.table_schema = t.table_schema
                  and s.table_name = t.table_name
where t.table_schema = schema()
order by t.table_name,
         s.index_name,
         s.seq_in_index;
```

The process is much clumsier with SQL Server, for which you must first call sp_helpstats with the name of your table and 'ALL', and then run dbcc show statistics for each statistic, the name of which is returned by the preceding stored procedure.

But what may be interesting to check are anomalies that may induce the query optimizer to err.

Optimizer Traps

Nonuniform distribution of values in a column is a good reason for the optimizer to compute execution costs from wrong premises, and therefore, to settle for the wrong execution plan. But there may be other, less obvious cases when the optimizer is led astray.

Extreme values

It may be useful to check the range of values for an indexed column, which is easy to do with the following:

```
select min(column_value), max(column_value)
from my_table;
```

When there is an index, minimum and maximum values can be read very quickly from the index. Such a query can lead to some interesting discoveries. With Oracle, for instance, more often than I'd like I find values in date columns referring to the first century AD, because people mistakenly entered dates as MM/DD/YY when Oracle was expecting MM/DD/YYYY (a problem that is much less likely to occur with SQL Server, for which the datetime type starts ticking in 1753, or with MySQL, which accepts dates from January 1, 1000 onward). With numeric columns, we may have values such as –99999999 used to circumvent the fact that a column is mandatory and the value unknown (a design issue, obviously), and so on. Keep in mind that when no other information is available, an optimizer assumes that values are uniformly spread between the lowest and highest values, and may grossly overestimate or underestimate the number of rows returned by a range scan (an inequality condition). As a result, it may decide to use an index when it shouldn't, or it may do the reverse. Correcting nonsensical (or bad data) values is a first step that may put the optimizer back in the saddle again.

What is true of lowest values is also true of highest values. It is common to use "far, far away dates" in a date column to mean "unexpired" or "current." You may also want to check for anomalies that extreme values will tell you nothing about. For instance, two programmers may use different standards for "far, far away dates": one programmer may use December 31, 2999, whereas the other programmer, who has a longer-term vision, uses the year 9999. If you ever encounter such a case, your optimizer will go through great pains to make sense of an overstretched date range. Even with histograms, two different peaks at remote dates may give the optimizer wrong ideas about the distribution. Whenever the optimizer encounters a value that isn't explicitly referenced in a histogram, it must extrapolate its distribution through a continuous function, and a very irregular distribution can lead to extrapolation that is wide of the mark. And needless to say, bugs are just waiting for one developer to test for "his" value when the other developer has set "her" value. You can easily test such a case by running something such as the following (unfortunately, this is a heavy query that you should run against a copy of production data):

```
select extract(year from date_column), count(*)
from my_table
group by extract(year from date_column)
```

Even if only a single date in the distant future is used in your database, using such a remote date to mean current value calls for histograms. Otherwise, as soon as data accumulates and past historical values weigh heavily in the database, every range scan on past values—that is, a query in which you have something such as this:

```
where expired_date < now( )
```

will look to the database, if you have no histogram, as though it is returning, say, a decade out of one or two millennia. If you really had data over one millennium, a decade would represent around 1% of all rows, when you actually want to return perhaps 99% of all rows in your table. The optimizer may want to use an index when a full scan would be more efficient, or it may choose the date column index over another index that *is* effective.

Temporary tables

It is also worth emphasizing the fact that temporary tables, the content of which is, by definition, very volatile, also contribute a lot to making the life of the optimizer spicier. This is particularly true when the only thing that points to their temporary nature is the use of TMP as a prefix or suffix in their name, and when they have not been created as temporary tables, but are only used (nuance) as temporary tables. Unfortunately, helpful hints in the name are totally lost on the optimizer. As a consequence, any table created as a regular table is treated as a regular table, whatever its name, and the fundamental rules apply. If, for instance, statistics were computed when the table was empty, the optimizer will stick to the idea that the table contains zero or very few rows, regardless of what happens, unless you ask the DBMS to keep the table under permanent watch, as you can do with Oracle when you ask for dynamic sampling or SQL Server with auto statistics, which obviously induces overhead.

With some products, temporary tables are visible only from the session that has created them; therefore, the mere presence of a table that contains TMP or TEMP in its name in information_schema.tables deserves investigation (actually, using temporary tables in itself deserves investigation; it can be justified, but sometimes it masks SQL deficiencies).

Indexing Review

Checking whether tables are properly indexed is probably one of the first steps you should take. Still, the results in Table 2-1 should convince you to remove from your mind simple rules such as "it is slow, so we should add indexes." Actually, and rather surprisingly, indexes are more often superfluous than missing.

The first call for improving the performance of an application is generally a matter of straightening up indexing. Indexes are often poorly understood, and in this section I will give you a number of examples to help you better understand how they work and how you can determine whether indexing needs review.

First, there are two types of indexes: indexes that exist as a consequence of database design, and performance indexes.

Indexes that derive from database design are indexes that enforce semantics—indexes on primary keys and unique columns. When you define a constraint on a table that says that one set of columns uniquely identifies a row in the column, you tell the DBMS that it should check, for each insertion, that the row doesn't already exist and that it should return an error if the key duplicates an existing key. Checking for the presence of a key in a tree during insertion is very efficient, and it happens that indexes are, most commonly, tree structures. Those indexes are therefore implementation tricks. Because columns that uniquely identify a row are often used to find and return that row, the implementation trick doubles as a rather convenient performance index, and all is for the best. Some products (such as the InnoDB engine with MySQL) also demand an index on foreign keys, a requirement that neither Oracle nor SQL Server imposes. Although indexing foreign keys is usually recommended as a "good practice," I don't share the view that all foreign keys should be systematically indexed. For one thing, in many cases a particular foreign key is the first column in the primary key, and is already indexed by the primary key index. But the real question is which table should drive the query—the table that contains the foreign key or the referencing table—because the indexing requirements are different in each case. I will discuss queries in much more detail in Chapter 5. For now, let's just say that any index on a foreign key, when it isn't mandatory, should be regarded as a performance index.

Performance indexes are indexes that are created to make searches faster; they include the regular B-tree indexes,* and other types of indexes such as bitmap indexes and hash indexes that you will encounter here and there. (I'm not including full-text indexes in this discussion, which can be very interesting for performance but are somewhat outside the DBMS core.) For the sake of simplicity, I'll stick to regular indexes until further notice.

We have seen that regular indexes sometimes make searches faster, sometimes make searches slower, and sometimes make no difference. Because they are maintained in real time, and because every row insertion, row deletion, or update of an indexed column implies inserting, deleting, or updating index keys, any index that makes no difference for searches is in fact a net performance loss. The loss is more severe when there is heavy contention during insertion, because it is not as easy to spread concurrent inserts over a tree-structured index as it is to spread them over a table; in some cases, writing to indexes is the real bottleneck. Some indexes *are* necessary, but indexing every column *just in case* isn't, to put it mildly, a very smart idea. In practice, poor indexing is much more common than it ought to be.

A Quick Look at Schema Indexing

Checking how tables in a schema are indexed takes a few seconds and can give you clues about existing or pending performance issues. When you don't have thousands of tables in the schema, running a query such as the following can be very instructive:

```
select t.table_name,
       t.table_rows,
       count(distinct s.index_name) indexes,
       case
         when min(s.unicity) is null then 'N'
         when min(s.unicity) = 0 then 'Y'
         else 'N'
       end unique_index,
       sum(case s.columns
             when 1 then 1
             else 0
           end) single_column,
```

---

* I don't want to get into the gory details about index structure; suffice it to say that B-trees are tree structures like any hierarchical structure you can think of, except that they are primarily designed to be self-reorganizing and to grow slowly in depth. Moreover, search times are identical for all keys.

```
      sum(case
              when s.columns is null then 0
              when s.columns = 1 then 0
              else 1
          end) multi_column
 from information_schema.tables t
      left outer join (select table_schema,
                              table_name,
                              index_name,
                              max(seq_in_index) columns,
                              min(non_unique) unicity
                       from  information_schema.statistics
                       where table_schema = schema()
                       group by table_schema,
                                table_name,
                                index_name) s
                  on s.table_schema = t.table_schema
                 and s.table_name = t.table_name
 where t.table_schema = schema()
 group by t.table_name,
          t.table_rows
 order by 3, 1;
```

If you are running Oracle, you may prefer the following:

```
select t.table_name,
       t.num_rows table_rows,
       count(distinct s.index_name) indexes,
       case
         when min(s.unicity) is null then 'N'
         when min(s.unicity) = 'U' then 'Y'
         else 'N'
       end unique_index,
       sum(case s.columns
              when 1 then 1
              else 0
          end) single_column,
       sum(case
              when s.columns is null then 0
              when s.columns = 1 then 0
              else 1
          end) multi_column
 from user_tables t
      left outer join (select ic.table_name,
                              ic.index_name,
                              max(ic.column_position) columns,
                              min(substr(i.uniqueness, 1, 1)) unicity
                       from  user_ind_columns  ic,
                             user_indexes i
                       where i.table_name = ic.table_name
                         and i.index_name = ic.index_name
                       group by ic.table_name,
                                ic.index_name) s
                  on s.table_name = t.table_name
 group by t.table_name,
          t.num_rows
 order by 3, 1;
```

This query displays for each table its number of rows, its number of indexes, whether there is a unique index, and how many indexes are single-column indexes and how many are multicolumn composite indexes. Such a query will not point to every mistake or give you wonderful ideas about how to magically increase performance, but it may provide you with a handful of pointers to potential issues:

Unindexed tables

Tables with a significant number of rows and no index will be easy to spot. Such tables may have their uses, in particular during database loads or massive operations involving data transformation. But they can also be big mistakes.

Tables without any unique index

A table without any unique index usually has no primary key constraint.* No primary key smells bad for the data, because the DBMS will do nothing to prevent you from inserting duplicate rows.

Tables with a single index

Note that having only one unique index on a table is not, in itself, a certificate of good design. If the primary key index is a single-column index, and if this column is a self-incrementing, system-generated number that can be produced by an identity or auto-increment column or by an Oracle sequence, having only one index is almost as bad as having none. The DBMS will not be any more helpful in preventing the insertion of duplicate rows, because whenever you insert the same data again, it will conveniently generate a new number that will make the new row different from all the other ones. Using a system-generated number can be justified as a convenient shorthand key to use elsewhere to reference a row, but in 99% of cases it should be complemented by a second unique index that bears on columns that really (as in "in real life") allow you to state that one row is special and is like no other.

Tables with many indexes

A very large number of indexes is rarely a good sign, except in the context of data marts where it is a justifiable and standard practice. In a regular, operational database (as opposed to a decision-support database), having almost as many indexes as you have columns should raise eyebrows. It is likely that at least some of the indexes are in the best of cases useless, and in the worst of cases harmful. Further investigation is required.

Tables with more than three indexes, all of them single-column indexes

My use of *three* here is arbitrary; you can replace it with *four* if you like. But the point is that having only single-column indexes may be a sign of a rather naive approach to indexing that deserves investigation.

Needless to say, the tables you need to watch more closely are those that you have seen appear again and again in queries that put a significant strain on the system.

---

* In some rare cases, primary key constraints may be enforced using a nonunique index.

A Detailed Investigation

In my experience, besides indexes that are plain useless, the most common indexing mistakes have to do with composite indexes. Composite indexes are indexes on several columns at once. To create the index, the DBMS scans the table, concatenates the values of the columns you want to index, calls the result the "key," associates to this new key the physical address of the row (as you would find a page number in a book index), sorts on the key, and builds on the sorted resultant list a tree that makes it quick and easy to reach a given key. Broadly, this is what a create index statement results in.

When two criteria are always used together, it makes little sense to use separate indexes even if both criteria are reasonably selective: having two indexes means that the optimizer either has to choose which is the best index to use, or has to use each index separately and merge the result—that is, return only those rows associated with both keys. In any case, this will be more complicated, and therefore slower, than simply searching one index (index maintenance during insertions and deletions will also be far less costly with fewer indexes).

To compare composite indexes to single-column indexes, suppose we want to query a table that records English plays from the late 16th and early 17th centuries. This table contains such information as the play title, its genre (comedy, tragedy, history, etc.), and the approximate year it was created. The column listing the genre may contain null values, because many plays were never printed, have been lost, and are known only in accounting books (when they were paid for) or the diaries of contemporaries; moreover, during the English Renaissance, many plays were still medieval in nature and were neither fish nor fowl, but just staged folk stories. Now, suppose we want to return plays that have been identified as comedies in our database and which were created between 1590 and 1595, and suppose we have an index on the genre and an index on the creation year.

I can symbolically represent the entries on the index on the genre in the following fashion:

```
            ->   The Fancies Chaste and Noble     Ford
            ->   A Challenge for Beautie          Heywood
            ->   The Lady's Trial                 Ford
  comedy    ->   A Woman is a Weathercock         Field
  comedy    ->   Amends for Ladies                Field
  comedy    ->   Friar Bacon and Friar Bungay     Greene
  comedy    ->   The Jew of Malta                 Marlowe
  comedy    ->   Mother Bombie                    Lyly
  comedy    ->   The Two Gentlemen of Verona      Shakespeare
  comedy    ->   Summer's Last Will and Testament Nashe
  ... many, many entries ...
  comedy    ->   The Spanish Curate               Massinger,Fletcher
  comedy    ->   Rule a Wife and Have a Wife      Fletcher
  comedy    ->   The Elder Brother                Massinger,Fletcher
  comedy    ->   The Staple of News               Jonson
  comedy    ->   The New Inn                      Jonson
  comedy    ->   The Magnetic Lady                Jonson
  comedy    ->   A Mayden-Head Well Lost          Heywood
  history   ->   Richard III                      Shakespeare
```

```
history    ->    Edward II                             Marlowe
history    ->    Henry VI, part 1                       Nashe,Shakespeare
....
```

This index points to the 87 plays in the table that are identified as comedies. Meanwhile, the index on the creation year looks something like this:

```
...
1589  ->  A Looking Glass for London and England    Greene
1589  ->  Titus Andronicus                          Shakespeare
1590  ->  Mother Bombie                             Lyly
1591  ->  The Two Gentlemen of Verona              Shakespeare
1591  ->  Richard III                               Shakespeare
1592  ->  Summer's Last Will and Testament          Nashe
1592  ->  Edward II                                 Marlowe
1592  ->  Henry VI, part 1                          Nashe,Shakespeare
1592  ->  Henry VI, part 2                          Nashe,Shakespeare
1592  ->  Henry VI, part 3                          Shakespeare,Nashe
1593  ->  The Massacre at Paris                     Marlowe
1594  ->  The Comedy of Errors                      Shakespeare
1594  ->  The Taming of the Shrew                   Shakespeare
1594  ->  The History of Orlando Furioso            Greene
1595  ->  A Midsummer Night's Dream                 Shakespeare
1595  ->  A Pleasant Conceited Comedy of George a Green  Greene
1595  ->  Love's Labour's Lost                      Shakespeare
1595  ->  Richard II                                Shakespeare
1595  ->  The Tragedy of Romeo and Juliet           Shakespeare
1596  ->  A Tale of a Tub                           Jonson
...
```

Here, we have only 17 plays that were created between 1590 and 1595—but a quick look at the titles is enough to tell us that some of the plays are not comedies!

What the DBMS can do, though, is read (from the index on the genre) the 87 references to comedies, read separately the 17 references to plays created between 1590 and 1595, and retain only the references that are common to both sets. Very roughly speaking, the "cost" will be reading 87 plus 17 index entries, and then sorting them to find their intersection.

We can compare this cost to the cost of accessing an index on both genre and creation year. Because the creation year is so much more selective than the genre, we might be tempted to build our composite index on (creation_year, genre) in this order:

```
...
1589|morality   ->  A Looking Glass for London and England  Greene
1589|tragedy    ->  Titus Andronicus                        Shakespeare
1590|comedy     ->  Mother Bombie                           Lyly
1591|comedy     ->  The Two Gentlemen of Verona            Shakespeare
1591|history    ->  Richard III                             Shakespeare
1592|comedy     ->  Summer's Last Will and Testament        Nashe
1592|history    ->  Edward II                               Marlowe
1592|history    ->  Henry VI, part 1                        Nashe,Shakespeare
1592|history    ->  Henry VI, part 2                        Nashe,Shakespeare
1592|history    ->  Henry VI, part 3                        Shakespeare,Nashe
1593|history    ->  The Massacre at Paris                   Marlowe
1594|comedy     ->  The Comedy of Errors                    Shakespeare
```

```
1594|comedy         ->   The Taming of the Shrew                           Shakespeare
1594|tragicomedy    ->   The History of Orlando Furioso                    Greene
1595|comedy         ->   A Midsummer Night's Dream                         Shakespeare
1595|comedy         ->   A Pleasant Conceited Comedy of George a Green     Greene
1595|comedy         ->   Love's Labour's Lost                              Shakespeare
1595|history        ->   Richard II                                        Shakespeare
1595|tragedy        ->   The Tragedy of Romeo and Juliet                   Shakespeare
1596|comedy         ->   A Tale of a Tub                                   Jonson
1596|comedy         ->   The Merchant of Venice                            Shakespeare
...
```

By reading this single index, the DBMS knows what to return and what to discard. However, on this particular query, this index isn't the most efficient one because the first column represents, for all practical purposes, the major sort key for the entries, and the second column the minor key. When the DBMS reads the index, the tree takes it to the first comedy that we know was created in 1590, which is John Lyly's *Mother Bombie*. From there, it reads all entries—comedies, tragedies, tragicomedies, and history plays—until it hits the first 1595 entry that isn't a comedy.

By contrast, if we index on (genre, creation_year), the DBMS can start, again, at *Mother Bombie* but can stop reading index entries when it encounters the first 1596 comedy. Instead of reading 15 index entries, it reads only the 8 entries that really point to rows that will have to be returned from the table:

```
...
comedy|<null>   ->   Amends for Ladies                                 Field
comedy|1589     ->   Friar Bacon and Friar Bungay                      Greene
comedy|1589     ->   The Jew of Malta                                  Marlowe
comedy|1590     ->   Mother Bombie                                     Lyly
comedy|1591     ->   The Two Gentlemen of Verona                       Shakespeare
comedy|1592     ->   Summer's Last Will and Testament                  Nashe
comedy|1594     ->   The Comedy of Errors                              Shakespeare
comedy|1594     ->   The Taming of the Shrew                           Shakespeare
comedy|1595     ->   A Midsummer Night's Dream                         Shakespeare
comedy|1595     ->   A Pleasant Conceited Comedy of George a Green     Greene
comedy|1595     ->   Love's Labour's Lost                              Shakespeare
comedy|1596     ->   A Tale of a Tub                                   Jonson
comedy|1596     ->   The Merchant of Venice                            Shakespeare
comedy|1597     ->   An Humorous Day's Mirth                           Chapman
comedy|1597     ->   The Case is Altered                               Jonson
comedy|1597     ->   The Merry Wives of Windsor                        Shakespeare
comedy|1597     ->   The Two Angry Women of Abington                   Porter
..
```

Of course, in this example, it wouldn't make much of a difference, but on some very big tables, the fact that one index goes straight to the point while the other muses would be noticeable. When a condition specifies a range condition (as in creation_year between 1590 and 1595) or a mere inequality on a column that belongs to a composite index, searches are faster when this column appears in the index after columns on which there is an equality condition (as in genre = 'comedy').

The bad news is that we cannot do everything we want with indexes. If we have an index on (genre, creation_year) and a frequent type of query happens to be "What plays were created in 1597?" our index will be of dubious use. The DBMS may choose to scan the index and jump from genre to genre (including the genre that is unknown or indefinable) to find a range of entries from the class of 1597. Or, because of the more complicated structure of indexes, the DBMS may consider it less costly and therefore faster to scan the table.

If the Elizabethan scholars I have to deal with are a rather impatient bunch and are as rowdy as some of the (rather colorful) playwrights from the era, my choice would probably be to have two indexes. Because this type of data will not be updated heavily, it makes sense to have on the one hand an index on (genre, creation_year) and on the other a single-column index on creation_year so that all queries run fast: queries that include the genre and queries that don't.

This kind of reasoning illustrates that it is very easy for indexing to be slightly wrong, but slightly wrong sometimes means a big performance penalty. The basic problem with composite indexes is always the order of columns. Suppose we have an index on columns C1, C2, and C3, in that order. Having a condition such as this:

```
where C1 = value1
  and C2 = value2
  and C3 = value3
```

is pretty much the same as asking you to find all the words in the dictionary whose first letter is *i*, second letter is *d*, and third letter is *e*—you will go straight to *idea* and read all the words up to (but excluding) *idiocy*. Now, suppose the condition is as follows:

```
where C2 = value2
  and C3 = value3
```

The equivalent dictionary search would be to find all the words with *d* and *e* as second and third letters. This is a much more difficult search to perform, because now we must check all sections from *A* to *Z* (not wasting too much time, perhaps, on *Q* and *X*) and look for the matching words.

As a final example, suppose now that we have the following:

```
where C1 = value1
  and C3 = value3
```

This is the same as saying "give me the words that start with *i*, the third letter of which is *e*." Knowing the first letter, we can make a reasonable use of the index, but in that case, we must scan all words starting with *i*, checking the third letter as we encounter it each time, whereas if we had been given the first and second letters, our search would have been far more efficient.

As you can see, with composite indexes it's exactly like knowing the first letters in a word to search a dictionary: if you miss a value to match for the first column, you cannot do much with your index. If you are given the values of the first column, even if you don't know the values for *all* columns, you can make reasonably efficient use of your index—how efficient depends on the selectivity of the columns for which a value is provided.

But as soon as a column is not referenced in the where clause, you cannot use the columns that follow it in the index, even when they are referenced in the where clause with equality conditions. Many poor uses of indexes come from incorrect ordering, where columns that contain important criteria are "buried" after columns that rarely appear in searches.

When reviewing indexes, you should therefore check a number of things:

- Single-column indexes on columns that also appear in the first position of a composite index are redundant, because the composite index can be used, perhaps a tad less efficiently, but efficiently nonetheless. You will often find redundant indexing in a case such as the classic enrollment of students: one student can take several courses, and several students attend one course. Therefore, an enrollment table will link a studentid to a courseid; the primary key for this table will be the studentid, plus the courseid, plus probably the term. But studentid and courseid are also foreign keys, respectively pointing to a students and a courses table. If you systematically index all foreign keys, you'll create an index on courseid (fine) and an index on studentid (redundant with the primary key, which starts with this column). There will be no performance penalty when querying, but there will be one when inserting rows.

- Indexes (particularly if they aren't defined as unique!) which are supersets of the primary key should come with rock-solid justification (there is no justification for not being defined as unique). Sometimes such indexes are created so as to find all the data required by a query in the index, and spare an access to the table itself. But it must be validated.

- Columns that *always* appear simultaneously in the where clause should be indexed by a composite index, not by separate single-column indexes.

- When columns *often* appear together, the columns that may appear without the others should appear first in a composite index, provided that they are selective enough to make the index search more efficient than a full scan. If all columns may appear separately and are reasonably selective, it makes sense to separately index some columns that don't appear in the first position in a composite index.

- You should check that whenever there is a range condition on a column that is always or very commonly associated with equality conditions on other columns, the latter columns appear first in the composite index.

- B-tree indexes on low cardinality columns are pointless if values are uniformly distributed, or if there is no value histogram (because then the optimizer assumes that values are uniformly distributed). If you have a gender column in the students table, for instance, it usually makes no sense to index it, because you can expect roughly as many male as female students in your population; you don't want to use an index to retrieve 50% of the rows. The rationale may be different, though, in a military academy where female students represent a small percentage of all cadets, and where being female is a selective criterion. But then, a value histogram is required for the DBMS to know it.

Indexes That Blur the Rules

As always, there are exceptions to general guidelines, mostly because of particular index types.

Bitmap indexes

Oracle, for instance, allows bitmap indexes, which are more particularly designed for decision-support systems. Bitmap indexes are useful, primarily for data that may be massively inserted but not—or rarely—updated (their weak point is that they poorly manage contention between concurrent sessions), and secondarily for columns with a low number of distinct values. The idea behind bitmap indexes is that if you have a number of conditions on several low-cardinality columns, combining bitmaps through logical ORs and ANDs will reduce the number of candidate rows very quickly and very efficiently. Although the implementation is different, the basic principle of bitmap indexes is closer to operations you can perform with full-text indexes* than to regular B-tree indexes, except that, as with regular B-tree indexes, the following is true:

- Bitmap indexes truly index column values, not parts of a column, like full-text indexes.
- Bitmap indexes participate fully in relational operations such as joins.
- Bitmap indexes are maintained (with the restrictions previously mentioned) in real time.

If you ever encounter bitmap indexes, follow these rules:

- If the system is transactional, do not use bitmap indexes on heavily updated tables.
- Do not isolate bitmap indexes. The power of bitmap indexes resides in how you combine and merge them. If you have a single bitmap index among several regular B-tree indexes, the optimizer will have trouble using this lone bitmap index efficiently.

Clustered indexes

You find another major type of exception in clustered indexes, which I've already mentioned more than once. Clustered indexes force the rows in the table to be stored in the same order as the keys in the index. Clustered indexes are a staple feature of both SQL Server and MySQL (with a storage engine such as InnoDB), and they have close cousins in Oracle's index-organized tables. In clustered indexes, keys take you directly to the data, not to the address of the data, because table and index are combined, which also saves storage. Because updating the key would mean physically moving the whole row to store it at the now-suitable location, the clustered index (obviously there can be only one per table) will usually be the primary key (don't tell me you update your primary keys) or a primary key candidate—that is, a combination of mandatory and unique columns.

---

* Full-text indexes are an integral part of SQL Server and MySQL, and they are available, although not as closely integrated, with Oracle.

There is one thing to check about clustered indexes: is the order of the rows appropriate for what you want to do? The three advantages of clustered indexes are that you're taken directly to the rows, rows are grouped together (as the name implies) for contiguous values of the key column(s), and they are presorted, which can save the DBMS a lot of work in the following scenarios:

- When using order by clauses

- When using group by clauses

- When using ranking functions such as rank( ) or row_number( )

It may also prove helpful with joins. If the columns that are supposed to match are in the same order in two tables, which may happen if the primary key of the first table is the first column in the composite primary key of the second table, finding correspondences is easy.

Also note that if you systematically use as the primary key a meaningless identity column (the auto-increment column for MySQL users) that neither is used as a sort key nor is a criterion for grouping or for joining, your clustered table brings no advantage over a regular table.

Indexes on expressions

Lastly, a brief word about indexes on computed columns (sometimes known as *function-based indexes*). As the example of a dictionary search pointed out, as soon as you are not searching for a word but a transformation of a word (such as "words that contain an *a* in the third position"), the only use of the dictionary will be as a word list that you'll have to scan, without any hope of searching it effectively. If you apply a function to a column and compare it to a constant, you make the index on this column unusable, which is why you should apply the inverse function to the constant instead. But if you feel inspired by Erato or Euterpe* and wonder what rhymes with "database," there is one solution: using a rhyming dictionary (although to be brutally honest, I fear I won't much enjoy reading your poetry). In a rhyming dictionary, entries are ordered differently from standard alphabetical order. Indexes on computed columns are to indexes on "raw" columns what rhyming dictionaries are to regular dictionaries. There is a restriction, however: the expression that is indexed must be deterministic—that is, it must always return the same value when fed the same arguments. Before rushing to redefine all the lookup functions that make your performances miserable as deterministic functions (because this is something that you declare for the instruction of the optimizer when you create your function), please read the next chapter. There may be interesting side effects. But indexes on computed columns or (truly) deterministic functions have saved more than one poorly designed and poorly written application.

---

* Both muses (lesser goddesses) of poetry in Greek mythology.

Parsing and Bind Variables

Besides statistics and indexing—both of which are independent from the application code proper—one point, which *is* directly relevant to the application code, should also be checked at a very early stage: whether statements are hardcoded or softcoded. *Hardcoded statements* are statements in which all constants are an integral part of the statement; *softcoded statements* are statements in which constants with a high degree of variability between successive executions are passed as arguments. I pointed out in Chapter 1 that hardcoded statements make it much more difficult to get a true idea of what keeps the DBMS server busy, and therefore, they may make us focus on the wrong issues if we aren't careful enough.

They may also inflict a serious performance penalty (this is particularly true with Oracle). To understand what loads a server, we must understand what happens at every stage, and a good place to start is to describe what happens when we issue an SQL statement. From a development viewpoint, we write an SQL statement to a character string variable. This statement may be a constant, or it may be dynamically built by the program. Then we call a function that executes the statement. We check the error code, and if there is no error and the statement was a select statement, we loop and fetch rows using another function until it returns nothing.

But what is happening on the server side?

SQL is a language specialized in storing, fetching, and modifying data. Like all languages, it must be translated to machine code, or at least to some intermediate, basic code. However, the translation is a heavier operation than with most languages. Consider the translation of synonyms, the control of access rights to tables, the interpretation of * in select *, and so on. All of these operations will require application of recursive queries to the data dictionary. Worse, consider the role played by the optimizer, and the choice of the best execution plan: identifying indexes, checking whether they are usable and beneficial, computing in which order to visit the numerous tables referenced in a complex join, the inclusion of views in an already daunting query, and so forth. Parsing an SQL query is a very complex, and therefore, costly operation. The less you do it, the better.

How to Detect Parsing Issues

There is an easier way to check for parsing issues than trying to sample what is being executed, provided that you have the privileges to query the right system views. With Oracle, v$ssystat will tell you all there is to know, including how much CPU time the DBMS has used and parsing has consumed since startup:

```
select sum(case name
            when 'execute count' then value
            else 0
         end) executions,
       sum(case name
            when 'parse count (hard)' then value
            else 0
```

```
                end) hard_parse,
        round(100 * sum(case name
                            when 'parse count (hard)' then value
                            else 0
                        end) /
                    sum(case name
                            when 'execute count' then value
                            else 0
                        end), 1) pct_hardcoded,
        round(100 * sum(case name
                            when 'parse time cpu' then value
                            else 0
                        end) /
                    sum(case name
                            when 'CPU used by this session' then value
                            else 0
                        end), 1) pct_cpu
    from v$sysstat
    where name in ('parse time cpu',
                    'parse count (hard)',
                    'CPU used by this session',
                    'execute count');
```

With MySQL, information_schema.global_status will provide you with very similar information, but for CPU consumption:

```
select x.queries_and_dml,
        x.queries_and_dml - x.executed_prepared_stmt hard_coded,
        x.prepared_stmt,
        round(100 * (x.queries_and_dml - x.executed_prepared_stmt)
                    / x.queries_and_dml,1) pct_hardcoded
from (select sum(case variable_name
                    when 'COM_STMT_EXECUTE' then 0
                    when 'COM_STMT_PREPARE' then 0
                    else cast(variable_value as unsigned)
                end) as queries_and_dml,
            sum(case variable_name
                    when 'COM_STMT_PREPARE' then cast(variable_value as unsigned)
                    else 0
                end) as prepared_stmt,
            sum(case variable_name
                    when 'COM_STMT_EXECUTE' then cast(variable_value as unsigned)
                    else 0
                end) as executed_prepared_stmt
        from information_schema.global_status
        where variable_name in ('COM_INSERT',
                                'COM_DELETE',
                                'COM_DELETE_MULTI',
                                'COM_INSERT_SELECT',
                                'COM_REPLACE',
                                'COM_REPLACE_SELECT',
                                'COM_SELECT',
                                'COM_STMT_EXECUTE',
                                'COM_STMT_PREPARE',
                                'COM_UPDATE',
                                'COM_UPDATE_MULTI')) x;
```

Note that because all values are cumulative, if you want to control a particular piece of the program you should take before and after snapshots and recompute the ratios.

SQL Server provides some parsing frequency counters directly. To give you an idea about the figures you should expect, in a corporate environment I have always seen with Oracle a ratio of parses to executions in the vicinity of 3% to 4% when this aspect of coding was satisfactory. I would have no qualms with 8% or 9%, but of course, the real question is how much this parsing is costing us (although the CPU indication provided by Oracle is a very good indicator), and, by derivation, how much we can hope to gain by correcting the code.

Estimating Performance Loss Due to Parsing

To get an estimate of how much we can lose to parsing, I ran a very simple test against Oracle, SQL Server, and MySQL. More specifically, I ran against one of the tables from the Chapter 1 example a JDBC program called *HardCoded.java*, of which the most important part is the following snippet:

```
start = System.currentTimeMillis( );
try {
    long      txid;
    float     amount;
    Statement st = con.createStatement( );
    ResultSet rs;
    String    txt;

    for (txid - 1000; txid <= 101000; txid++){
        txt = "select amount"
            + " from transactions"
            + " where txid=" + Long.toString(txid);
        rs = st.executeQuery(txt);
        if (rs.next( )) {
            amount = rs.getFloat(1);
        }
    }
    rs.close( );
    st.close( );
} catch(SQLException ex){
      System.err.println("==> SQLException: ");
      while (ex != null) {
          System.out.println("Message:    " + ex.getMessage ( ));
          System.out.println("SQLState:   " + ex.getSQLState ( ));
          System.out.println("ErrorCode: " + ex.getErrorCode ( ));
          ex = ex.getNextException( );
          System.out.println("");
      }
}
stop = System.currentTimeMillis( );
System.out.println("HardCoded - Elapsed (ms)\t" + (stop - start));
```

This program executes 100,000 times in a loop a simple query that fetches a value from the single row associated with the primary key value; you'll notice that the loop index is converted to a string, and then it is merely concatenated to the text of the query before the statement is passed to the DBMS server for execution.

If you repeatedly execute a query, it makes a lot of sense to write it as you would write a function: you want a piece of code that takes parameters and is executed repeatedly with different arguments (there is nothing peculiar to SQL here; we could say the same of any language). Whenever you execute a similar statement with constants that vary with every execution, you should not "hardcode" those constants, but rather proceed in three steps:

1. Prepare a statement with place markers for the constants.

2. Bind values to the statements—that is, provide pointers to variables that will be substituted at runtime with the place markers (hence the name of *bind variable* commonly used with Oracle).

3. Execute the statement.

When you need to reexecute the statement with different values, all you need to do is to assign new values to the variables and repeat step 3.

I therefore rewrote *HardCoded.java*, using a prepared statement instead of the dynamically built hardcoded one, but in two different ways:

* In *FirmCoded.java* I created in each iteration of the loop a new prepared statement with a placeholder for txid, bound the current value of txid to the statement, executed it, fetched the amount value, and closed the statement before incrementing txid.

* In *SoftCoded.java* I created the prepared statement once, and just changed the parameter value before reexecuting the statement and fetching the amount value in the loop.

I plotted in Figure 2-1 the relative performance of *FirmCoded* and *SoftCoded* compared to *HardCoded* for each database management system in my scope.

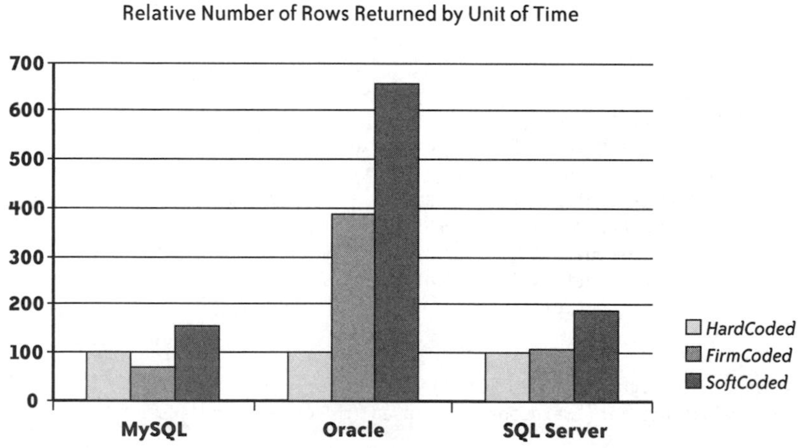

FIGURE 2-1. The performance penalty of hardcoding

The differences are very interesting to consider, particularly in the case of *FirmCoded.java*: with Oracle there is a big performance boost, whereas with MySQL there is a noticeable performance penalty. Why is that? Actually, the MySQL Connector/J (the JDBC driver) documentation states that prepared statements are implemented by the driver and the same documentation makes a difference between client-side prepared statements and server-side prepared statements. It is not, actually, a language or driver issue: I rewrote all three programs in C, and although everything ran faster than in Java, the performance ratio was strictly identical among *HardCoded*, *FirmCoded*, and *SoftCoded*. The difference between MySQL and Oracle lies in the way the server caches statements. MySQL caches query results: if identical queries that return few rows are executed often (which is typically the pattern we can see on a popular website that uses a MySQL-based content management system, or CMS), the query is executed once, its result is cached, and as long as the table isn't modified, the result is later returned from the cache every time the same query is handed to the server. Oracle also has a query cache, although it has been introduced belatedly (with Oracle 11*g*); however, for decades it has used a statement cache, where execution plans, instead of results, are saved. If a similar (byte for byte) query has already been executed against the same tables and is still in the cache, it is reused even by another session as long as the environment is identical.*

With Oracle, each time a new query is passed to the server, the query is checksummed, the environment is controlled, and the cache is searched; if a similar query is found, we just have this "soft parse" and the query is executed. Otherwise, the real parsing operation takes place and we have a costly "hard parse." In *FirmCoded*, we replace hard parses with soft parses, and in *SoftCoded* we get rid of soft parses altogether. If I run the various programs through the Unix time command, as I did in Figure 2-2, I can see that the difference in elapsed time takes place entirely on the server side, because CPU consumption on the client side (the sum of sys and user) remains more or less the same. Actually, because *FirmCoded* executes multiple allocations and de-allocations of a prepared statement object, it is the program variant that consumes the most resources on the client side.

By contrast, with MySQL when we prepare the statement we associate it with a particular plan, but if the query cache is active (it isn't by default), the checksumming takes place after parameters have been substituted to see whether the result can be fetched from the cache. And as long as the bind variables are different, a statement that is "prepared" is hard-parsed. As a result, in *FirmCoded*, where statements are prepared to be executed only once, there is no performance benefit at all. We plainly see the performance penalty due to a costlier client side. As soon as the statement is reexecuted with different values, as is the case with *SoftCoded*, the link between the statement to run and its execution plan is preserved, and there is a significant performance benefit, if not quite as spectacular as with Oracle.

* A session can locally tweak some parameters that affect the way a statement will be executed.

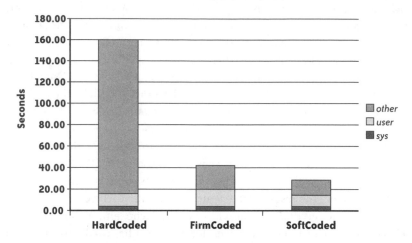

Where Time Is Spent with Oracle

FIGURE 2-2. What the Unix time command says about where time is spent

SQL Server lies somewhere in between, and even if in the light of results it looks closer to MySQL than to Oracle, its internal mechanisms are actually much closer to Oracle (execution plans can be shared). What blurs the picture is the fact that, on as simple a query as in my example, SQL Server performs *simple parameterization* of the hardcoded statement— when it analyzes a hardcoded statement and if it looks safe enough (with a primary key, it's pretty safe), the DBMS just rips the constant off and passes it as a parameter. In the case of SQL Server, the hardcoded statements were, through internal DBMS mechanisms, transmogrified into something similar to the prepared statements of *FirmCoded.java*; as a result, the original performance was in fact much better than with Oracle. *FirmCoded.java* was slightly better, though, because each time we prepared the statement, we saved that additional processing of ripping constant values off before checking whether the statement had already been executed. I should emphasize, though, that simple parameterization is not performed aggressively, but quite the contrary, and therefore it "works" in only simple cases.

The first (and intermediate) conclusion is that hardcoding statements borders on the suicidal with Oracle, is to be avoided with SQL Server, and inflicts a severe performance penalty on any DBMS whenever a single session repeatedly runs statements that have the same pattern.

Somehow, using prepared statements with Oracle and with SQL Server is altruistic: if all sessions use prepared statements, everyone benefits, because only one session will go through the hard parse. By contrast, with MySQL it's a more selfish affair: one session will significantly benefit (50% in my example) if it reexecutes the same query, but other sessions will not. Beware that I am talking here of database sessions; if you are using an application server that pools several user sessions and you make them share a smaller number of database sessions, user sessions may mutually benefit.

Correcting Parsing Issues

Even developers with some experience often end up hardcoding statements when their statements are dynamically built on the fly—it just seems so natural to concatenate values after concatenating pieces of SQL code.

First, when you concatenate constant values, and particularly strings entered into web application forms, you're taking a huge risk if you're not extra careful (if you've never heard *SQL* being associated with *injection*, it is more than time to use your favorite web search engine).

Second, many developers seem to believe that hardcoding a statement doesn't make much difference when "everything is so dynamic," especially as there are practical limits on the number of prepared statements. But even when users can pick any number of criteria among numerous possibilities, the number of combinations can be big (it's 2 raised to the power of the number of criteria), but wide arrays of possible combinations are usually compounded by the fact that some combinations are extremely popular and others are very rarely used. As a result, the real diversity comes from the values that are entered and associated to a criterion, much more than from the choice of criteria.

Switching from hardcoded to "softcoded" statements doesn't usually require much effort. When using a prepared statement, the previous code snippet for the hardcoded statement appears as follows:

```
start = System.currentTimeMillis();
try {
    long      txid;
    float     amount;
    PreparedStatement st = con.prepareStatement("select amount"
                                    + " from transactions"
                                    + " where txid=?");
    ResultSet rs;

    for (txid = 1000; txid <= 101000; txid++){
        st.setLong(1, txid);
        rs = st.executeQuery();
        if (rs.next()) {
            amount = rs.getFloat(1);
        }
    }
    rs.close();
    st.close();
} catch(SQLException ex){
        System.err.println("==> SQLException: ");
        while (ex != null) {
            System.out.println("Message:   " + ex.getMessage ());
            System.out.println("SQLState:  " + ex.getSQLState ());
            System.out.println("ErrorCode: " + ex.getErrorCode ());
            ex = ex.getNextException();
            System.out.println("");
        }
}
stop = System.currentTimeMillis();
System.out.println("SoftCoded - Elapsed (ms)\t" + (stop - start));
```

Modifying the code is very easy when, as in this case, the number of values to "parameter-ize" is constant. The difficulty, though, is that when statements are dynamically built, usually the number of conditions varies, and as a matter of consequence the number of candidate parameters varies with it. It would be very convenient if you could concatenate a piece of SQL code that contains a place marker, bind the matching variable, and go on your way. Unfortunately, this isn't how it works (and you would run into difficulties when reexecuting the statement, anyway): the statement is first prepared and then the values bound to it, but you cannot prepare the statement before it is fully built.

However, because the building of a statement is usually directed by fields that were entered by a user, it isn't very difficult to run twice through the list of fields—once to build the statement with placeholders and once to bind the actual values to placeholders.

WHAT IF ONE VALUE MUST BE BOUND SEVERAL TIMES?

Some languages allow you to use a named marker (e.g., if you are coding in C# or Visual Basic, you can call a place marker @name). If you refer several times to the variable in your statement, you need, in a .NET context, to call the SqlCommand method Parameters.AddWithValue("@name", ...) just once to associate the same value to all occurrences of @name in the statement. Some languages, though, allow only a generic place marker (such as ?), and it's the position of place markers that counts. When each parameter occurs only once, it doesn't make much difference with named place markers. But when you need to reference a single parameter several times, binding it as many times as it appears may become a clumsy affair. For instance, if you want to get values as of a particular date, you can generate a statement that looks like this:

```
select whatever
from list of tables
where ...
    and effective_date <= ?
    and until_date > ?
 ...
```

where the ? placeholder is supposed to take, in both cases, the same value.

Often you can easily work around such a difficulty by cheating a little, and pushing inside the query a dummy subquery that allows you to refer to what it returns. Thus, on Oracle:

```
select whatever
from list of tables
    , (select ?  as val from dual) as mydate
where ...
    and effective_date <= mydate.val
    and until_date > mydate.val
 ...
```

Replacing hardcoded statements with softcoded statements isn't an enormous rewriting effort, but it isn't something you can do mechanically either, which is why people are often tempted by the easiest solution of letting the DBMS do the job.

Correcting Parsing Issues the Lazy Way

You have seen that SQL Server attempts to correct parsing issues on its own. This attempt is timid, and you can make it much more daring by setting the database PARAMETERIZATION parameter to FORCED. As you might have expected, an equivalent feature exists in Oracle with the CURSOR_SHARING parameter, the default value of which is EXACT (i.e., reuse execution plans only when statements are strictly identical), but can be set to SIMILAR (which is very close to the default value of SIMPLE for the SQL Server PARAMETERIZATION parameter) or to FORCE. There are, though, a number of minor differences; for instance, the parameter can be set with Oracle either database-wide* or within the scope of a session. Oracle also behaves slightly more aggressively, when asked to do so, than SQL Server. For instance, SQL Server would leave the following code snippet alone:

```
and char_column like 'pattern%'
```

whereas Oracle will turn it into this:

```
and char_column like :"SYS_B_n" || '%'
```

Similarly, SQL Server will leave a statement that already contains at least a single parameter to its own destiny, whereas Oracle will happily parameterize it further. But by and large, the idea behind the feature is the same: having the DBMS do what developers should have done in the first place.

I ran my tests a second time with Oracle, after executing (with the privileges of a database administrator) the following command:

```
alter system set cursor_sharing=similar;
```

As I indicated, this setting instructs Oracle to behave as SQL Server does without having to be told. And if I replace the figures previously obtained with Oracle with the new result, I get improvement ratios that are much more in line with what we got with SQL Server, because for both SQL Server and Oracle, if statements are still hardcoded in the program in *HardCoded.java*, they are no longer hardcoded when they are executed (see Figure 2-3).

From a practical point of view, if we are running on Oracle and we notice parsing issues, one of our first sanity checks should be to verify the setting of the cursor_sharing parameter and, if it happens to be exact, to set it to similar and examine whether it improves performance.

---

* Don't forget that *database* doesn't mean the same as in the SQL Server and MySQL worlds, where you would talk of a *server*.

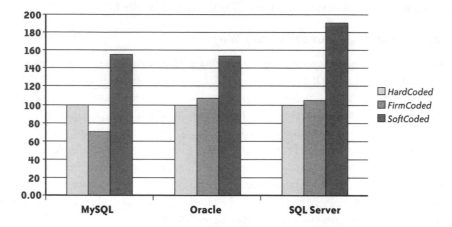

FIGURE 2-3. Performance penalty with behind-the-scenes softening enabled

Correcting Parsing Issues the Proper Way

Why bother (besides to protect against SQL injection) with using prepared statements if the DBMS can do it for us? First, we can see with both the Oracle and SQL Server examples that if the automated parameterization process is only slightly less efficient than prepared statements, statements that are prepared once and are executed many times are at least 1.5 times faster than statements that are parameterized before each execution. Second, having AutoCorrect under the Tools option of the menu bar in your word processor doesn't mean you should happily ignore grammar and let auto-correction go amiss. Third, the less aggressive type of system-enabled parameterization errs on the side of caution and will, with real-world applications, alleviate only some of the pain; the more aggressive type can throw you into deep trouble.

You should be careful not to replace every constant with a place marker. When you have a column with a low cardinality (i.e., a small number of different values), passing the values at runtime can actually be harmful if the values are not uniformly distributed; in plain English, you can have bad surprises if one value is very common and the others are comparatively rare (a common occurrence with columns that record a status). The case when it hurts is when the column with few values is indexed because the rare values are extremely selective. When the optimizer decides what the best execution plan is likely to be, and if, when scanning the statement, it encounters something such as the following:

```
and status = ?
```

and if the status column is indexed, it has to decide whether it should be using this index (possibly giving it preference over another index). In a join, it can influence the decision of visiting the table to which status belongs before others. At any point, the goal of the optimizer is to funnel what will become the result set as quickly as possible, which means filtering out the rows that cannot possibly belong to the result set as early as possible.

The problem with place markers is that they provide no clue about the actual value that will be passed at runtime. At this stage, there are several possibilities, which depend on what the optimizer knows about the data (statistics that are often routinely collected as part of database administration):

- No statistics have ever been collected, and the optimizer knows nothing at all about what the column contains. In that case, the only thing it knows is that the index isn't unique. If the optimizer has the choice between a nonunique index and a unique index, it will prefer the unique index because one key value can, at most, return one row with a unique index. If the optimizer only has a choice between nonunique indexes, it depends on your luck.* Hence, the importance of statistics.

- Statistics are not extremely precise, and all the optimizer knows is that the column contains few distinct values. In such a case, it will generally ignore the index, which can be quite unfortunate when the condition on status happens to be most selective.

- Statistics are precise, and the optimizer also knows, through frequency histograms, that some values are very selective and others are not selective at all. When confronted with the place marker, the optimizer will have to choose from the following:

  — Unbridled optimism, or assuming that the value that is passed will always be very selective, and therefore, favoring an execution plan that gives preeminence to the condition on status. In spite of the nice alliteration, you are unlikely to meet optimistic optimizers, because optimism can backfire.

  — Playing it safe, which means ignoring the index, because statistically, it is likely to be of dubious use. We are back to the case where the optimizer knows only that there are few distinct values and nothing else, and once again, this may be the wrong tactic when the condition on status happens to be the most selective one in the query.

  — Being clever, which means indiscreetly peeping at the value that is passed the first time (this is known as *bind variable peeking* with Oracle). If the value is selective, the index will be used; if not, the index will be ignored. This is all very good, but what if in the morning we use selective values, and then the pattern of queries changes during the day and we end up querying with the most common value later on? Or what if the reverse occurs? What if for some reason a query happens to be parsed again, with values leading to a totally different execution plan, which will be applied for a large number of executions? In that case, users will witness a seemingly random behavior of queries—sometimes fast and sometimes slow. This is rarely a popular query behavior with end-users.

  — Being even cleverer and, knowing that there may be a problem with one column, checking this column value each time (in practice, this means behaving as though this value were hardcoded).

---

* All right, luck can sometimes be helped.

As you see, place markers are a big problem for optimizers when they take the place of values that are compared to indexed columns containing a small number of unevenly distributed values. Sometimes optimizers will make the right choice, but very often, even when they try to be clever, they will make the wrong bet, or they will select in a seemingly erratic way a plan that may in some cases stand out as very bad.

For low-cardinality columns storing unevenly distributed values, the best way to code, if the distribution of data is reasonably static and there is no risk of SQL injection, is by far to hardcode the values they are compared to in a where clause. Conversely, all uniformly distributed values that change between successive executions *must* be passed as arguments.

Handling Lists in Prepared Statements

Unfortunately, one case occurs often (particularly in dynamically built statements) but is particularly tricky to handle when you are serious about properly preparing statements: in (...) clauses, where the ... is a comma-separated list, not a subquery.

In some cases, in clauses are easy to deal with:

- When we are checking a status column or any column that can take one of a few possible values, the in clause should stay hardcoded for the same reason you just saw.

- When there is a high variability of values, but when the number of items in the list is constant, we can easily use prepared statements as usual.

The difficulty arises when the values vary wildly, and the number of items in the list varies wildly, too. Even if you use prepared statements and carefully use markers for each value in the list, two statements that differ only in terms of the number of items in the list are distinct statements that need to be parsed separately. With prepared statements, there is no notion of the "variable list of arguments" that some languages allow.

Lists wouldn't be too much of an issue if all you had was a single condition in the where clause with an in criterion taking its values from a drop-down box in an HTML form; even if you can select multiple entries, the number of items you may have in your list is limited, and it is not a big deal to have, say, 10 different statements in the cache: one for a single-value list, one for a two-value list, and so on up to a 10-value list.

But now suppose that this list is just one out of five different criteria that can be dynamically added to build up the query. You must remember that having five possible criteria means we can have 32 (2^5) combinations, and having 32 different prepared statements is perfectly reasonable. But if one of these five criteria is a list that can take any number of values between 1 and 10, that list is, by itself, equivalent to 10 criteria, and our five criteria are actually equivalent to 14. As such, $2^{14} = 16,284$, and we no longer are in the same order of magnitude as before. And of course, the bigger the maximum possible number of items in the list, the worse the number of combinations. Possibilities explode, and the benefit of using prepared statements dwindles.

With this in mind, there are three ways to handle lists in prepared statements, and I discuss them in the next three subsections.

Passing the list as a single variable

By using some tricky SQL, you can split a string and make it look like a table that can be selected from or joined to other tables later. To explain further I will use a simple example in MySQL that you can easily adapt to another SQL dialect. Suppose our program is called by an HTML form in which there is a drop-down list from which you can select multiple values. All you know is that 10 values, at most, can be returned.

The first operation is to concatenate all selected values into a string, using a separator (in this case, a comma), and to both prefix and postfix the list with the same separator, as in this example:

```
',Doc,Grumpy,Happy,Sneezy,Bashful,Sleepy,Dopey,'
```

This string will be my parameter. From here, I will multiply this string as many times as the maximum number of items I expect, by using a Cartesian join as follows:

```
select pivot.n, list.val
from (select 1 as n
      union all
      select 2 as n
      union all
      select 3 as n
      union all
      select 4 as n
      union all
      select 5 as n
      union all
      select 6 as n
      union all
      select 7 as n
      union all
      select 8 as n
      union all
      select 9 as n
      union all
      select 10 as n) pivot,
     (select ? val) as list;
```

There are several ways to obtain something similar to pivot. For instance, I could use an ad hoc table for a larger number of rows. If I substitute the string to the placeholder and run the query, I get the following result:

```
mysql> \. list0.sql
+----+------------------------------------------------+
| n  | val                                            |
+----+------------------------------------------------+
|  1 | ,Doc,Grumpy,Happy,Sneezy,Bashful,Sleepy,Dopey, |
|  2 | ,Doc,Grumpy,Happy,Sneezy,Bashful,Sleepy,Dopey, |
|  3 | ,Doc,Grumpy,Happy,Sneezy,Bashful,Sleepy,Dopey, |
|  4 | ,Doc,Grumpy,Happy,Sneezy,Bashful,Sleepy,Dopey, |
|  5 | ,Doc,Grumpy,Happy,Sneezy,Bashful,Sleepy,Dopey, |
|  6 | ,Doc,Grumpy,Happy,Sneezy,Bashful,Sleepy,Dopey, |
|  7 | ,Doc,Grumpy,Happy,Sneezy,Bashful,Sleepy,Dopey, |
|  8 | ,Doc,Grumpy,Happy,Sneezy,Bashful,Sleepy,Dopey, |
```

```
|  9 | ,Doc,Grumpy,Happy,Sneezy,Bashful,Sleepy,Dopey, |
| 10 | ,Doc,Grumpy,Happy,Sneezy,Bashful,Sleepy,Dopey, |
+----+-------------------------------------------------+
10 rows in set (0.00 sec)
```

However, there are only seven items in my list. Therefore, I must limit the number of rows to the number of items. The simplest way to count the items is to compute the length of the list, remove all separators, compute the new length, and derive the number of separators from the difference. Because by construction I have one more separator than number of items, I easily limit my output to the right number of rows by adding the following condition to my query:

```
where pivot.n < length(list.val) - length(replace(list.val, ',', ''));
```

Now, I want the first item on the first row, the second item on the second row, and so on. If I rewrite my query as shown here:

```
select pivot.n, substring_index(list.val, ',', 1 + pivot.n)
from (select 1 as n
      union all
      select 2 as n
      union all
      select 3 as n
      union all
      select 4 as n
      union all
      select 5 as n
      union all
      select 6 as n
      union all
      select 7 as n
      union all
      select 8 as n
      union all
      select 9 as n
      union all
      select 10 as n) pivot,
    (select ? val) as list
where pivot.n < length(list.val) - length(replace(list.val, ',', ''));
```

I get the following result with my example string:

```
mysql> \. list2.sql
+---+-------------------------------------------------+
| n | substring_index(list.val, ',', 1 + pivot.n)     |
+---+-------------------------------------------------+
| 1 | ,Doc                                            |
| 2 | ,Doc,Grumpy                                     |
| 3 | ,Doc,Grumpy,Happy                               |
| 4 | ,Doc,Grumpy,Happy,Sneezy                        |
| 5 | ,Doc,Grumpy,Happy,Sneezy,Bashful                |
| 6 | ,Doc,Grumpy,Happy,Sneezy,Bashful,Sleepy         |
| 7 | ,Doc,Grumpy,Happy,Sneezy,Bashful,Sleepy,Dopey   |
+---+-------------------------------------------------+
7 rows in set (0.01 sec)
```

I am very close to the final result, which I obtain by applying substring_index( ) a second time. I want substring_index( ) to now return the last item in each row, which I make it do by replacing the first line in my query with this:

```
select pivot.n,
       substring_index(substring_index(list.val, ',', 1 + pivot.n), ',', -1)
```

This gives me the following:

```
mysql> \. list3.sql
+---+---------------------------------------------------------------------+
| n | substring_index(substring_index(list.val, ',', 1 + pivot.n), ',', -1) |
+---+---------------------------------------------------------------------+
| 1 | Doc                                                                 |
| 2 | Grumpy                                                              |
| 3 | Happy                                                               |
| 4 | Sneezy                                                              |
| 5 | Bashful                                                             |
| 6 | Sleepy                                                              |
| 7 | Dopey                                                               |
+---+---------------------------------------------------------------------+
7 rows in set (0.00 sec)

mysql>
```

As you may have noticed, although the query is more complicated than the average SQL textbook query, it works as shown here with any list that contains up to 10 items, and can be easily accommodated to handle bigger lists. The text of the statement remains identical and will not be reparsed, even when the number of items in the list changes.

Passing list values as a single string is a very good and efficient solution for small lists. Its limitation is the length of the character string: you may hit a constraint either in the wrapper language or in SQL (Oracle has the shortest limit, at 4,000 characters); if your list contains several hundred items, another solution may be more appropriate.

Batching lists

One solution is to operate by batches, trying to keep lists to a fixed number of items. What allows us to use such a method is the fact that in( ) ignores duplicates in the list, whether it is an explicit list or the result of a subquery. Suppose we get our parameters in an array that, as in the previous example, can contain up to 10 values. If I try to softcode the statement, I may write something such as this:

```
my_condition = "where name in"
loop for i in 1 to count(myarray)
    if i > 1 then my_condition = my_condition + "("
                else my_condition = my_condition + ","
    my_condition = my_condition + "?"
end loop
my_condition = my_condition + ")"
```

Then I'll loop again to bind each value to its place marker, and I'll get as many different statements as I may have items in the list. What I can do instead is build a statement that can handle up to 10 items in the list:

```
my_condition = "where name in (?,?,?,?,?,?,?,?,?,?)"
```

Then I can prepare the statement by executing the suitable database call, and systematically bind 10 parameters by repeating some of the actual parameters to complete the 10 items:

```
loop for i in 1 to 10
     j = 1 + modulo(i, count(array))*
     bind(stmt_handler, i, array(j))
end loop
```

If need be, we can have several list sizes, with one statement to accommodate, say, lists with from 1 to 20 items, another statement for lists with from 21 to 40 items, and so on. This way, when we get lists containing any number of items up to 100, we are sure to keep in the cache, at most, 5 different statements instead of 100.

Using a temporary table

With very large lists, the simplest solution is probably to use a temporary table, and to replace the explicit list with a subquery that selects from this temporary table—once again, the text of the query will remain the same regardless of the number of rows in the temporary table. The downside to this method is the cost of insertion: it adds more interaction with the database. However, the real question concerns the origin of the data that is used to populate the list. For huge lists, it's not unusual for the items to come from a query. If this is the case, insert ... select ... into a temporary table will take place entirely on the server, and will save fetching the data into the application program. At this point, you may be wondering whether a temporary table is really necessary, and whether a simple subquery or join wouldn't do the trick much more efficiently. If the data comes from an external file and if this file can be sent to the server that hosts the database, you can use various utilities to load a temporary table almost painlessly. (Oracle's external tables, MySQL's load data infile statement, and SQL Server Integration Services all provide developers with tools that can eliminate a lot of programming.)

Bulk Operations

Besides indexing, statistics, and parsing rate, which are general points affecting one particular application or all applications accessing the database, there are other types of processes that you should check when performance isn't as good as expected. For instance, one factor that can slow down performance considerably when fetching (or inserting) a large number of rows is the number of round trips, particularly when there is a wide area network (WAN) between the application server and the database (yes, it happens).

---

* The first value will not be the first entry in the array, but it works fine nevertheless.

Unfortunately, I am touching on a topic that is dependent not only on the DBMS, but also on the language that is used to access that DBMS. I am therefore going to give a broad sketch to point at possible issues and give some examples. The principle is very simple: suppose you have to move a heap of sand. Operating row by row is like moving the heap of sand with a teaspoon. Perhaps using a shovel or a wheelbarrow would be more efficient.

Implementations vary. Some leave more to the imagination than others, but in all cases, when you fetch data from a server in a cursor loop you issue calls that say, in effect, "send me more data." At a very low level, you send on the network a packet that contains this command. In return, the DBMS sends back another packet that either contains the data you require or simply says "I'm done." Each time, you have a round trip and, as a matter of consequence, some network latency. The same types of exchanges occur when you insert row after row of data. Packets that are exchanged have a fixed size, and sending a full packet is neither more expensive nor slower than sending a mostly empty packet; exchanging fuller packets will mean fewer exchanges for the same amount of data. When you insert or return massive amounts of data—for instance, to create a file that is to be sent elsewhere for further processing by another system—it makes little sense to send row after row to the server, or to fetch row after row from the server, even when the procedural part of your program actually processes one row at a time. Some products and programmatic environments allow you to batch operations; this is typically the case with, for instance, T-SQL, JDBC, and SQLJ, which allow you to group several insert statements before sending them to the server, or the SqlPipe object in the .NET Framework. Others allow you to insert from or fetch into arrays, as is the case with Oracle and PL/SQL or the OCI C/C++ interface. MySQL takes a slightly different approach with streaming; it sends an uninterrupted flow of data without being explicitly prompted for it. If you use the C or PHP libraries, for instance, you will get the entire result set at once, which is fine for a small to moderately sized result set, but may lead to memory shortages when you really need to return a lot of data, in which case you must switch to another mode.

In some cases, batching is implicitly performed by the client side of your application. For instance, you may code this:

```
while fetch_one_row_from_database( )
      do something
```

and behind your back the client side performs this:

```
while fetch_one_row_from_array( )
      do something

fetch_one_row_from_array {
    increase index;
    if index > array_size
          fetch_array_size_rows_at_once_from_database
          set index to point to first array entry
    if buffer[index] is empty
          return done
    else
          return buffer(index)
```

This is typically what can happen in a JDBC program, in PHP database interface functions, or in some C/C++ client libraries. What few developers remember is that the array size is sometimes under their control, and that the default value isn't always the most suitable for what they have to do.

Figure 2-4 shows how performance is affected by setting the "fetch size" in the case of a JDBC program that dumps the contents of the transactions table used in Chapter 1 to a CSV file. Don't try to compare the various products with one another because all tests weren't run on the same machine, and I have normalized the number of rows returned by unit of time into a "throughput index." MySQL and SQL Server (i.e., their JDBC drivers) clearly ignore the settings, but Oracle is extremely sensitive to the parameter. Increasing the fetch size from its default value of 10 to 100 doubles the throughput on this example with very little effort (and both the JDBC program and the database were running on the same machine). When I wrote that MySQL ignores the settings, that was not quite true: I was able to push the MySQL throughput by about 15% by creating the statement of type *forward only* and *read only*, and by setting the fetch size to Integer.MIN_VALUE, which triggered a switch to a faster (in that case) streaming mode (which happens to also be supported by SQL Server's TDS protocol).

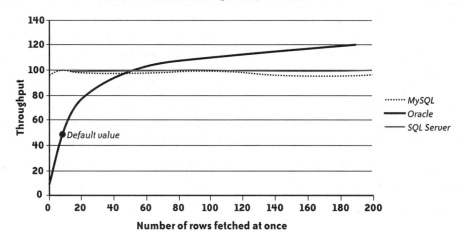

FIGURE 2-4. Changing the fetch size in a JDBC program

All the cases I have mentioned so far take a rather conservative approach to bulk operations, by mostly buffering data to optimize transfers. You may also encounter bulk operations that go beyond buffering and boldly bypass regular SQL operations, which for massive processes can also be very interesting: for instance, bulk copy operations with SQL Server's SQL Native Client, or the direct path-loading functions of Oracle's C call interface. But in that case, we are very far from quick, simple changes.

Transaction Management

Another important point to check is how transactions are managed. Transactions are supposed to be a break-or-pass suite of statements, opened either implicitly by the first statement that changes the database, or explicitly, and ended with either a commit, which makes the change permanent if the server were to crash, or a rollback, which cancels all changes to the database since the beginning of the transaction (or an optional, intermediary savepoint). The end of the transaction releases the locks acquired by the session on the table, page, or row that was changed, depending on the grain of locking. In practice, if the server crashes in the middle of a transaction, any changes are lost because they were not necessarily written to disk (if they were, they will be rolled back when the database starts).

Committing takes time, because the only way to ensure that the changes will be permanent—even if the database crashes—is to record all updates to a file in nonvolatile memory, and not to return before the data is actually written. Commit changes very often, and you'll realize that a significant part of your time is taken up by these waits.

Committing often is critical in online transaction processing (OLTP) environments, because if locks are held for longer than necessary, concurrent transactions are serialized and pile up, waiting for the previous transaction to complete and unlock the resource. It's somewhat different during nightly batch updates when there is no concurrency and one process inserts, purges, or updates data on a grand scale. If you are unsure about how often your data loading or upgrading batch program commits in the course of its run, this is definitely a point to check. The default with some languages (hi, JDBC!) is to be in a so-called "auto-commit" mode—that is, to commit after every change to the database, which, as Figure 2-5 shows, is extremely painful to all database products. (I normalized the number of rows updated by unit of time in a massive update to two million rows.)

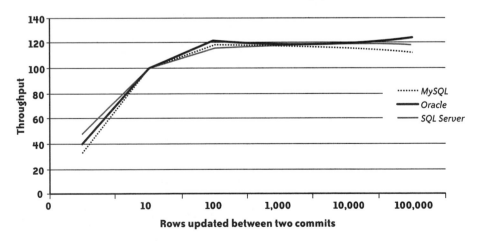

FIGURE 2-5. Influence of commit rate over update throughput

I should add that when you are operating in auto-commit mode, you are not only severely impairing your batch programs, but also sacrificing the concept of transactions, because the logical unit of work becomes the SQL statement. This can present some interesting situations. Suppose you want to transfer money from your checking account to your savings account. First you update your checking account to subtract the amount you want to transfer, and then update your savings account to add that same amount. Now picture a computer crash between the two updates. Oops. That's what transactions were invented for: if the two updates are in the same transaction, the first update will be canceled. If not, expect to spend some time on the phone with your bank.

We will return to transaction and commit frequency in Chapter 6, but as far as "quick wins" are concerned, this is all I will say on this topic for the moment. It is now time to take a look at views and stored functions.

## CHAPTER THREE

User Functions and Views

**But the answer is that with few tools and many tasks to do
much fudging is in fact necessary.**

—Henry W. Fowler (1858–1933) and Francis G. Fowler (1871–1918)

The King's English, Chapter IV

STORED OBJECTS IN A DATABASE ARE A PRIME TARGET FOR REFACTORING, FOR TWO REASONS: FIRST, they are often involved in some glaring performance issues, and second, their source code being inside the database makes them often more immediately "accessible" than procedural code, which is spread among umpteen source files. As with indexes and statistics, you can sometimes improve performance significantly by refactoring user-written functions and views without "touching the code"—even if the functions and views are actually part of the code.

Stored functions and views often serve the same purpose, which is to centralize in one place some SQL code that will be required often. If you manage to significantly improve a stored object that is widely used, the performance benefits you will receive will ripple much farther than the problem process that rang the first bell. Conversely, you must bring to the refactoring exercise of stored objects both care and attention proportionate to its possible wider effects.

Although stored procedures are often hailed as a feature that distinguishes a mature, corporate-grade DBMS product from a "small product," the availability of user-written functions lends itself easily to abuse. Developers who have been groomed in traditional programming "good practices" usually start by writing functions for often-performed operations (including validity checks that could sometimes be implemented by declarative integrity constraints). It isn't by chance that I included two utility functions in the example I used in Chapter 1: lookup functions are a common feature, and a common reason for poor performance. The systematic application of what is good practice with procedural languages often leads to dreadful performance with SQL code. SQL isn't a procedural language; it is a (somewhat wishfully) declarative language, which operates primarily against tables, not rows. In the procedural world, you use functions to record a sequence of operations that is often executed with mostly two aims in mind:

- Ensuring that all developers will use the same carefully controlled code, instead of multiplying, sometimes incorrectly, lines of code that serve the same purpose

- Easing maintenance by ensuring that all the code is concentrated in one place and that changes will have to be applied only once

If you want to record a complex SQL statement and satisfy the same requirements that functions satisfy in the procedural world, you should use views, which are the real SQL "functions." As you will see in this chapter, this is not to say that views are always performance-neutral. But when you're given the choice, you should try to think "view" before thinking "user-written function" when coding database accesses.

User-Defined Functions

When you are accustomed to procedural languages, it is tempting to employ user-defined functions extensively. Few developers resist temptation. We can roughly divide user-written functions and procedures into three categories:

Database-changing procedures
  These weld together a succession of SQL change operations (i.e., mostly inserts, updates, and deletes, plus the odd select here and there) that perform a unitary business task.

Computation-only functions
  These may embed if-then-else logic and various operations.

Lookup functions
  These execute queries against the database.

Database-changing procedures, which are an otherwise commendable practice, often suffer the same weaknesses as any type of procedural code: several statements where one could suffice, loops, and so on. In other words, they are not bad by nature—quite the opposite, actually—but they are sometimes badly implemented. I will therefore ignore them for the time being, because what I will discuss in the following chapters regarding code in general also applies to this type of stored procedure.

Improving Computation-Only Functions

Computation-only functions are (usually) pretty harmless, although it can be argued that when you code with SQL, it's not primarily in functions that you should incorporate computations, unless they are very specific:* computed columns in views are the proper place to centralize simple to moderately complex operations. Whenever you call a function, a context switch slows down execution, but unless your function is badly written (and this isn't specific to databases), you cannot hope for much performance gain by rewriting it. The only case when rewriting can make a significant difference is when you can make better use of primitive built-in functions. Most cases I have seen of poor usage of built-in functions were custom string or date functions, especially when some loop was involved.

I will give you an example of a user-written function in Oracle that is much more efficient when it makes extensive use of built-in functions: the counting of string patterns. Counting repeating patterns is an operation that can be useful in a number of cases, and you'll find an application of this operation at the end of this chapter. Let's state the problem in these terms: we are given a string haystack and a pattern needle, and we want to return how many times needle occurs in haystack.

One way to write this function is the way I wrote it in function1:

```
create or replace function function1(p_needle   in varchar2,
                                     p_haystack in varchar2)
return number
is
  i   number := 1;
  cnt number := 0;
begin
  while (i <= length(p_haystack))
  loop
    if (substr(p_haystack, i, length(p_needle)) = p_needle)
    then
      cnt := cnt + 1;
    end if;
    i := i + 1;
  end loop;
  return cnt;
end;
/
```

This is standard code that uses two built-in functions, length( ) and substr( ). We can improve it a little, if we don't want to count overlapping patterns, by increasing the index by the length of needle instead of by 1 each time we find a match.

However, we can write it a different way (function2) by using the Oracle-specific function instr( ), which returns the position of a substring within a string. instr( ) takes two additional parameters: the start position within the string and the occurrence (first, second, etc.)

---

* In which case it is likely that SQL will not be the language of choice: with SQL Server, complex computations would typically be coded in managed code, or in other words, in a .NET language called from within the database.

of the substring we search. function2 takes advantage of the occurrence parameter, increasing it until nothing is found:

```
create or replace function function2(p_needle   in varchar2,
                                      p_haystack in varchar2)
return number
is
  pos        number;
  occurrence number := 1;
begin
  loop
    pos := instr(p_haystack, p_needle, 1, occurrence);
    exit when pos = 0;
    occurrence := occurrence + 1;
  end loop;
  return occurrence - 1;
end;
/
```

I removed the loop in function3 by comparing the length of the initial searched string haystack to the length of the string after replacing all occurrences of needle with an empty string; I just need to divide the difference by the length of needle to determine how many times the pattern occurs. Contrary to the previous functions, I no longer use any Oracle-specific implementation. (You may remember that I used this method in the preceding chapter to count separators in a string that contained a list of values I wanted to bind.)

```
create or replace function function3(p_needle   in varchar2,
                                      p_haystack in varchar2)
return number
is
begin
  return (length(p_haystack)
          - length(replace(p_haystack, p_needle, '')))
          /length(p_needle);
end;
/
```

To compare functions, I created a table and populated it with 50,000 strings of random lowercase letters, with a random length of between 5 and 500:

```
create table test_table(id number,
                        text varchar2(500))
/
begin
  dbms_random.seed(1234);
  for i in 1 .. 50000
  loop
    insert into test_table
    values(i, dbms_random.string('L', dbms_random.value(5, 500)));
  end loop;
  commit;
end;
/
```

Finally, I compared all three functions by counting in my test tables how many strings contain more than 10 occurrences of the letters *s*, *q*, and *l*, respectively:

```
select count(*)
from test_table
where functioni('s', text) > 10
/
select count(*)
from test_table
where functioni('q', text) > 10
/
select count(*)
from test_table
where functioni('l', text) > 10
/
```

I ran this test with each of the three functions, summed up elapsed times (all three nearly identical), and divided 150,000 (the total number of rows I scanned) by the total elapsed time to compare the number of rows scanned per second in all three cases. You can see the result of the experiment in Figure 3-1.

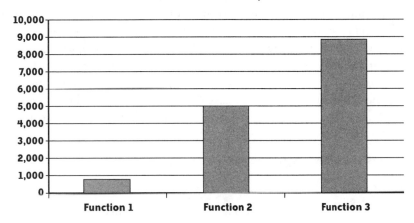

FIGURE 3-1. Three different ways to implement pattern counting with Oracle

The original function that loops on strings is about 10 times less efficient than the function that makes creative use of replace( ), with the loop on instr( ) halfway between the two others. It would probably not be a waste of your time to carefully read the documentation regarding the built-in functions provided with your DBMS; reinventing the wheel, even if your code avoids gross inefficiencies, doesn't pay. But suffice it to say that as the respective throughputs show, improving a function of moderate complexity can bring ample rewards in a batch program.

Improving Functions Further

The Oracle and SQL Server optimizers know one particular kind of function: *deterministic* functions. A function is deterministic if it always returns the same value when you call it with the same parameters. SQL Server decides by itself whether a function is deterministic. Oracle relies on your stating that it is by adding the deterministic keyword after the declaration of the type of value returned by the function (MySQL 5.1 knows the keyword but the optimizer ignores it). If a function is deterministic, the DBMS "remembers" a number of associations between the parameters and the returned value, and returns the result without actually calling the function whenever it is invoked with the same parameters. This caching of function results can bring impressive performance gains, but it is beneficial only when we call the function with relatively few different parameters. The previous example of a function looking for patterns would not benefit from being declared deterministic (even if it is), because one of the parameters, the text string to scan, is different each time. However, in many cases the same parameters are used again and again. This is particularly true when we apply functions to dates, because very often processes are applied to a relatively narrow range of dates, with the same date occurring many times.

You must be very careful about determinism; sometimes a function isn't deterministic for a reason that comes from an unexpected corner. A typical example is the function that returns the number representing a day in the week, something you obtain by applying to your date column to_char(*date_column*, 'D') with Oracle, datepart(dw, *date_column*) with SQL Server, or dayofweek(*date_column*) with MySQL. Except in the case of MySQL, where the function returns the ISO day-of-week number, the function is not deterministic because it depends on internationalization settings and local conventions. And as you can see in the following Oracle example, conventions may be different even in countries that are geographically very close:

```
SQL> alter session set nls_territory=spain;

Session altered.

SQL> select to_char(to_date('1970/01/01', 'YYYY/MM/DD'), 'D')
  2  from dual;

TO_CHAR(TO_DATE('1970/01/01','YYYY/MM/DD'),'D')
-------------------------------------------------------------------------
4

SQL> alter session set nls_territory=portugal;

Session altered.

SQL> select to_char(to_date('1970/01/01', 'YYYY/MM/DD'), 'D')
  2  from dual;

TO_CHAR(TO_DATE('1970/01/01','YYYY/MM/DD'),'D')
-------------------------------------------------------------------------
5
```

```
SQL> alter session set nls_territory=morocco;

Session altered.

SQL> select to_char(to_date('1970/01/01', 'YYYY/MM/DD'), 'D')
  2  from dual;

TO_CHAR(TO_DATE('1970/01/01','YYYY/MM/DD'),'D')
---------------------------------------------------------------------------
6
```

Oracle has a workaround with a conversion to the *name* of the day, which optionally takes a parameter that specifies the language in which the name must be returned:

```
ORACLE-SQL> alter session set nls_language=american;

Session altered.

SQL> select to_char(to_date('1970/01/01', 'YYYY/MM/DD'),
  2                 'DAY', 'NLS_DATE_LANGUAGE=ITALIAN')
  3  from dual;

TO_CHAR(TO_DATE('1970/01/01','YYYY/MM/DD'),'DAY','NLS_DATE_LANGUAGE=ITALIAN
---------------------------------------------------------------------------
GIOVEDI

SQL> select to_char(to_date('1970/01/01', 'YYYY/MM/DD'), 'DAY')
  2  from dual;

TO_CHAR(TO_DATE('1970/01/01','YYYY/MM/DD'),'DAY')
---------------------------------------------------------------------------
THURSDAY

SQL> alter session set nls_language=german;

Session altered.


SQL> select to_char(to_date('1970/01/01', 'YYYY/MM/DD'),
  2                 'DAY', 'NLS_DATE_LANGUAGE=ITALIAN')
  3  from dual;

TO_CHAR(TO_DATE('1970/01/01','YYYY/MM/DD'),'DAY','NLS_DATE_LANGUAGE=ITALIAN
---------------------------------------------------------------------------
GIOVEDI

SQL> select to_char(to_date('1970/01/01', 'YYYY/MM/DD'), 'DAY')
  2  from dual;

TO_CHAR(TO_DATE('1970/01/01','YYYY/MM/DD'),'DAY')
---------------------------------------------------------------------------
DONNERSTAG
```

The regular manner with SQL Server to cast in bronze what will be returned by datepart(dw, ...) is to call set datefirst, which cannot be done in a function. There is a way out, though: comparing what the function returns with what the *same function applied to a known date* returns. From the results kindly provided by Oracle, we know that January 1, 1970 was a Thursday; if the function returns the same thing we get with January 3, 1970, we have a Saturday, and so on.

Keeping in mind how to return with Oracle a truly deterministic identification of days, I can now write a function that returns 1 if a date corresponds to a weekend day (i.e., Saturday or Sunday) and 0 otherwise. To see the benefits of using Oracle to declare a function as deterministic, I will create two identical functions, one that isn't declared deterministic and one that is:

```
SQL> create or replace function weekend_day(p_date in date)
  2  return number
  3  is
  4    wday    char(3);
  5  begin
  6    wday := substr(to_char(p_date, 'DAY',
  7                      'NLS_DATE_LANGUAGE=AMERICAN'), 1, 3);
  8    if (wday = 'SAT') or (wday = 'SUN')
  9    then
 10        return 1;
 11    else
 12        return 0;
 13    end if;
 14  end;
 15  /

Function created.

Elapsed: 00:00:00.04
SQL> create or replace function weekend_day_2(p_date in date)
  2  return number
  3  deterministic
  4  is
  5    wday    char(3);
  6  begin
  7    wday := substr(to_char(p_date, 'DAY',
  8                      'NLS_DATE_LANGUAGE=AMERICAN'), 1, 3);
  9    if (wday = 'SAT') or (wday = 'SUN')
 10    then
 11        return 1;
 12    else
 13        return 0;
 14    end if;
 15  end;
 16  /

Function created.

Elapsed: 00:00:00.02
```

Now, suppose we have a table that records sales, associating to each sale a date and an amount, and say that we want to compare the total amount sold during weekends with the total amount sold during the rest of the week for the past month. Let's run the query twice, with the nondeterministic function first and the deterministic function afterward:

```
SQL> select sum(case weekend_day(sale_date)
  2              when 1 then 0
  3              else sale_amount
  4          end) week_sales,
  5          sum(case weekend_day(sale_date)
  6              when 0 then 0
  7              else sale_amount
  8          end) week_end_sales
  9  from sales
 10  where sale_date >= add_months(trunc(sysdate), -1)
 11  /

WEEK_SALES WEEK_END_SALES
---------- --------------
 191815253      73131546.8
```

Elapsed: 00:00:11.27

```
SQL> select sum(case weekend_day_2(sale_date)
  2              when 1 then 0
  3              else sale_amount
  4          end) week_sales,
  5          sum(case weekend_day_2(sale_date)
  6              when 0 then 0
  7              else sale_amount
  8          end) week_end_sales
  9  from sales
 10  where sale_date >= add_months(trunc(sysdate), -1)
 11  /

WEEK_SALES WEEK_END_SALES
---------- --------------
 191815253      73131546.8
```

Elapsed: 00:00:11.24

The results are not that convincing. Why? Actually, my query violates one of the conditions I specified for the efficiency of deterministic functions: being called with the same parameters again and again. The Oracle date type is equivalent to the datetime type of other DBMS products: it contains a time element, to a precision of one second. Needless to say, I was careful when generating my test data to generate values of sale_date at various times of the day. Let's suppress the time element by applying the trunc( ) function to the data, which sets time to 00:00:00, and let's try again:

```
SQL> select sum(case weekend_day(trunc(sale_date))
  2              when 1 then 0
  3              else sale_amount
  4          end) week_sales,
  5          sum(case weekend_day(trunc(sale_date))
  6              when 0 then 0
  7              else sale_amount
  8          end) week_end_sales
  9  from sales
 10  where sale_date >= add_months(trunc(sysdate), -1)
 11  /
```

```
WEEK_SALES WEEK_END_SALES
---------- --------------
 191815253      73131546.8

Elapsed: 00:00:12.69
SQL> select sum(case weekend_day_2(trunc(sale_date))
  2             when 1 then 0
  3             else sale_amount
  4           end) week_sales,
  5           sum(case weekend_day_2(trunc(sale_date))
  6             when 0 then 0
  7             else sale_amount
  8           end) week_end_sales
  9  from sales
 10  where sale_date >= add_months(trunc(sysdate), -1)
 11  /

WEEK_SALES WEEK_END_SALES
---------- --------------
 191815253      73131546.8

Elapsed: 00:00:02.58
```

Under suitable circumstances, the deterministic function allows the query to run five times faster.

You must be aware that declaring with Oracle that a function is deterministic isn't something to be taken lightly.

To explain, imagine that we have a table of employees, and that employees may be assigned to projects through a table called project_assignment that links an employee number to a project identifier. We could issue a query such as the following to find out which projects are currently assigned to people whose last name is "Sharp":

```
SQL> select e.lastname, e.firstname, p.project_name, e.empno
  2  from employees e,
  3       project_assignment pa,
  4       projects p
  5  where e.lastname = 'SHARP'
  6    and e.empno = pa.empno
  7    and pa.project_id = p.project_id
  8    and pa.from_date < sysdate
  9    and (pa.to_date >= sysdate or pa.to_date is null)
 10  /

LASTNAME             FIRSTNAME             PROJECT_NAME        EMPNO
-------------------- --------------------- ------------------ ----------
SHARP                REBECCA               SISYPHUS                 2501
SHARP                REBECCA               DANAIDS                  2501
SHARP                MELISSA               DANAIDS                  7643
SHARP                ERIC                  SKUNK                    7797
```

A similar type of query returns the only "Crawley" and the project to which he is assigned:

```
SQL> select e.lastname, e.firstname, p.project_name
  2  from employees e,
  3         project_assignment pa,
  4         projects p
  5  where e.lastname = 'CRAWLEY'
  6    and e.empno = pa.empno
  7    and pa.project_id = p.project_id
  8    and pa.from_date < sysdate
  9    and (pa.to_date >= sysdate or pa.to_date is null)
 10  /

LASTNAME             FIRSTNAME            PROJECT_NAME
-------------------- -------------------- --------------------
CRAWLEY              RAWDON               SISYPHUS
```

Now let's suppose that for some obscure reason someone has written a lookup function that returns the name associated with an employee number capitalized in a more glamorous way than the full uppercase used in the tables:

```
SQL> create or replace function NameByEmpno(p_empno in number)
  2  return varchar2
  3  is
  4       v_lastname varchar2(30);
  5  begin
  6       select initcap(lastname)
  7       into v_lastname
  8       from employees
  9       where empno = p_empno;
 10       return v_lastname;
 11  exception
 12       when no_data_found then
 13            return '*** UNKNOWN ***';
 14  end;
 15  /
```

Someone else now decides to use this function to return the employee/project association without explicitly joining the employees table:

```
SQL> select p.project_name, pa.empno
  2  from projects p,
  3       project_assignment pa
  4  where pa.project_id = p.project_id
  5    and namebyempno(pa.empno) = 'Sharp'
  6    and pa.from_date < sysdate
  7    and (pa.to_date >= sysdate or pa.to_date is null)
  8  /

PROJECT_NAME              EMPNO
-------------------- ----------
SKUNK                      7797
SISYPHUS                   2501
DANAIDS                    7643
DANAIDS                    2501
```

Analysis reveals that indexing the function would make the query faster:

```
SQL> create index my_own_index on project_assignment(namebyempno(empno))
  2  /
create index my_own_index on project_assignment(namebyempno(empno))
                                                               *
ERROR at line 1:
ORA-30553: The function is not deterministic
```

Undaunted, our developer modifies the function, adds the magical deterministic keyword, and successfully creates the index.

I would really have loved to elaborate on the romantic affair that developed around the coffee machine, but I'm afraid that O'Reilly is not the proper publisher for that kind of story. Suffice it to say that one day, Mr. Crawley proposed to Miss Sharp and his proposal was accepted. A few months later, the marriage led to a data change at the hands of someone in the HR department, following a request from the new Mrs. Crawley:

```
SQL> update employees set lastname = 'CRAWLEY' where empno = 2501;

1 row updated.

SQL> commit;

Commit complete.
```

What happens to the project queries now? The three-table join no longer sees any Rebecca Sharp, but a Rebecca Crawley, as can be expected:

```
SQL> select e.lastname, e.firstname, p.project_name
  2  from employees e,
  3       project_assignment pa,
  4       projects p
  5  where e.lastname = 'SHARP'
  6    and e.empno = pa.empno
  7    and pa.project_id = p.project_id
  8    and pa.from_date < sysdate
  9    and (pa.to_date >= sysdate or pa.to_date is null)
 10  /

LASTNAME             FIRSTNAME            PROJECT_NAME
-------------------- -------------------- --------------------
SHARP                MELISSA              DANAIDS
SHARP                ERIC                 SKUNK

SQL> select e.lastname, e.firstname, p.project_name
  2  from employees e,
  3       project_assignment pa,
  4       projects p
  5  where e.lastname = 'CRAWLEY'
  6    and e.empno = pa.empno
  7    and pa.project_id = p.project_id
  8    and pa.from_date < sysdate
  9    and (pa.to_date >= sysdate or pa.to_date is null)
 10  /
```

```
LASTNAME              FIRSTNAME             PROJECT_NAME
--------------------  --------------------  --------------------
CRAWLEY               REBECCA               SISYPHUS
CRAWLEY               RAWDON                SISYPHUS
CRAWLEY               REBECCA               DANAIDS
```

For the query that uses the function, and the function-based index, nothing has changed:

```
SQL> select p.project_name, pa.empno
  2  from projects p,
  3          project_assignment pa
  4  where pa.project_id = p.project_id
  5    and namebyempno(pa.empno) = 'Crawley'
  6    and pa.from_date < sysdate
  7    and (pa.to_date >= sysdate or pa.to_date is null)
  8  /

PROJECT_NAME          EMPNO
--------------------  ----------
SISYPHUS                    2503

SQL> select p.project_name, pa.empno
  2  from projects p,
  3          project_assignment pa
  4  where pa.project_id = p.project_id
  5    and namebyempno(pa.empno) = 'Sharp'
  6    and pa.from_date < sysdate
  7    and (pa.to_date >= sysdate or pa.to_date is null)
  8  /

PROJECT_NAME          EMPNO
--------------------  ----------
SKUNK                       7797
SISYPHUS                    2501
DANAIDS                     7643
DANAIDS                     2501
```

The reason is simple: indexes store key values and addresses; they duplicate some information, and DBMS products routinely return data from indexes when the only information needed from the table is contained in the index. The table has been updated, but not the index. Our present key is stored in the index. We have said that the function is deterministic and that it always returns the same value for the same set of parameters. That means the result should never change. Therefore, the DBMS believes this assertion, doesn't attempt to rebuild or invalidate the index when the base table is changed (which would be totally impractical anyway), and returns wrong results.

Obviously, the previous function could not be deterministic because it was a lookup function, querying the database. Fortunately, we sometimes have other means to improve lookup functions, and we will explore them now.

Improving Lookup Functions

Lookup functions can provide fertile ground for spectacular improvement. By embedding database access inside a precompiled function, the original developer wanted to turn the function into a building block. Rather than a building block, you should have another image in mind: a black box, because that's what the function will look like to the optimizer. Whenever you call a lookup function inside a query, the queries that run inside the function are insulated from what happens outside, even if they are hitting the same tables as the calling statement; in particular, there are strong odds that if you aren't careful, queries that are hidden inside a function will be executed every time the function is called.

Estimating how many times a function may be called is the key to estimating how much it contributes to poor performance. This is true of any function, but more so of lookup functions, because even a fast database access is comparatively much costlier than the computation of a mathematical or string expression. And here you must once again distinguish between two cases, namely:

- Functions that are referenced inside the select list, and are therefore called once for every row that belongs to the result set.

- Functions that are referenced inside the where clause, and can be called any number of times between (in the best of cases) the total number of rows returned and (at worst) the total number of rows tested against the conditions expressed in the where clause. The actual number of calls basically depends on the efficiency of the *other* criteria in the where clause to screen out rows before we have to compute the function for a more refined search.

If we consider the very worst case, a lookup function that happens to be the only criterion inside the where clause, we end up with what is, in effect, a straightjacketed nested loop: a table will be scanned, and for each row the function will be called and will access another table. Even if the SQL query in the function is very fast, you will kill performance. I called the loop *straightjacketed* because the optimizer will be given no chance to choose a different plan, such as joining the two tables (the one to which the function is applied and the one that is queried in the function) through merging or hashing. Worse, in many cases the lookup function will always be called with the same parameters to always return the same values, not truly deterministic, but "locally deterministic," within the scope of the user session or batch run.

Now I will use two different examples of lookup functions, and I will show you how you can improve them in some cases, even when they look rather plain.

Example 1: A calendar function

The first function is called NextBusinessDay( ), takes a date as a single parameter, and returns a date that is computed in the following manner:

- If the parameter is a Friday, we add three days to it (we are in a country where neither Saturday nor Sunday is a business day).

- If the parameter is a Saturday, we add two days.

- Otherwise, we add one day.

- We then check the result against a table that contains all the dates of public holidays for the range of dates of interest. If we find a public holiday that matches the date we have found, we iterate. Otherwise, we are done.

Being aware of the number-of-the-day-in-the-week issue, here is how I can code the function, first with Oracle:

```
create or replace function NextBusinessDay(this_day in date)
return date
as
   done      boolean := false;
   dow       char(3);
   dummy     number;
   nextdate date;
begin
   nextdate := this_day;
   while not done
   loop
      dow := substr(to_char(nextdate, 'DAY',
                          'NLS_DATE_LANGUAGE=AMERICAN'), 1, 3);
      if (dow = 'FRI')
      then nextdate := nextdate + 3;
      elsif (dow = 'SAT')
          then nextdate := nextdate + 2;
      else nextdate := nextdate + 1;
      end if;
      begin
        select 1
        into dummy
        from public_holidays
        where day_off = nextdate;
      exception
        when no_data_found then
            done := true;
      end;
   end loop;
   return nextdate;
end;
/
```

Then with SQL Server:

```
create function NextBusinessDay(@this_day date)
returns date
as
begin
   declare @done      bit;
   declare @dow       char(1);
   declare @dummy     int;
   declare @nextdate date;
```

```
   set @nextdate = @this_day;
   set @done = 0;
   while @done = 0
   begin
      set @dow = datepart(dw, @nextdate);
      if @dow = datepart(dw, convert(date, '01/02/1970', 101))
        set @nextdate = @nextdate + 3;
      else
        if @dow = datepart(dw, convert(date, '01/03/1970', 101))
          set @nextdate = @nextdate + 2;
        else
          set @nextdate = @nextdate + 1;
      set @dummy = (select 1
                    from public_holidays
                    where day_off = @nextdate);
      if coalesce(@dummy, 0) = 0
      begin
        set @done = 1;
      end;
   end;
   return @nextdate;
end;
```

And finally with MySQL (for which I don't need to worry about what dayofweek( ) returns):

```
delimiter //
create function NextBusinessDay(this_day datetime)
returns date
reads sql data
begin
  declare done      boolean default 0;
  declare dow       smallint;
  declare dummy     smallint;
  declare nextdate date;
  declare continue handler for not found set done = 1;
  set nextdate = date(this_day);
  while not done do
     set dow = dayofweek(nextdate);
     case dow
       when 6 then set nextdate = date_add(nextdate, interval 3 day);
       when 7 then set nextdate = date_add(nextdate, interval 2 day);
       else        set nextdate = date_add(nextdate, interval 1 day);
     end case;
     select 1
     into dummy
     from public_holidays
     where day_off = nextdate;
  end while;
  return nextdate;
end;
//
delimiter ;
```

I use the same one-million-row table containing sales dates as I did when I added up the sales that took place on weekend days and sales from other weekdays. Then I simply run a select NextBusinessDay(sale_date)... over all the rows of my table.

For reasons that will soon be obvious, I mostly used Oracle for my tests.

On my machine, the simple test took about two and a half minutes to return all one million rows—a throughput of 6,400 rows per second. Not dismal, but the statistics kindly provided by Oracle* report two million recursive calls; these calls comprise the function call and the query inside the function. It's a mighty number when you consider that we have only 121 different days in the table. Because rows were presumably entered chronologically,[†] in most cases the result of the function applied to a row will be exactly the same as the result for the previous row.

How can I improve performance without touching the code that calls the function? One possibility, if the DBMS supports it, is to ask the SQL engine to cache the result of the function. Caching the function result is not as stringent as defining the function as deterministic: it just says that as long as the tables on which the function relies are not modified, the function can cache results and can return them again when it is called with the same parameters. Such a function will not allow us, for instance, to create an index on its result, but it will not reexecute when it is not needed.

Oracle introduced the caching of function results in Oracle 11*g*; MySQL 5.1 doesn't cache the result of queries that are called in a function, and SQL Server 2008 doesn't allow caching that is any more explicit than specifying that a function returns null when input is null (which can speed up evaluation in some cases). With Oracle, I have therefore re-created my function, simply modifying its heading in the following way:

```
create or replace function NextBusinessDay(this_day in date)
return date
result_cache relies_on(public_holidays)
as ...
```

The optional relies_on clause simply tells Oracle that the cached result may need to be flushed if the public_holidays table is modified.

Running the same test as before yielded a very bad result: my throughput went down by 30% or so, to 4,400 rows per second. The reason is exactly the same as we already saw in the case of the deterministic function: because the dates also store a time part that varies, the function is almost never called with the same parameter. We get no benefit from the cache, and we pay the overhead due to its management.

---

* set autotrace traceonly stat, under SQL*Plus.

† I generated random data and then ordered it by date to create a realistic case.

If I don't want to modify the original code, I can cheat. I can rename my previous cached function as Cached_NextBusinessDay( ) and rewrite the function that is called in the statement as follows:

```
create or replace function NextBusinessDay(this_day in date)
return date
as
begin
  return(Cached_NextBusinessDay(trunc(this_day)));
end;
```

Running the same query, my table scan took a little more than 30 seconds, or a throughput of 31,700 rows per second, almost five times my initial throughput. This ratio is in the same neighborhood as the ratio obtained by stating that a function was deterministic, without all the constraints linked to having a truly deterministic function. If you want to improve lookup functions, caching their result is the way to go.

But what if my DBMS doesn't support caching function results? We still have some tricks we can apply by taking advantage of the fact that rows are, more or less, stored in chronological order. For instance, every version of Oracle since Oracle 7 (released in the early 1990s) supports using variables in a package to cache the previous results. Packaged variables aren't shared among sessions. You first define your function inside a package:

```
create or replace package calendar
is
    function NextBusinessDay(this_day in date)
    return date;
end;
/
```

Then you create the package body, in which two variables, duly initialized, store both the last input parameter and the last result. You must be careful that the lifespan of the cache is the duration of the session; in some cases, you may have to build an aging mechanism. In the function, I check the current input parameter against the past one and return the previous result without any qualms if they are identical; otherwise, I run the query that is the costly part of the function:

```
create or replace package body calendar
is

    g_lastdate   date := to_date('01/01/0001', 'DD/MM/YYYY');
    g_lastresult date := NULL;

    function NextBusinessDay(this_day in date)
    return date
    is
        done      boolean := false;
        dow       char(3);
        dummy     number;
    begin
        if (this_day <> g_lastdate)
        then
          g_lastdate := this_day;
```

```
      g_lastresult := this_day;
      while not done
      loop
         dow := substr(to_char(g_lastresult, 'DAY',
                        'NLS_DATE_LANGUAGE=AMERICAN'), 1, 3);
         if (dow = 'FRI')
         then g_lastresult := g_lastresult + 3;
         elsif (dow = 'SAT')
              then g_lastresult := g_lastresult + 2;
         else g_lastresult := g_lastresult + 1;
         end if;
         begin
            select 1
            into dummy
            from public_holidays
            where day_off = g_lastresult;
         exception
            when no_data_found then
               done := true;
         end;
      end loop;
   end if;
   return g_lastresult;
 end;

end;
```

Finally, to keep the interface identical, I rewrite the initial function as a mere wrapper function that calls the function in the package, after removing the time part from the date:

```
create or replace function NextBusinessDay(this_day in date)
return date
as
begin
  return calendar.NextBusinessDay(trunc(this_day));
end;
```

The good news for people who are running older Oracle versions is that in this case (i.e., when I process dates in more or less chronological order), I get an even better result than when I let Oracle manage the cache: my test run was almost 10% faster, achieving a throughput of 34,868 rows per second. However, keep in mind that the Oracle cache is not dependent on the order of the dates, but simply on there having been a limited number of dates. Figure 3-2 summarizes the variations of throughput by rewriting my NextBusinessDay( ) function in different ways.

It is interesting to note that the result_cache clause can either noticeably degrade or boost performance depending on whether it has been used in the wrong or right circumstances.

Can we apply any of the improvement methods that work with Oracle to other products? It depends. Explicitly asking for the function result to be cached is, at the time of this writing, something specific to Oracle, as are packages. Unfortunately, SQL Server offers no way to manually cache the result of functions written in T-SQL, because it only knows of local variables that exist only for the duration of the function call, and because temporary tables, which are the closest you can come to global variables, cannot be referenced in a function.

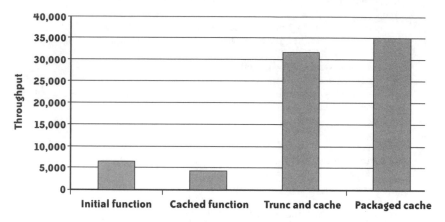

FIGURE 3-2. How the throughput of the same Oracle lookup function varies

Although MySQL 5.1 can cache the result of queries, it cannot cache the result of queries run from inside a function or procedure. However, contrary to T-SQL, MySQL allows referencing global session variables inside a function, and session variables can be used for buffering results. The only snag is that, whereas Oracle's packaged variables are private when defined in the package body and invisible outside the package, the MySQL session variables are accessible to any function. Giving them very common names (e.g., @var1) is therefore courting disaster, and if you want to stay on the safe side you should use long, unwieldy names that minimize the risk of accidental collision. In the following example, I systematically use <function name>$ as a prefix:

```
delimiter //
create function NextBusinessDay(this_day datetime)
returns date
reads sql data
begin
 declare done      boolean default 0;
 declare dow       smallint;
 declare dummy     smallint;
 declare continue handler for not found set done = 1;
 if (ifnull(@NextBusinessDay$last_date, '1769-08-15') <> date(this_day))
 then
  set @NextBusinessDay$last_date = date(this_day);
  set @NextBusinessDay$last_business_day = date(this_day);
  while not done do
   set dow = dayofweek(@NextBusinessDay$last_business_day);
   case dow
    when 6 then
      set @NextBusinessDay$last_business_day =
          date_add(@NextBusinessDay$last_business_day, interval 3 day);
    when 7 then
      set @NextBusinessDay$last_business_day =
          date_add(@NextBusinessDay$last_business_day, interval 2 day);
    else set @NextBusinessDay$last_business_day =
          date_add(@NextBusinessDay$last_business_day, interval 1 day);
```

```
   end case;
   select 1
   into dummy
   from public_holidays
   where day_off = @NextBusinessDay$last_business_day;
 end while;
 end if;
 return @NextBusinessDay$last_business_day;
end;
//
delimiter ;
```

As you can see in Figure 3-3, implementing in MySQL the same ideas as with Oracle also brings a significant performance improvement when scanning chronologically ordered rows.

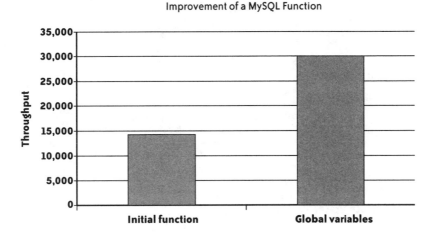

Improvement of a MySQL Function

FIGURE 3-3. Using variables to cache the result of a MySQL function

Example 2: A conversion function

The second function, called FxConvert( ),* takes two parameters—an amount and a currency code—and returns the amount converted into a predefined reference currency at the most recent available conversion rate. Here I am using the tables used in the Chapter 1 example. You can use FxConvert( ) as a prototype for transcoding functions.

Here is the original code for Oracle:

```
create or replace function FxConvert(p_amount   in number,
                                     p_currency in varchar2)
return number
is
  n_converted    number;
begin
```

---

* FX is a common abbreviation for Foreign eXchange.

```
    select p_amount * a.rate
    into n_converted
    from currency_rates a
    where (a.iso, a.rate_date) in
        (select iso, max(rate_date) last_date
         from currency_rates
         where iso = p_currency
         group by iso);
    return n_converted;
exception
  when no_data_found then
        return null;
end;
/
```

Here is the code for SQL Server:

```
create function fx_convert(@amount   float,
                           @currency char(3))
returns float
as
begin
  declare @rate  float;
  set @rate = (select a.rate
                 from currency_rates a
                    inner join (select iso,
                                       max(rate_date) last_date
                                from currency_rates
                                where iso = @currency
                                group by iso) b
                      on a.iso = b.iso
                      and a.rate_date = b.last_date);
  return coalesce(@rate, 0) * @amount;
end;
```

And here is the code for MySQL:

```
delimiter //
create function FxConvert(p_amount float, p_currency char(3))
returns float
reads sql data
begin
  declare converted_amount float;
  declare continue handler for not found set converted_amount = 0;
  select a.rate * p_amount
  into converted_amount
  from currency_rates a
        inner join (select iso, max(rate_date) last_date
                    from currency_rates
                    where iso = p_currency
                    group by iso) b
              on a.iso = b.iso
              and a.rate_date = b.last_date;
  return converted_amount;
end;
//
delimiter ;
```

Let's start, as we did before, with Oracle. We have basically two ways to improve the function: either use the result_cache keyword for Oracle 11*g* and later, or use packaged variables and "manually" handle caching.

If I want result_cache to be beneficial, I need to modify the function so as to have a limited number of input parameters; because there may be a large number of different amounts, the amount value must be taken out of the equation. I therefore redefine the function as a wrapper of the real function for which results will be cached:

```
create or replace function FxRate(p_currency in varchar2)
return number
result_cache relies_on(currency_rates)
is
  n_rate     number;
begin
  select rate
  into n_rate
  from (select rate
        from currency_rates
        where iso = p_currency
        order by rate_date desc)
  where rownum = 1;
  return n_rate;
exception
  when no_data_found then
      return null;
end;
/
create or replace function FxConvert(p_amount   in number,
                                     p_currency in varchar2)
return number
is
begin
  return p_amount * FxRate(p_currency);
end;
/
```

If I want to handle caching through packaged variables, I cannot use two variables as I did in the NextBusinessDay() example. I was implicitly relying on the fact that the function was successively evaluated for the same date. In this example, even if I have a limited number of currencies, the currency codes will be alternated instead of having long runs of identical codes that would benefit from "remembering" the previous value.

Instead of simple variables, I use a PL/SQL associative array, indexed by the currency code:

```
create or replace package fx
as

  function rate(p_currency in varchar2)
  return number;

end;
/
```

```
create or replace package body fx
as
  type t_rates is table of number
                  index by varchar2(3);
  a_rates  t_rates;
  n_rate   number;

  function rate(p_currency in varchar2)
  return number
  is
    n_rate number;
  begin
    begin
      n_rate := a_rates(p_currency);
    exception
      when no_data_found then
        begin
          select a.rate
          into a_rates(p_currency)
          from currency_rates a
          where (a.iso, a.rate_date) in
              (select iso, max(rate_date) last_date
               from currency_rates
               where iso = p_currency
               group by iso);
          n_rate := a_rates(p_currency);
        end;
    end;
    return n_rate;
  end;

end;
/
create or replace function FxConvert(p_amount   in number,
                                     p_currency in varchar2)
return number
is
begin
  return p_amount * fx.rate(p_currency);
end;
/
```

I tested the alternative versions of the function by running the following query against my two-million-row transactions table, using as a reference for 100 the number of rows scanned per second by the original function:

```
select sum(FxConvert(amount, curr))
from transactions;
```

Figure 3-4 shows the result.

At this point, I should put these performance gains into perspective. If you cannot touch the code, the rewrites I just presented can indeed result in an impressive improvement: the simple split of the function to use a result cache improved speed by a factor of 30 on my machine, and the more elaborate use of an array cache inside a package improved

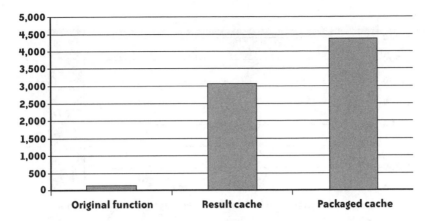

Oracle Performance Gain

FIGURE 3-4. Comparison of alternative ways to write a currency-conversion function with Oracle

speed by a factor of 45. But remember that the function is a black box, and if you really want an impressive improvement with Oracle, there is no such thing as rewriting the test query as follows:

```
select sum(t.amount * r.rate)
from transactions t
      inner join
          (select a.iso, a.rate
           from (select iso,
                        max(rate_date) last_date
                 from currency_rates
                 group by iso) b
                inner join currency_rates a
                  on a.iso = b.iso
                  and a.rate_date = b.last_date) r
  on r.iso = t.curr;
```

You'll probably find this query more difficult to read than the one that uses the function, but in fact, the subquery that follows the first inner join is nothing more than the subquery in the function. I am using an inner join because the function ignores currencies for which the rate is unknown, and therefore, we need not bother about the few lines referring to very exotic currencies. Figure 3-5, which is Figure 3-4 with the replacement of the function call by the join, probably doesn't need any comment.

What about the other products?

We have seen that unfortunately, options are very limited with T-SQL functions. I already mentioned that T-SQL doesn't know of session variables. You could cheat and use managed code (a .NET language routine called by the SQL engine) to do the trick; for instance, you could use static variables in C#. Take such an idea out of your mind, however; in their great wisdom, Microsoft developers have decided that "assemblies" (i.e., interfaces between T-SQL and .NET language code) have, by default, a PERMISSION_SET value of SAFE.

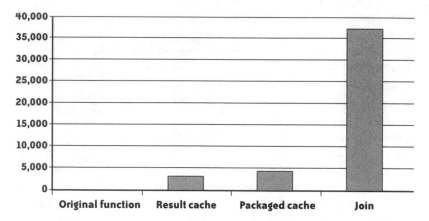

Oracle Performance Gain

FIGURE 3-5. An Oracle comparison of various rewrites of a function to a simple join

Therefore, if you try to use static variables in a managed code function, you'll get the following error message:

```
CREATE ASSEMBLY failed because type '...' in safe assembly '...' has
a static field '...'. Attributes of static fields in safe assemblies
must be marked readonly in Visual C#, ReadOnly in Visual Basic, or
initonly in Visual C++ and intermediate language.
```

If you don't want to play it safe, you can have static variables. But the problem is that in a DLL, they are shared by all sessions. When queries run concurrently, anything can happen.

To demonstrate this (and for once I will *not* give the code), I tested a C# function that converts currencies using two static variables and "remembers" the exchange rate and last currency encountered (in this case, this method is inefficient, but efficiency wasn't my goal). I summed the converted amounts in my two-million-row transactions table.

If you run the query when you are the only connected session, you get, more slowly, the same result as the T-SQL function; that is:

```
782780436669.151
```

Now, running the same query using the C#-with-static-variables function against the same data in three concurrent sessions yielded the following results:

```
782815864624.758
782797493847.697
782816529963.717
```

What happened? Each session simply overwrote the static variables in turn, messing up the results—a good example of uncoordinated concurrent access to the same memory area.

If refactoring a function, and one function alone, is not an option with SQL Server, replacing a lookup function with a join is often possible. The comparison of the query that calls the function with the query that uses the join, though not as impressive as with Oracle, is nevertheless impressive enough to give good hopes of improving speed when a function that can be merged inside the query is used. The result of my tests is shown in Figure 3-6.

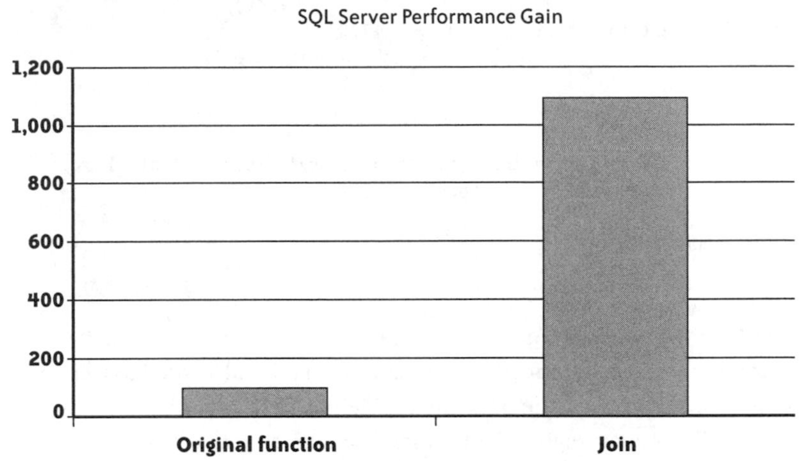

FIGURE 3-6. An SQL Server performance comparison of repeatedly calling a simple lookup function versus a join

As we have seen, with MySQL you can use session variables. However, in the case of currencies, and noting the need to remember *several* exchange rates, we must be a little creative because MySQL knows no array variable. Instead of using an array, I concatenate the currency codes into one string and the matching exchange rates into another; built-in functions allow me to identify the position of one code in the string and to isolate the matching exchange rate, converting the string into a *float* value by adding 0.0 to it. To stay on the safe side, I define a maximum length for my strings:

```
delimiter //
create function FxConvert(p_amount float, p_currency char(3))
returns float
reads sql data
begin
  declare pos       smallint;
  declare rate      float;
  declare continue handler for not found set rate = 0;
  set pos = ifnull(find_in_set(p_currency,
                          @FxConvert$currency_list), 0);

  if pos = 0
  then
    select a.rate
    into rate
    from currency_rates a
         inner join (select iso, max(rate_date) last_date
                     from currency_rates
                     where iso = p_currency
                     group by iso) b
```

```
                on a.iso = b.iso
                and a.rate_date = b.last_date;
        if (ifnull(length(@FxConvert$rate_list), 0) < 2000
                and ifnull(length(@FxConvert$currency_list), 0) < 2000)
        then
          set @FxConvert$currency_list = concat_ws(',',
                                                @FxConvert$currency_list,
                                                p_currency);
          set @FxConvert$rate_list = concat_ws('|',
                                              @FxConvert$rate_list,
                                              rate);
        end if;
      else
        set rate = 0.0 + substring_index(substring_index(@FxConvert$rate_list,
                            '|', pos), '|', -1);
      end if;
      return p_amount * rate;
    end;
    //
    delimiter ;
```

I won't pretend that the resultant code is elegant or that hand-crafted associative arrays are very easy to maintain. But the performance gain is here, and interestingly, the rewritten function performs even slightly better than the join, as you can see in Figure 3-7.

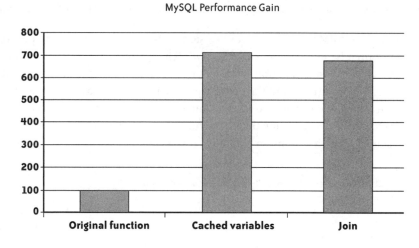

FIGURE 3-7. Substantially rewriting the conversion function with MySQL

Improving Functions Versus Rewriting Statements

As the preceding currency conversion example shows, it is sometimes much more efficient to rewrite a statement to get rid of the function entirely. Instead of executing a call, you can reinject the database accesses you find in the function as joins or subqueries, which may be easy if the function is simple, or more difficult if the function includes procedural logic. (I will discuss how you can graft procedural logic into a statement in more detail in Chapter 6.) There are two major advantages to getting rid of functions:

- You will modify a single query. This is a localized change; it makes it easier to check correctness and test for nonregression.

- By reinjecting ancillary SQL statements into the main statement, you turn the database optimizer into your ally. The optimizer will have the full vision of what you are trying to achieve, and will try to optimize globally instead of optimizing each part independently.

The disadvantages are as follows:

- The improvement that you will bring will benefit only that particular process, even if the function is used in many places.

- You are defeating the initial purpose of the function, which is to centralize code for ease of maintenance.

Your choices are also sometimes limited by political reasons: if you are asked to refactor application A, and you find out that you could tremendously improve performance by reworking function F, which queries tables from a different functional domain, you may not have direct access to these tables. And if function F is also a cornerstone, in another functional domain, of applications B and C, for which no performance issue has so far been reported, touching F can trigger vicious turf wars if personal rivalries step in. In that case, adding a layer as a special wrapper function called FA that calls the original function F is often the best solution if you can limit in FA the number of calls to F.

I stated at the beginning of this chapter that views are the SQL equivalent of functions; in many cases—and the currency conversion is a good example—creating a view over the join that replaces the function would have provided a simple and efficient interface. But even views can sometimes have a negative impact on performance, as you will see next.

Views

I have often found views to be implicated in performance issues. Once again, views are the real SQL equivalent of functions. But in the same way as deeply nested functions and clumsy parameter passing sometimes take their toll on performance, in many cases performance issues can be traced back to views.

What Views Are For

Views can serve several purposes. At their simplest (and most innocent), they can serve as a security device, narrowing the vision of data to some columns, or to some rows, or to some combination of rows and columns. Because all DBMS products feature information functions that retrieve data specific to the current user (such as the login name or system username), a generic view can be built that returns data dependent on the privileges of the invoker. Such a view merely adds filtering conditions to a base table and has no measurable impact on performance.

But views can also be repositories for complicated SQL operations that may have to be reused. And here it becomes much more interesting, because if we don't keep in mind the fact that we are operating against a view and not a base table, in some cases we may suffer a severe performance penalty.

In this section, I will show how even a moderately complex view can impact performance through two examples drawn on two of the tables I used in Chapter 1: the transactions table, which contains amounts for many transactions carried out in different currencies, and the currency_rates table, which stores the exchange rate for the various currencies at various dates.

Performance Comparison with and Without a Complex View

First let's create a "complex" view that is no more than an aggregate of transactions by currency (in the real world, there likely would be an additional condition on dates, but the absence of this condition changes nothing in this example):

```
create view v_amount_by_currency
as select curr, round(sum(amount), 0) amount
    from transactions
    group by curr;
```

I haven't picked a view that aggregates values at random; the problem with aggregating and filtering lies in whether you first aggregate a large volume of data and then filter on the result, or whether you filter first so as to aggregate a much smaller amount of data. Sometimes you have no choice (when you want to filter on the result of the aggregation, which is the operation performed by the having clause), but when you have the choice, what you do first can make a big difference in performance.

The question is what happens when you run a query such as the following:

```
select *
from v_amount_by_currency
where curr = 'JPY';
```

You have two options. You can apply filtering after the aggregate, like so:

```
select curr, round(sum(amount), 0) amount
from transactions
group by curr
having curr = 'JPY';
```

Or you can push the filtering inside the view, which behaves as though the query were written as follows:

```
select curr, round(sum(amount), 0) amount
from transactions
where curr = 'JPY'
group by curr;
```

You can consider this last query to be the "optimal" query, which I will use as a reference.

What happens when we query through the view actually depends on the DBMS (and, of course, on the DBMS version). MySQL 5.1 runs the view statement and then applies the filter, as the explain command shows:

```
mysql> explain select * from v_amount_by_currency
    -> where curr = 'JPY';
+----+-------------+--------------+-//--------+------------------------------+
| id | select_type | table        | //        |                              |
+----+-------------+--------------+-//--------+------------------------------+
|  1 | PRIMARY     | <derived2>   | //    170 | Using where                  |
|  2 | DERIVED     | transactions | //2000421 | Using temporary; Using filesort |
+----+-------------+--------------+-//--------+------------------------------+
2 rows in set (3.20 sec)
```

There is a MySQL extension to the create view statement, algorithm=merge, that you can use to induce MySQL to merge the view inside the statement, but group by makes it inoperative.

On the Oracle side, the execution plan shows that the optimizer is smart enough to combine the view and the filtering condition, and to filter the table as it scans it, before sorting the result and performing the aggregation:

```
---------------------------------------------------------------------...
| Id  | Operation            | Name         | Rows  | Bytes | Cost (%CPU)| ...
---------------------------------------------------------------------...
|   0 | SELECT STATEMENT     |              |     1 |    12 | 2528    (3)| ...
|   1 |  SORT GROUP BY NOSORT|              |     1 |    12 | 2528    (3)| ...
|*  2 |   TABLE ACCESS FULL  | TRANSACTIONS |  276K | 3237K | 2528    (3)| ...
---------------------------------------------------------------------...

Predicate Information (identified by operation id):
---------------------------------------------------
    2 - filter("CURR"='JPY')
```

This is in marked contrast to how Oracle behaves when it encounters a having clause in a regular statement. The upbeat Oracle optimizer assumes that developers know what they are writing and that having is always to be applied after the aggregate. Like the Oracle optimizer, the SQL Server optimizer pushes the where condition applied to the view inside the view. However, being less confident in human nature than its Oracle counterpart, the SQL Server optimizer is also able to push a condition that can be applied before aggregation inside the where clause when it appears in a having clause.

Figure 3-8 shows how the view performs comparatively to the "optimal" query that filters before aggregation and the query that uses having when it shouldn't. There is a severe penalty with MySQL both when the view is used and when the having clause is misused; there is a stronger penalty with Oracle when filtering is wrongly performed through having, but there is hardly any impact when using the view. Performance is identical in all three cases with SQL Server.

Take note, though, that the MySQL penalty also comes from my having mischievously applied my condition to the column that controls the grouping: the currency column. I would have experienced no (or hardly any) penalty if my condition had been applied to the aggregated amount, because in that case the where applied to the view would have been strictly equivalent to a having clause.

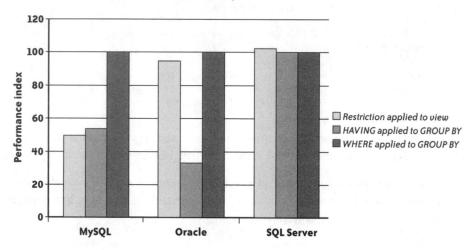

Views and Performance: Complex View

FIGURE 3-8. How a query against a complex view can compare to a query against a table

All things considered, the complexity of the previous view was rather moderate. So, I have refined my analysis by creating a "more complex" view that refers to a secondary utility view. Let's start with this utility view, which returns for each currency the most recent exchange rate:

```
create view v_last_rate
as
select a.iso, a.rate
from currency_rates a,
     (select iso, max(rate_date) last_date
      from currency_rates
      group by iso) b
where a.iso= b.iso
and a.rate_date = b.last_date;
```

I can now build the more complex view, which returns the converted amount per currency, but isolates the currencies that are most important to the bank's business and groups together as OTHER all currencies that represent a small fraction of business:

```
create view v_amount_main_currencies
as
select case r.iso
         when 'EUR' then r.iso
         when 'USD' then r.iso
         when 'JPY' then r.iso
         when 'GBP' then r.iso
         when 'CHF' then r.iso
         when 'HKD' then r.iso
         when 'SEK' then r.iso
         else 'OTHER'
```

```
            end currency,
        round(sum(t.amount*r.rate), 0) amount
from transactions t,
     v_last_rate r
where r.iso = t.curr
group by case r.iso
            when 'EUR' then r.iso
            when 'USD' then r.iso
            when 'JPY' then r.iso
            when 'GBP' then r.iso
            when 'CHF' then r.iso
            when 'HKD' then r.iso
            when 'SEK' then r.iso
            else 'OTHER'
          end;
```

Now I run the same test as with the simpler aggregate, by comparing the performance of the following code snippet to the performance of two functionally equivalent queries that still use the utility view:

```
select currency, amount
from v_amount_main_currencies
where currency = 'JPY';
```

First I place the condition on the currency in the having clause:

```
select t.curr, round(sum(t.amount) * r.rate, 0) amount
from transactions t,
     v_last_rate r
where r.iso = t.curr
group by t.curr, r.rate
having t.curr = 'JPY';
```

Then I place the condition on the currency in the where clause:

```
select t.curr, round(sum(t.amount) * r.rate, 0) amount
from transactions t,
     v_last_rate r
where r.iso = t.curr
  and t.curr = 'JPY'
group by t.curr, r.rate;
```

You can see the result in Figure 3-9. As you might have expected, the MySQL engine goes on computing the aggregate in the view, and then performs the filtering (as it does with having). The resultant performance is rather dismal in comparison to the query that hits the table with the filtering condition where it should be.

But the interesting and new fact in this rather hostile case is that even the Oracle and SQL Server optimizers cannot really keep query performance with the view on a par with the performance that can be obtained when correctly querying the table: the query against the view takes almost twice as long to run as the optimal query against the table.

The sample views I used are still simple views compared to some freak views I have come across; even a very smart optimizer will lose its footing when the view becomes quite complicated or when there are views stacked on one another.

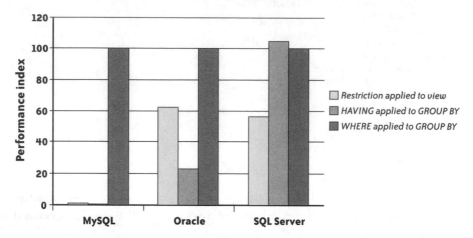

Views and Performance: More Complex View

Legend:
- Restriction applied to view
- HAVING applied to GROUP BY
- WHERE applied to GROUP BY

FIGURE 3-9. Performance comparison with a more complex view

The optimizer isn't necessarily to blame; sometimes it simply cannot decide what to do to improve performance.

Suppose, for instance, that we have a view defined as a join:

```
create view v(c1, c2, c3, c4, c5) as
select a.c1, a.c2, a.c3, b.c4, b.c5
from a, b
where a.c6 = b.c6
```

Now suppose that in a query all we require are columns c1 and c2, which both come from table a.

Do we need the join with table b? The answer may be either yes or no:

No

> We do not need the join with table b if c6 is both a mandatory column and a foreign key that must always have a match in table b. For instance, we can imagine that table a contains purchases, that c6 contains the customer code, and that c4 and c5 contain information such as customer name and customer town.

Yes

> We do need the join with table b if c6 is a column that can be null or that doesn't necessarily refer to a row from table b, because if this is the case, the join not only provides additional information (c4 and c5), but also serves as an implicit additional filtering criterion by requiring that a.c6 is not null (if it were null, there would be no match because null is never equal to anything, not even null), and that it corresponds to an existing row in table b.

In other words, sometimes the join just provides additional columns, where this:

```
select c1, c2 from v
```

will return exactly the same rows as this:

```
select c1, c2 from a
```

And other times the query against the view will return fewer rows than the select from the table, because the join provides an additional filtering condition. In many cases, a human being will be able to decide what is or isn't necessary to identify the proper result set, while the optimizer, very often because it lacks relevant information, will not be able to do so. In cases of doubt, the DBMS will always take the safest option: if you refer to the view, the optimizer will suppose, if it cannot decide otherwise, that the view may return a result set that is different from the result set returned by a simpler query, and it will use the view.

The more complex the view, the more ambiguities you may come across. Even a super-clever optimizer will be unable to decide how best to amalgamate the view to the query in all cases; moreover, a complex query means a very big number of options that it cannot explore in a limited amount of time. There is always a threshold where the optimizer gives up and the DBMS engine executes the view "as is" inside another query.

Earlier I mentioned joins that return columns that are unused in the query, which under certain conditions can translate into useless additional work. There are many other cases, especially when the query joins a view to a table that is already referenced inside a view. For instance, let's suppose the query is built over an outer join:

```
select a.c1, a.c2, a.c3, b.c4, b.c5
from a
    left outer join b
        on b.c6 = a.c3
```

And let's further suppose that this view is joined (with an inner join) inside a query to b, to return other information from b that doesn't appear in the view. The inner join in the query is a stronger condition than the outer join in the view. In the context of the query, the outer join in the query might as well have been an inner join: rows for which there is no match between a and b will be returned by the view, but will be filtered out in the query. Every additional row returned because of the outer join is a waste in the context of the query—and an inner join might just have been much more efficient than an outer join.

You find very similar cases with views that are built as the union of several queries; you regularly find them used in queries that apply such filtering criteria that the result set can contain rows coming from only a small subset of the view, and we could have spared several possibly costly select statements.

A different, but no less perverse, effect of views on unsuspecting programmers is to induce them to base searches or joins on columns that are computed on the fly. Say, for instance, that one column in a table contains, for historical reasons, a Unix timestamp (the number of seconds elapsed since January 1, 1970, at 0:00 a.m.); this is the only table in the schema that doesn't contain a regular SQL date, and therefore a developer decided to map over this table a simple view that masks the timestamp and converts it to a regular SQL date.

If an unsuspecting programmer innocently writes a condition such as the following:

```
where view_date_column = convert_to_date('date string')
```

this is what is really executed:

```
where convert_from_unix_timestamp(timestamp) = convert_to_date('date string')
```

Here we have a fine example of the dreaded case of the function applied to the indexed column, which prevents the use of the index. Unless an index has been computed—as Oracle and SQL Server may allow—on the converted timestamp,* any date condition applied to the view is certain to not take advantage of an existing index on the raw timestamp.

Similarly, some developers are sometimes tempted to hide the ugliness of a very poor database design under views, and to make a schema look more normalized than it really is by splitting, for instance, a single column that contains multiple pieces of information. Such a Dorian Grayish attempt is pretty sure to backfire: filters and joins would be based not on real, indexed columns but on derived columns.

Refactoring Views

Many views are harmless, but if monitoring proves that some of the "problem queries" make use of complex views, these views should be one of your first targets. And because complex, underperforming views are often combinations of several views, you shouldn't hesitate to rewrite views that are built on other views when they appear in problem queries; in many cases, you will be able to improve the performance of queries without touching them by simply redefining the views they reference. Views that are very complex should be made as simple as possible for the optimizer to work efficiently—not *apparently* simple, but simple in the sense that any trace of "fat" and unnecessary operations should be eliminated. If there is one place where the SQL code should be lean and mean, it is inside views. Rewriting views is, of course, the same skill as rewriting queries, which we will review in Chapter 5.

When you have doubts about views, querying the data dictionary can help you to spot complex views that you should rewrite. With MySQL, we can search the views' text for the name of another view in the same schema, and for some keywords that indicate complexity. The following query counts for each view how many views it contains, as well as the number of subqueries—union, distinct or group by (here is the pattern counting in action):

```
select y.table_schema,
       y.table_name,
       y.view_len,
       y.referenced_views                        views,
       cast((y.view_len - y.wo_from) / 4  - 1 as unsigned) subqueries,
       cast((y.view_len - y.wo_union) / 5 as unsigned)    unions,
```

---

* Remember that this requires the conversion function to be deterministic, and a Unix timestamp lacks the time zone information.

```
            cast((y.view_len - y.wo_distinct) / 8 as unsigned)  distincts,
            cast((y.view_len - y.wo_group) / 5 as unsigned)      groups
    from (select x.table_schema,
                 x.table_name,
                 x.view_len,
                 cast(x.referenced_views as unsigned) referenced_views,
                 length(replace(upper(x.view_definition), 'FROM', '')) wo_from,
                 length(replace(upper(x.view_definition), 'UNION', '')) wo_union,
                 length(replace(upper(x.view_definition), 'DISTINCT', '')) wo_distinct,
                 length(replace(upper(x.view_definition), 'GROUP', '')) wo_group
          from (select v1.table_schema,
                       v1.table_name,
                       v1.view_definition,
                       length(v1.view_definition) view_len,
                       sum(case
                              when v2.table_name is not null
                              then (length(v1.view_definition)
                                    - length(replace(v1.view_definition,
                                                     v2.table_name, '')))
                                   /length(v2.table_name)
                              else 0
                           end) referenced_views
                from information_schema.views v1
                     left outer join information_schema.views v2
                               on v1.table_schema = v2.table_schema
                where v1.table_name <> v2.table_name
                group by v1.table_schema,
                         v1.table_name,
                         v1.view_definition) x
          group by x.table_schema,
                   x.table_name) y
    order by 1, 2;
```

The fact that Oracle stores the text of views in a `long` column prevents us from directly
looking for keywords inside the view definition. We could do it with a little help from a
PL/SQL stored procedure and conversion to a more amenable `clob` or a very large `varchar2`.
However, we can get a very interesting indicator of view complexity thanks to the user_
dependencies view that can be queried recursively when views depend on views:

```
col "REFERENCES" format A35
col name format A40
select d.padded_name name,
       v.text_length,
       d."REFERENCES"
from (select name,
             lpad(name, level + length(name)) padded_name,
             referenced_name || ' (' || lower(referenced_type) || ')' "REFERENCES"
      from user_dependencies
      where referenced_type <> 'VIEW'
      connect by prior referenced_type = type
          and prior referenced_name = name
      start with type = 'VIEW') d
     left outer join user_views v
          on v.view_name = name;
```

SQL Server allows both possibilities: querying `information_schema.views` or listing the hierarchy of dependencies available through `sys.sql_dependencies`. Although, to be frank, getting rid of duplicate rows and listing dependencies in a legible order requires a good deal of back-bending. The following query, which lists dependencies, is intended for a mature audience only:

```
with recursive_query(level,
                     schemaid,
                     name,
                     refschemaid,
                     refname,
                     reftype,
                     object_id,
                     ancestry) as
(select 1 as level,
        x.schema_id as schemaid,
        x.name,
        o.schema_id as refschemaid,
        o.name as refname,
        o.type_desc as reftype,
        o.object_id,
        cast(x.rn_parent + '.'
             + cast(dense_rank() over (partition by x.rn_parent
                                       order by o.object_id) as varchar(5))
             as varchar(50)) as ancestry
 from (select distinct cast(v.rn_parent as varchar(5)) as rn_parent,
                       v.name,
                       v.schema_id,
                       v.object_id,
                       d.referenced_major_id,
                       cast(dense_rank() over (partition by v.rn_parent
                                               order by d.object_id)
                            as varchar(5)) as rn_child
       from (select row_number() over (partition by schema_id
                                       order by name) as rn_parent,
                    schema_id,
                    name,
                    object_id
             from sys.views) v
            inner join sys.sql_dependencies d
                on v.object_id = d.object_id) x
       inner join sys.objects o
             on o.object_id = x.referenced_major_id
 union all
 select parent.level + 1 as level,
        parent.refschemaid as schemaid,
        parent.refname as name,
        o.schema_id as refschemaid,
        o.name as refname,
        o.type_desc as reftype,
        o.object_id,
        cast(parent.ancestry + '.'
             + cast(dense_rank() over (partition by parent.object_id
                                       order by parent.refname) as varchar(5))
             as varchar(50)) as ancestry
 from sys.objects o
```

```
        inner join sys.sql_dependencies d
                on d.referenced_major_id = o.object_id
        inner join recursive_query parent
                on d.object_id = parent.object_id)
select a.name,
       len(v.view_definition) view_length,
       a.refname,
       a.reftype
from (select distinct space((level - 1) * 2) + name as name,
                      name as real_name,
                      schemaid,
                      refname,
                      lower(reftype) as reftype,
                      ancestry
       from recursive_query) as a
     inner join sys.schemas s
            on s.schema_id = a.schemaid
     left outer join information_schema.views v
            on v.table_schema = s.name
           and v.table_name = a.real_name
order by a.ancestry;
```

The queries that explore dependencies between objects will also tell you whether views depend on user functions.

The different possibilities we explored in Chapter 2 and in this chapter are probably all we can do without either reorganizing the database or (hardly) touching the application code. If at this stage we are still unsatisfied with performance, we must start to rewrite the code. But before getting our hands dirty, let's consider some tools that will help us to proceed with confidence.

## CHAPTER FOUR

Testing Framework

—*George Bernard Shaw (1856–1950)*

Pygmalion, Act III

BEFORE I EMBARK ON THE TOPIC OF SURGICALLY REMODELING **SQL** STATEMENTS AND PROGRAMS, I
need to discuss a topic of great practical importance: how to define a framework for testing, an environment to check that rewrites are not only faster, but also functionally equivalent. In theory, you should be able to mathematically prove that a relational construct is
equivalent to another construct. Actually, many features of the SQL language are not relational in the strictest sense (there's order by to start with; there is no order in a mathematical relation), and in practice, quirks in database design make some queries bear only a
faint resemblance to what they'd look like in an ideal world. As a result, you have to
resort to the usual tactics of program development: comparing what you get to what you
expected on as wide a variety of cases as possible. Except that such a comparison is much
more difficult with tables than with scalar values or even arrays.

Because refactoring is, by nature, an iterative process (changing little thing after little
thing until performance is deemed acceptable), we need tools to make iterations as short
as possible. In this chapter, I will address first the issue of generating test data, and then
that of checking correctness.

Generating Test Data

Among the important steps of a refactoring project, the generation of test data is probably the one that is easiest to underestimate. I have encountered cases when it took much longer to generate quality data than to correct and test the SQL accesses. The problem with SQL is that however poorly you code, a query on a 10-row table will always respond instantly, and in most cases results will be displayed as soon as you press Enter even on a 10,000-row table. It's usually when you have accumulated enough data in your database that performance turns sluggish. Although it is often possible to compare the relative performance of alternative rewrites on tables of moderate size, it is very difficult to predict on which side of the acceptability threshold we will be without testing against the target volume.

There are several cases when you need to generate test data:

* When you are working remotely and when the production data is much too voluminous to be sent over the network or even shipped on DVDs

* When the production data contains sensitive information, whether it is trade secrets or personal data such as medical records or financial information, which you are not allowed to access

* When refactoring is a preemptive strike anticipating a future data increase that has not yet taken place in production

* And even when, for various reasons, you just need a smaller but consistent subset of the production data that the production people are unable to provide;* in such a case, producing your own data is often the simplest and fastest way to get everything you need before starting your work

Even when tools do exist, it is sometimes hard to justify their purchase unless you have a recurrent need for them. And even when your bosses are quite convinced of the usefulness of tools, the complicated purchase circuit of big corporations doesn't necessarily fit within the tight schedule of a refactoring operation. Very often, you have to create your own test data.

Generating at will any number of rows for a set of tables is an operation that requires some thought. In this section, I will show you a number of ways you can generate around 50,000 rows in the classic Oracle sample table, emp, which comprises the following:

empno
: The primary key, which is an integer value

ename
: The surname of the employee

---

* Commercial products are available for extracting consistent data sets from production databases, but unfortunately, if you are a consultant (like I am), you cannot expect all of your customers to have bought them; otherwise, the absence of referential integrity constraints may seriously hamper their capabilities.

job

    A job description

mgr

    The employee number of the manager of the current employee

hiredate

    A date value in the past

sal

    The salary, a float value

comm

    Another float value that represents the commission of salespeople, null for most
    employees

deptno

    The integer identifier of the employee's department

Multiplying Rows

The original Oracle emp table contains 14 rows. One very simple approach is the multiplication of rows via a Cartesian product: create a view or table named ten_rows that, when queried, simply returns the values 0 through 9 as column num.

Therefore, if you run the following code snippet without any join condition, you will append into emp 14 rows times 10 times 10 times 10 times 4, or 56,000 new rows:

```
insert into emp
select e.*
from emp e,
     ten_rows t1,
     ten_rows t2,
     ten_rows t3,
     (select num
      from ten_rows
      where num < 4) t4
```

Obviously, primary keys object strongly to this type of method, because employee numbers that are supposed to be unique are going to be cloned 4,000 times each. Therefore, you have to choose one solution from among the following:

- Disabling all unique constraints (in practice, dropping all unique indexes that implement them), massaging the data, and then re-enabling constraints.

- Trying to generate unique values during the insertion process. Remembering that ten_rows returns the numbers 0 through 9 and that the original employee numbers are all in the 7,000s, something such as this will do the trick:

```
insert into emp(empno, ename, job, mgr, hiredate, sal, comm, deptno)
select 8000 + t1.num * 1000 + t2.num * 100 + t3.num * 10 + t4.num,
       e.ename, e.job, e.mgr, e.hiredate, e.sal, e.comm, e.deptno
from emp e,
     ten_rows t1,
```

```
     ten_rows t2,
     ten_rows t3,
     (select num
      from ten_rows
      where num < 4) t4
```

- Alternatively, you can use a sequence with Oracle or computations using a variable with MySQL or SQL Server (if the column has not been defined as an auto-incrementing identity column).

Your primary key constraint will be satisfied, but you will get rather poor data. I insisted in Chapter 2 on the importance of having up-to-date statistics. The reason is that the continuous refinement of optimizers makes it so that the value of data increasingly shapes execution plans. If you multiply columns, you will have only 14 different names for more than 50,000 employees and 14 different hire dates, which is totally unrealistic (to say nothing of the 4,000 individuals who bear the same name and are vying for the job of president). You saw in Chapter 2 the relationship between index selectivity and performance; if you create an index on ename, for instance, it is unlikely to be useful, whereas with real data it might be much more efficient. You need realistic test data to get realistic performance measures.

Using Random Functions

Using random functions to create variety is a much better approach than cloning a small sample a large number of times. Unfortunately, generating meaningful data requires a little more than randomness.

All DBMS products come with at least one function that generates random numbers, usually real numbers between 0 and 1. It is easy to get values in any range by multiplying the random value by the difference between the maximum and minimum values in the range, and adding the minimum value to the result. By extending this method, you can easily get any type of numerical value, or even any range of dates if you master date arithmetic.

The only trouble is that random functions return uniformly distributed numbers—that means that statistically, the odds of getting a value at any point in the range are the same. Real-life distributions are rarely uniform. For instance, salaries are more likely to be spread around a mean—the famous bell-shaped curve of the Gaussian (or "normal") distribution that is so common. Hire dates, though, are likely to be distributed otherwise: if we are in a booming company, a lot of people will have joined recently, and when you walk back in time, the number of people hired before this date will dwindle dramatically; this is likely to resemble what statisticians call an *exponential distribution*.

A value such as a salary is, generally speaking, unlikely to be indexed. Dates often are. When the optimizer ponders the benefit of using an index, it matters how the data is spread. The wrong kind of distribution may induce the optimizer to choose a way to execute the query that it finds fitting for the test data—but which isn't necessarily what it will do on real data. As a result, you may experience performance problems where there will be none on production data—and the reverse.

SQL SERVER AND RANDOM FUNCTIONS

SQL Server must be gently coaxed to produce random values, for reasons that are directly related to caching and the optimization of functions. Basically, if you run the following code, you will get a random value between 0 and 1:

```
select rand( );
```

However, if you run this next code snippet, you will get one random value repeated 10 times, which isn't exactly what you want when you need to generate data:

```
select rand( )
from ten_rows;
```

Actually, SQL Server "caches" the result of the rand( ) function and serves the same value with each row. This behavior may surprise you; after all, rand( ) seems to be the archetypal nondeterministic function that should be evaluated for each call (even if serious statisticians consider computer-generated "random" numbers to be deterministic).[a]

You can work around this feature by wrapping the T-SQL function within your own user-defined function. But here, you bump into a new difficulty: if you directly refer to rand( ) inside your own function, SQL Server suddenly remembers that the function is not *that* deterministic and complains. A second level of workaround is to hide rand( ) within a view, and then to query the view inside your function.

Let's do it all over again. First you create a view:

```
create view random(value)
as select rand( );
```

Then you create a function that queries the view:

```
create function randuniform( )
returns real
begin
   declare @v    real;

   set @v = (select value from random);
   return @v;
end;
```

And then you run a query that calls the function:

```
select dbo.randuniform( ) rnd
from ten_rows;
```

And it will magically work.

---

[a] One of the pioneers of computer science and the father of one method of random number generation, John von Neumann once jocularly commented about the sinful state of people trying to produce randomness through arithmetical means.

Fortunately, generating nonuniform random data from a uniform generator such as the one available in your favorite DBMS is an operation that mathematicians have studied extensively. The following MySQL function, for instance, will generate data distributed as a bell curve around mean *mu* and with standard deviation *sigma** (the larger the *sigma*, the flatter the bell):

```
delimiter //
create function randgauss(mu      double,
                          sigma double)
returns double
not deterministic
begin
  declare v1    double;
  declare v2    double;
  declare radsq double;
  declare v3    double;

  if (coalesce(@randgauss$flag, 0) = 0) then
    repeat
      set v1 := 2.0 * rand() - 1.0;
      set v2 := 2.0 * rand() - 1.0;
      set radsq := v1 * v1 + v2 * v2;
    until radsq < 1 and radsq > 0
    end repeat;
    set v3 := sqrt(-2.0 * log(radsq)/radsq);
    set @randgauss$saved := v1 * v3;
    set @randgauss$flag := 1;
    return sigma * v2 * v3 + mu;
  else
    set @randgauss$flag := 0;
    return sigma * @randgauss$saved + mu;
  end if;
end;
//
delimiter ;
```

The following SQL Server function will generate a value that is exponentially distributed; parameter lambda commands how quickly the number of values dwindles. If lambda is high, you get fewer high values and many more values that are close to zero. For example, subtracting from the current date a number of days equal to 1,600 times randexp(2) gives hire dates that look quite realistic:

```
create function randexp(@lambda  real)
returns real
begin
  declare @v    real;

  if (@lambda = 0) return null;
  set @v = 0;
  while @v = 0
```

---

* *mu* (μ) and *sigma* (Σ) are the names of the Greek letters traditionally used to represent mean and standard deviation—that is, the measure of the spread around the mean.

```
  begin
    set @v = (select value from random);
  end;
  return -1 * log(@v) / @lambda;
end;
```

Remember that the relative order of rows to index keys may also matter a lot. If your data isn't stored in a self-organizing structure such as a clustered index, you may need to sort it against a key that matches the order of insertion to correctly mimic real data.

We run into trouble with the generation of random character strings, however.

Oracle comes with a PL/SQL package, dbms_random, which contains several functions, including one that generates random strings of letters, with or without digits, with or without exotic but printable characters, in lowercase, uppercase, or mixed case. For example:

```
SQL> select dbms_random.string('U', 10) from dual;

DBMS_RANDOM.STRING('U',10)
----------------------------------------------------------------------
PGTWRFYMKB
```

Or, if you want a random string of random length between 8 and 12 characters:

```
SQL> select dbms_random.string('U',
  2                            8 + round(dbms_random.value(0, 4)))
  3  from dual;

DBMS_RANDOM.STRING('U',8+ROUND(DBMS_RANDOM.VALUE(0,4)))
----------------------------------------------------------------------
RLTRWPLQHEB
```

Writing a similar function with MySQL or SQL Server is easy; if you just want a string of up to 250 uppercase letters, you can write something such as this:

```
create function randstring(@len int)
returns varchar(250)
begin
  declare @output  varchar(250);
  declare @i       int;
  declare @j       int;

  if @len > 250 set @len = 250;
  set @i = 0;
  set @output = '';
  while @i < @len
  begin
    set @j = (select round(26 * value, 0) from random);
    set @output = @output + char(ascii('A') + @j);
    set @i = @i + 1;
  end;
  return @output;
end;
```

You can easily adapt this SQL Server example to handle lowercase or mixed case.

But if you want to generate strings, such as a job name, which must come out of a limited number of values in the correct proportions, you must rely on something other than randomly generated strings: you must base test data distribution on existing data.

Matching Existing Distributions

Even when data is ultra-confidential, such as medical records, statistical information regarding the data is very rarely classified. People responsible for the data will probably gladly divulge to you the result of a group by query, particularly if you write the query for them (and ask them to run it at a time of low activity if tables are big).

Suppose we want to generate a realistic distribution for jobs. If we run a group by query on the sample emp table, we get the following result:

```
SQL> select job, count(*)
  2 from emp
  3 group by job;

JOB         COUNT(*)
--------- ----------
CLERK           4
SALESMAN        4
PRESIDENT       1
MANAGER         3
ANALYST         2
```

If you had many more rows on which to base the distribution of the test data, you could directly use the output of such a query. With just 14 rows, it is probably wiser to use the preceding result as a mere starting point. Let's ignore the coveted job of president for the time being; it will always be possible to manually update one row later. What I want is the distribution of data shown in Figure 4-1.

Generating such a distribution is easy if we associate one job name to one range of values between 0 and 100: all we need to do is to generate a random number uniformly distributed in this interval. If it falls between 0 and 35, we'll return CLERK; if it falls between 35 and 70, we'll return SALESMAN; between 70 and 80, MANAGER; and between 80 and 100, ANALYST. From a practical point of view, all we need to do is compute cumulated frequencies.

Now I will show you in detail how to set this up on something more sophisticated than job names: family names. Of course, I could generate random strings, but somehow, DXGB-BRTYU doesn't look like a credible surname. How can I generate a realistic-looking list of people? The answer, as is so often the case, is to search the Internet. On many government websites, you can find some statistical information that makes for wonderful data sources. If you want to generate American family names, for instance, the Genealogy section of the *http://www.census.gov* website is the place to start.* You'll find on this site the most common American family names, with their ranking and the number of bearers.

---

* Wikipedia offers an article on the most common surnames for other countries: *http://en.wikipedia.org/wiki/Common_surnames*.

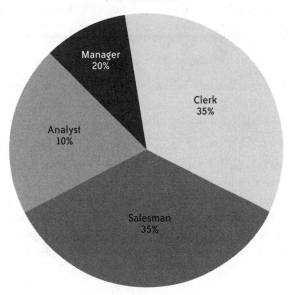
Job Distribution

FIGURE 4-1. Target job distribution for the test data

If you want to generate a relatively small number of different names, you can download *Top1000.xls*, which contains the 1,000 most common American names according to the last census (a bigger, more complete file is also available if you want a larger selection of common names). Download this file and save it as a *.csv* file. Here are the first lines from the file:

```
name;rank;count;prop100k;cum_prop100k;pctwhite;pctblack;pctapi;\..
   .. (first line cont'd) ..\pctaian;pct2prace;pcthispanic
SMITH;1;2376206;1727,02;1727,02;73,35;22,22;0,40;0,85;1,63;1,56
JOHNSON;2;1857160;1349,78;3076,79;61,55;33,80;0,42;0,91;1,82;1,50
WILLIAMS;3;1534042;1114,94;4191,73;48,52;46,72;0,37;0,78;2,01;1,60
BROWN;4;1380145;1003,08;5194,81;60,71;34,54;0,41;0,83;1,86;1,64
JONES;5;1362755;990,44;6185,26;57,69;37,73;0,35;0,94;1,85;1,44
MILLER;6;1127803;819,68;7004,94;85,81;10,41;0,42;0,63;1,31;1,43
DAVIS;7;1072335;779,37;7784,31;64,73;30,77;0,40;0,79;1,73;1,58
GARCIA;8;858289;623,80;8408,11;6,17;0,49;1,43;0,58;0,51;90,81
RODRIGUEZ;9;804240;584,52;8992,63;5,52;0,54;0,58;0,24;0,41;92,70
WILSON;10;783051;569,12;9561,75;69,72;25,32;0,46;1,03;1,74;1,73
...
```

Although we really need the name and cumulated proportion (available here as the fifth field, cum_prop100k, or cumulated proportion per 100,000), I will use the first three fields only to illustrate how I can massage the data to get what I need.

First I will create the table name_ref as follows:

```
create table name_ref(name      varchar(30),
                      rank      int,
                      headcount bigint,
                      cumfreq   bigint,
                      constraint name_ref_pk primary key(name));
```

The key column from which to pick a name is cumfreq, which represents the cumulated frequency. For data in this column, I chose to use integer values. If these values were percentages, integers would not be precise enough, and I would need decimal values. But like the U.S. government, I am going to use "per-100,000" values instead of "per-100" values, which will provide me with enough precision to allow me to work with integers.

At this stage, I can load the data into my table using the standard commands provided by my DBMS: BULK INSERT with SQL Server, LOAD with MySQL, and the SQL*Loader utility (or external tables) with Oracle (you will find the precise commands for each DBMS in the downloadable code samples described in Appendix A).

Once the original data is loaded, I must first compute cumulated values, normalize them, and then turn cumulated values into per-100,000 values. Because my population is limited in this example to the 1,000 most common names in America, I will get cumulated frequencies that are significantly higher than the real values; this is a systemic error I could minimize by using a bigger sample (such as the list of names with more than 100 bearers, available from the same source). I can compute normalized cumulated frequencies pretty easily in two statements with MySQL:

```
set @freq = 0;
update name_ref
set cumfreq = greatest(0, @freq := @freq + headcount)
order by rank;
update name_ref
set cumfreq = round(cumfreq * 100000 / @freq);
```

Two different statements will perform the same operation with SQL Server:

```
declare @maxfreq real;
set @maxfreq = (select sum(headcount) from name_ref);
update name_ref
set cumfreq = (select round(sum(n2.headcount)
                           * 100000 / @maxfreq, 0)
               from name_ref n2
               where name_ref.rank >= n2.rank);
```

And I can do it in a single statement with Oracle:

```
update name_ref r1
set r1.cumfreq = (select round(100000 * r2.cumul / r2.total)
                  from (select name,
                               sum(headcount) over (order by rank
                                   range unbounded preceding) cumul,
                               sum(headcount) over () total
                        from name_ref) r2
                  where r2.name = r1.name);
```

The preceding code snippets represent good illustrations of syntactical variations when one treads away from the most basic SQL queries. Some of these operations (particularly in the case of SQL Server) aren't very efficient, but since this is a one-off operation on (presumably) a development database, I can indulge in a little inefficiency.

At this point, all that remains to do is to create an index on the cumfreq column that will drive my queries, and I am ready to generate statistically plausible data (if not quite statistically correct data, because I ignore the "long tail," or all the names outside the 1,000 most common ones). For each name I want to pick, I need to generate a random number between 0 and 100,000, and return the name associated with the smallest value of cumfreq that is greater than (or equal to) this random number.

To return one random name with SQL Server, I can run the following (using the view that calls rand( )):

```
select top 1 n.name
from name_ref n,
     random r
where n.cumfreq >= round(r.value * 100000, 0)
order by n.cumfreq;
```

You can apply these techniques to generate almost any type of data. All you need is to find lists of items associated to a weight (sometimes you may find a rank, but you can create a weight from it by assigning a large weight to the first rank, then 0.8 times this weight to the second rank, then 0.8 times the weight of the second rank to the third rank, etc.). And obviously, any group by on existing data will give you what you need to seed the generation of test data that follows existing ratios.

Generating Many Rows

When we want to generate test data we usually don't want a single value, but rather a large number. Inserting many random values is, surprisingly, sometimes more difficult than you might think. On MySQL, we get the expected result when we call the query that returns one random name from the select list of a query that returns several rows:

```
mysql> select (select name
    ->           from name_ref
    ->           where cumfreq >= round(100000 * rand( ))
    ->           limit 1) name
    -> from ten_rows;
+-----------+
| name      |
+-----------+
| JONES     |
| MARTINEZ  |
| RODRIGUEZ |
| WILSON    |
| THOMPSON  |
| BROWN     |
| ANDERSON  |
| SMITH     |
| JACKSON   |
| JONES     |
+-----------+
10 rows in set (0.00 sec)

mysql>
```

Unfortunately, SQL Server returns the same name 10 times, even with our special wrapper for the rand( ) function:

```
select (select top 1 name
        from name_ref
        where cumfreq >= round(dbo.randuniform( ) * 100000, 0)
        order by cumfreq) name
from ten_rows;
```

The following Oracle query behaves like the SQL Server query:*

```
select (select name
        from (select name
              from name_ref
              where cumfreq >= round(dbms_random.value(0, 100000)))
        where rownum = 1) name
from ten_rows;
```

In both cases, the SQL engine tries to optimize its processing by caching the result of the subquery in the select list, thus failing to trigger the generation of a new random number for each row. You can remedy this behavior with SQL Server by explicitly linking the subquery to each different row that is returned:

```
select (select top 1 name
        from name_ref
        where cumfreq >= round(x.rnd * 100000, 0)
        order by cumfreq) name
from (select dbo.randuniform( ) rnd
      from ten_rows) x;
```

This isn't enough for Oracle, though. For one thing, you may notice that with Oracle we have two levels of subqueries inside the select list, and we need to refer to the random value in the innermost subquery. The Oracle syntax allows a subquery to refer to the current values returned by the query just above it, but no farther, and we get an error if we reference in the innermost query a random value associated to each row returned by ten_rows. Do we absolutely need two levels of subqueries? The Oracle particularity is that the pseudocolumn rownum is computed as rows are retrieved from the database (or from the result set obtained by a nested query), during the phase of identification of rows that will make up the result set returned by the current query. If you filter by rownum after having sorted, the rownum will include the "ordering dimension," and you will indeed retrieve the *n* first or last rows depending on whether the sort is ascending or descending. If you filter by rownum in the same query where the sort takes place, you will get *n* rows (the *n* first rows from the database) and sort them, which will usually be a completely different result. Of course, it might just happen that the rows are retrieved in the right order (because either Oracle chooses to use the index that refers to rows in the order of key values, or it scans the table in which rows have been inserted by decreasing frequency). But for that to happen would be mere luck.

* On Oracle 11*g* at least.

If we want to spur Oracle into reexecuting for each row the query that returns a random name instead of lazily returning what it has cached, we must also link the subquery in the select list to the main query that returns a certain number of rows, but in a different way—for instance, as in the following query:

```
SQL> select (select name
  2            from (select name
  3                    from name_ref
  4                   where cumfreq >= round(dbms_random.value(0, 100000)))
  5           where rownum = 1
  6             and -1 < ten_rows.num) ename
  7  from ten_rows
  8  /

ENAME
------------------------------
PENA
RUSSELL
MIRANDA
SWEENEY
COWAN
WAGNER
HARRIS
RODRIGUEZ
JENSEN
NOBLE

10 rows selected.
```

The condition on –1 being less than the number from ten_rows is a dummy condition—it's always satisfied. But Oracle doesn't know that, and it has to reevaluate the subquery each time and, therefore, has to return a new name each time.

But this doesn't represent the last of our problems with Oracle. First, if we want to generate a larger number of rows and join several times with the ten_rows table, we need to add a dummy reference in the select list queries to *each* occurrence of the ten_rows table; otherwise, we get multiple series of repeating names. This results in very clumsy SQL, and it makes it difficult to easily change the number of rows generated. But there is a worse outcome: when you try to generate all columns with a single Oracle query, you get data of dubious randomness.

For instance, I tried to generate a mere 100 rows using the following query:

```
SQL> select empno,
  2         ename,
  3         job,
  4         hiredate,
  5         sal,
  6         case job
  7           when 'SALESMAN' then round(rand_pack.randgauss(500, 100))
  8           else null
  9         end comm,
 10         deptno
 11  from (select 1000 + rownum * 10 empno,
```

```
 12                (select name
 13                 from (select name
 14                       from name_ref
 15                       where cumfreq >= round(100000
 16                                  * dbms_random.value(0, 1)))
 17                  where rownum = 1
 18                    and -1 < t2.num
 19                    and -1 < t1.num) ename,
 20                (select job
 21                 from (select job
 22                       from job_ref
 23                       where cumfreq >= round(100000
 24                                  * dbms_random.value(0, 1)))
 25                  where rownum = 1
 26                    and -1 < t2.num
 27                    and -1 < t1.num) job,
 28                round(dbms_random.value(100, 200)) * 10 mgr,
 29                sysdate - rand_pack.randexp(0.6) * 100 hiredate,
 30                round(rand_pack.randgauss(2500, 500)) sal,
 31                (select deptno
 32                 from (select deptno
 33                       from dept_ref
 34                       where cumfreq >= round(100000
 35                                  * dbms_random.value(0, 1)))
 36                  where rownum = 1
 37                    and -1 < t2.num
 38                    and -1 < t1.num) deptno
 39          from ten_rows t1,
 40               ten_rows t2)
 41  /

 EMPNO ENAME        JOB       HIREDATE        SAL       COMM     DEPTNO
------- ------------ --------- --------- ---------- ---------- ----------
   1010 NELSON       CLERK     04-SEP-07       1767                    30
   1020 CAMPBELL     CLERK     15-NOV-07       2491                    30
   1030 BULLOCK      SALESMAN  11-NOV-07       2059        655         30
   1040 CARDENAS     CLERK     13-JAN-08       3239                    30
   1050 PEARSON      CLERK     03-OCT-06       1866                    30
   1060 GLENN        CLERK     09-SEP-07       2323                    30
...
   1930 GRIMES       SALESMAN  05-OCT-07       2209        421         30
   1940 WOODS        SALESMAN  17-NOV-07       1620        347         30
   1950 MARTINEZ     SALESMAN  03-DEC-07       3108        457         30
   1960 CHANEY       SALESMAN  15-AUG-07       1314        620         30
   1970 LARSON       CLERK     04-SEP-07       2881                    30
   1980 RAMIREZ      CLERK     07-OCT-07       1504                    30
   1990 JACOBS       CLERK     17-FEB-08       3046                    30
   2000 BURNS        CLERK     19-NOV-07       2140                    30

100 rows selected.
```

Although surnames look reasonably random, and so do hire dates, salaries, and commissions, I have never obtained, in spite of repeated attempts, anything other than SALESMAN or CLERK for a job—and department 30 seems to have always sucked everyone in.

However, when I wrote a PL/SQL procedure, generating each column in turn and inserting row after row, I experienced no such issue and received properly distributed, random-looking data. I have no particular explanation for this behavior. The fact that data is correct when I used a procedural approach proves that the generation of random numbers isn't to blame. Rather, it's function caching and various optimization mechanisms that, in this admittedly particular case, all work against what I'm trying to do.

You may have guessed from the previous chapters (and I'll discuss this topic in upcoming chapters as well) that I consider procedural processing to be something of an anomaly in a relational context. But the reverse is also true: when we are generating a *sequence* of random numbers, we are in a procedural environment that is pretty much alien to the set processing of databases. We must pick the right tool for the job, and the generation of random data is a job that calls for procedures.

The downside to associating procedural languages to databases is their relative slowness; generating millions of rows will not be an instant operation. Therefore, it is wise to dump the tables you filled with random values if you want to compare with the same data several operations that change the database; it will make reloads faster. Alternatively, you may choose to use a "regular" language such as C++ or Java, or even a powerful scripting language such as Perl, and generate a flat file that will be easy to load into the database at high speed. Generating files independently from the database may also allow you to take advantage of libraries such as the Gnu Statistical Library (GSL) for sophisticated generation of random values. The main difficulty lies in the generation of data that matches predefined distributions, for which a database and the SQL language are most convenient when your pool of data is large (as with surnames). But with a little programming, you can fetch this type of data from your database, or from an SQLite* or Access file.

Dealing with Referential Integrity

Generating random data while preserving referential integrity may be challenging. There are few difficulties with preserving referential integrity among different tables; you just need to populate the reference tables first (in many cases, you don't even need to generate data, but rather can use the real tables), and then the tables that reference them. You only need to be careful about generating the proper proportions of each foreign key, using the techniques I have presented. The real difficulties arise with dependencies *inside* a table. In the case of a table such as emp, we have several dependencies:

comm
> The existence of a commission is dependent on the job being SALESMAN; this relationship is easy to deal with.

---

* SQLite is one of my favorite tools whenever I need to organize personal data, whether it is reference data, as in this case, or collected performance data.

`mgr`

The manager identifier, `mgr`, must be an existing employee number (or `null` for the president). One relatively easy solution if you are generating data using a procedure is to state that the manager number can be only one of the (say) first 10% of employees. Because employee numbers are generated sequentially, we know what range of employee numbers we must hit to get a manager identifier. The only difficulty that remains, then, is with the managers themselves, for which we can state that their manager can only be an employee that has been generated before them. However, such a process will necessarily lead to a lot of inconsistencies (e.g., someone with the `MANAGER` job having for a manager someone with the `CLERK` job in another department).

Generally speaking, the less cleanly designed your database is, the more redundant information and hidden dependencies you will get, and the more likely you will be to generate inconsistencies when populating the tables. Take the `emp` table, for instance. If the manager identifier was an attribute of a given job in a given department that is an attribute of the function (which it is, actually; there is no reason to update the records of employees who remain in their jobs whenever their manager is promoted elsewhere), and is not an attribute of the person, most difficulties would vanish. Unfortunately, when you refactor you have to work with what you have, and a full database redesign, however necessary it may be at times, is rarely an option. As a result, you must evaluate data inconsistencies that are likely to derive from the generation of random values, consider whether they may distort what you are trying to measure, and in some cases be ready to run a few normative SQL updates to make generated data more consistent.

Generating Random Text

Before closing the topic of data generation, I want to say a few words about a particular type of data that is on the fringe of database performance testing but that can be important nonetheless: random text. Very often, you find in databases text columns that contain not names or short labels, but XML data, long comments, or full paragraphs or articles, as may be the case in a website content management system (CMS) or a Wiki that uses a database as a backend. It may sometimes be useful to generate realistic test data for these columns, too: for instance, you may have to test whether `like '%pattern%'` is a viable search solution, or whether full-text indexing is required, or whether searches should be based on keywords instead.

Random XML data requires hardly any more work than generating numbers, dates, and strings of characters: populating tables that more or less match the XML document type definition (DTD) and then querying the tables and prefixing and suffixing values with the proper tags is trivial. What is more difficult is producing real, unstructured text. You always have the option of generating random character strings, where spaces and punctuation marks are just characters like any others. This is unlikely to produce text that looks like real text, and it will make text-search tests difficult because you will have no real word to search for. This is why "randomized" real text is a much more preferable solution.

In design examples, you may have encountered paragraphs full of Latin text, which very often start with the words *lorem ipsum.** *Lorem ipsum*, often called *lipsum* for short, is the generic name for filler text, designed to look like real text while being absolutely meaningless (although it looks like Latin, it means nothing), and it has been in use by typographers since the 16th century. A good way to generate *lipsum* is to start with a real text, tokenize it (including punctuation marks, considered as one-letter words), store it all into (guess what) an SQL table, and compute frequencies. However, text generation is slightly subtler than picking a word at random according to frequency probabilities, as we did with surnames. Random text generation is usually based on *Markov chains*—that is, random events that depend on the preceding random events. In practice, the choice of a word is based on its length and on the length of the two words just output. When the seeding text is analyzed, one records the relative lengths of three succeeding words. To choose a new word, you generate a random number that selects a length, based on the lengths of the two preceding words; then, from among the words whose length matches the length just selected, you pick one according to frequency.

I wrote two programs that you will find on this book's website (*http://www.oreilly.com/catalog/9780596514976*); instructions for their use are in Appendix B. These programs use SQLite as a backend. The first one, mklipsum, analyzes a text and generates an SQLite datafile. This file is used by the second program, lipsum, which actually generates the random text.

You can seed the datafile with any text of your choice. The best choice is obviously something that looks similar to what your database will ultimately hold. Failing this, you can give a chic classical appearance to your output by using Latin. You can find numerous Latin texts on the Web, and I'd warmly recommend Cicero's *De Finibus*, which is at the root of the original "lorem ipsum." Otherwise, a good choice is a text that already looks randomized when it is not, such as a teenager's blog or the marketing fluff of an "Enterprise Software" vendor. Lastly, you may also use the books (in several languages) available from *http://www.gutenberg.org*. Beware that the specific vocabulary and, in particular, the character names, of literary works will give a particular tone to what you generate. Texts generated from *Little Women*, *Treasure Island*, or *Paradise Lost* will each have a distinct color; you're on safer ground with abstract works of philosophy or economy.

I will say no more about the generation of test data—but don't forget that phase in your estimate of the time required to study how to improve a process, as it may require more work than expected.

---

* You can find examples on such a site as *http://www.oswd.org*, which offers open source website designs.

Comparing Alternative Versions

Because refactoring involves some rewriting, when the sanity checks and light improvements you saw in Chapters 2 and 3 are not enough, you need methods to compare alternative rewrites and decide which one is best. But before comparing alternative versions based on their respective performance, we must ensure that our rewrites are strictly equivalent to the slow, initial version.[*]

Unit Testing

Unit testing is wildly popular with methodologies often associated with refactoring; it's one of the cornerstones of Extreme Programming. A unit is the smallest part of a program that can be tested (e.g., procedure or method). Basically, the idea is to set up a context (or "fixture") so that tests can be repeated, and then to run a test suite that compares the actual result of an operation to the expected result, and that aborts if any of the tests fail.

Using such a framework is very convenient for procedural or object languages. It is a very different matter with SQL,[†] unless all you want to check is the behavior of a select statement that returns a single value. For instance, when you execute an update statement, the number of rows that may be affected ranges from zero to the number of rows in the table. Therefore, you cannot compare "one value" to "one expected value," but you must compare "one state of the table" to "one expected state of the table," where the state isn't defined by the value of a limited number of attributes as it could be with an instance of an object, but rather by the values of a possibly very big set of rows.

We might want to compare a table to another table that represents the expected state; this may not be the most convenient of operations, but it is a process we must contemplate.

Comparing Crudely

If you are rewriting a query that returns very few rows, a glance at the result will be enough to check for correctness. The drawback of this method is that glances are hard to embed in automated test suites, and they can be applied neither to queries that return many rows nor to statements that modify the data.

The second simplest functional comparison that you can perform between two alternative rewrites is the number of rows either returned by a select statement or affected by an insert, delete, or update statement; the number of rows processed by a statement is a standard value returned by every SQL interface with the DBMS, and is available either through some kind of system variable or as the value returned by the function that calls for the execution of the statement.

---

[*] Actually, I have seen cases when rewrites have revealed some bugs in the original code, and therefore the result was not strictly identical in the old and new versions. But we can probably ignore such unusual cases.

[†] It is worth mentioning that most unit testing frameworks available for database servers are actually designed for stored procedures—in other words, the procedural extension of the language.

Obviously, basing one's appraisal of functional equivalence on identical numbers of rows processed isn't very reliable. Nevertheless, it can be effective enough as a first approximation when you compare *one* statement to *one* statement (which means when you don't substitute one SQL statement for several SQL statements). However, it is easy to derail a comparison that is based solely on the number of rows processed. Using aggregates as an example, the aggregate may be wrong because you forgot a join condition and you aggregate a number of duplicate rows, and yet it may return the same number of rows as a correct query. Similarly, an update of moderate complexity in which column values are set to the result of subqueries may report the same number of rows updated and yet be wrong if there is a mistake in the subquery.

If a statement rewrite applied to the same data processes a different number of rows than the original statement, you can be certain that one of the two is wrong (not necessarily the rewrite), but the equality of the number of rows processed is, at best, a very weak presumption of correctness.

In other cases, the comparison of the number of rows processed is simply irrelevant: if, through SQL wizardry, you manage to replace several successive updates to a table with a single update, there will be no simple relationship between the number of rows processed by each original update and the number of rows processed by your version.

Comparing Tables and Results

Comparing the number of operations is one thing, but what matters is the data. We may want to compare tables (e.g., how the same initial data was affected by the initial process and the refactored version) or result sets (e.g., comparing the output of two queries). Because result sets can be seen as virtual tables (just like views), I will consider how we can compare tables, keeping in mind that whenever I refer to a table name in the from clause, it could also be a subquery.

What to compare

Before describing comparison techniques, I'd like to point out that in many cases, not all table columns are relevant to a comparison, particularly when we are comparing different ways to change the data. It is extremely common to record information such as a timestamp or who last changed the data inside a table; if you successively run the original process and an improved one, timestamps cannot be anything but different and must therefore be ignored. But you can find trickier cases to handle when you are confronted with alternate keys—in other words, database-generated numbers (through sequences with Oracle, identity columns with SQL Server, or auto-increment columns with MySQL).

Imagine that you want to check whether the rewriting of a process that changes data gives the same result as the original slow process. Let's say the process is applied to table T. You could start by creating T_COPY, an exact copy (indexes and all) of T. Then you run the original process, and rename the updated T to T_RESULT. You rename T_COPY to T, run your improved process, and want to compare the new state of T to T_RESULT. If you are using an

Oracle database, and if some sequence numbers intervene in the process, in the second run you will have sequence numbers that follow those that were generated during the first run. Naturally, you could imagine that before running the improved process, you drop all sequences that are used and re-create them starting with the highest number you had before you ran the initial process. However, this seriously complicates matters, and (more importantly) you must remember that the physical order of rows in a table is irrelevant. That also means that processing rows in a different order is perfectly valid, as long as the final result is identical. If you process rows in a different order, your faster process may not assign the same sequence number to the same row in all cases. The same reasoning holds with identity (auto-increment) columns. Strictly speaking, the rows will be different, but as was the case with timestamps, logically speaking they will be identical.

If you don't want to waste a lot of time hunting down differences that are irrelevant to business logic, you must keep in mind that columns that are automatically assigned a value (unless it is a default, constant value) don't really matter. This can be all the more disturbing as I refer hereafter to primary key columns, as there are literally crowds of developers (as well as numerous design tools) that are honestly convinced that the database design is fine as long as there is some unique, database-generated number column in every table, called id. It must be understood that such a purposely built "primary key" can be nothing but a practical shorthand way of replacing a "business-significant" key, often composed of several columns, that uniquely identifies a row. Therefore, let me clearly state that:

- When I use * in the following sections, I'm not necessarily referring to all the columns in the table, but to all the "business relevant" columns.

- When I refer to *primary key columns*, I'm not necessarily referring to the column(s) defined as "primary key" in the database, but to columns that, from a business perspective, uniquely identify each row in the table.

Brute force comparison

One simple yet efficient way to compare whether two tables contain identical data is to dump them to operating system files, and then to use system utilities to look for differences.

At this point, we must determine how we must dump the files:

DBMS utilities

All DBMS products provide tools for dumping data out of the database, but those tools rarely fill our requirements.

For instance, with MySQL, `mysqldump` dumps full tables; as you have seen, in many cases we may have a number of different values for technical columns and yet have functionally correct values. As a result, comparing the output of `mysqldump` for the same data after two different but functionally equivalent processes will probably generate many false positives and will signal differences where differences don't matter.

SQL Server's bcp doesn't have the limitations of mysqldump, because with the queryout parameter it can output the result of a query; bcp is therefore usable for our purpose.

Oracle, prior to Oracle 10.2, was pretty much in the same league as MySQL because its export utility, exp, was only able to dump all the columns of a table; contrary to mysqldump, the only output format was a proprietary binary format that didn't really help the "spot the differences" game. Later versions indirectly allow us to dump the result of a query by using the data pump utility (expdp) or by creating an external table of type oracle_datapump as the result of a query. There are two concerns with these techniques, though: the format is still binary, and the file is created on the server, sometimes out of reach of developers.

To summarize, if we exclude bcp, and in some simple cases mysqldump, DBMS utilities are not very suitable for our purpose (to their credit, they weren't designed for that anyway).

DBMS command-line tools

Running an arbitrary query through a command-line tool (sqlplus, mysql, or sqlcmd) is probably the simplest way to dump a result set to a file. Create a file containing a query that returns the data you want to check, run it through the command-line utility, and you have your data snapshot.

The snag with data snapshots is that they can be very big; one way to work around storage issues is to run the data through a checksumming utility such as md5sum. For instance, you can use a script such as the following to perform such a checksum on a MySQL query:

```
#
#    A small bash-script to checksum the result
#    of a query run through mysql.
#
#    In this simplified version, connection information
#    is supposed to be specified as <user>/<password>:<database>
#
#    An optional label (-l "label") and timestamp (-t)
#    can be specified, which can be useful when
#    results are appended to the same file.
#
usage="Usage: $0 [-t][-l label] connect_string sql_script"
#
ts=''
while getopts "tl:h" options
do
  case $options in
    t )  ts=$(date +%Y%m%d%H%M%S);;
    l )  label=$OPTARG;;
    h )  echo $usage
         exit 0;;
    \? ) echo $usage
         exit 0;;
    * )  echo $usage
         exit 1;;
  esac
done
```

```
shift $(($OPTIND - 1))
user=$(echo $1 | cut -f1 -d/)
password=$(echo $1 | cut -f2 -d/ | cut -f1 -d:)
database=$(echo $1 | cut -f2 -d:)
mysum=$(mysql -B --disable-auto-rehash -u${user} -p${password} \
        -D${database} < $2 | md5sum | cut -f1 -d' ')
echo "$ts        $label  $mysum"
```

On a practical note, beware that MD5 checksumming is sensitive to row order. If the table has no clustered index, a refactored code that operates differently may cause the same data set to be stored to a table in a different row order. If you want no false positives, it is a good idea to add an order by clause to the query that takes the snapshot, even if it adds some overhead.

There is an obvious weakness with checksum computation: it can tell you whether two results are identical or different, but it won't tell you where the differences are. This means you will find yourself in one of the following two situations:

- You are very good at "formal SQL," and with a little prompting, you can find out how two logically close statements can return different results without actually running them (9 times out of 10, it will be because of null values slipping in somewhere).

- You still have to hone your SQL skills (or you're having a bad day) and you need to actually "see" different results to understand how you can get something different, in which case a data dump can harmoniously complement checksums when they aren't identical (of course, the snag is that you need to run the slow query once more to drill in).

In short, you need different approaches to different situations.

SQL comparison, textbook version

Using a command-line utility to either dump or checksum the contents of a table or the result of a query presumes that the unit you are testing is a full program. In some cases, you may want to check from within your refactored code whether the data so far is identical to what would have been obtained with the original version. From within a program, it is desirable to be able to check data using either a stored procedure or an SQL statement.

The classical SQL way to compare the contents of two tables is to use the except set operator (known as minus in Oracle). The difference between tables A and B is made of the rows from A that cannot be found in B, plus the rows from B that are missing from A:

```
(select * from A
 except
 select * from B)
union
(select * from B
 except
 select * from A)
```

Note that the term "missing" also covers the case of "different." Logically, each row consists of the primary key, which uniquely identifies the row, plus a number of attributes.

A row is truly missing if the primary key value is absent. However, because in the preceding SQL snippet we consider *all* the relevant columns, rows that have the same primary key in both tables but different attributes will simultaneously appear as missing (with one set of attributes) from one table and (with the other set of attributes) from the other table.

If your SQL dialect doesn't know about except or minus (which is the case with MySQL*), the cleanest implementation of this algorithm is probably with two outer joins, which requires knowing the names of the primary key columns (named pk1, pk2, ... pkn hereafter):

```
select A.*
from A
     left outer join B
          on A.pk1 = B.pk1
          ...
          and A.pkn = B.pkn
where B.pk1 is null
union
select B.*
from B
     left outer join A
          on A.pk1 = B.pk1
          ...
          and A.pkn = B.pkn
where A.pk1 is null
```

Now, if you consider both code samples with a critical eye, you will notice that the queries can be relatively costly. Comparing all rows implies scanning both tables, and we cannot avoid that. Unfortunately, the queries are doing more than simply scanning the tables. When you use except, for instance, there is an implicit data sort (something which is rather logical, when you think about it: comparing sorted sets is easy, so it makes sense to sort both tables before comparing them). Therefore, the SQL code that uses except actually scans and sorts each table *twice*. Because the tables contain (hopefully) the same data, this can hurt when the volume is sizable. A purist might also notice that, strictly speaking, the union in the query (which implicitly asks for removing duplicates and causes a sort) could be a union all, because the query is such that the two parts of the union cannot possibly return the same row. However, because we don't expect many differences (and we hope for none), it wouldn't make the query run much faster, and getting an implicitly sorted result may prove convenient.

The version of the code that explicitly references the primary key columns performs no better. As you saw in Chapter 2, using an index (even the primary key index) to fetch rows one by one is much less efficient than using a scan when operating against many rows. Therefore, even if the writing is different, the actual processing will be roughly similar in both cases.

---

* Although MaxDB, available from the same provider, implements it.

SQL comparison, better version

On a site that is popular with Oracle developers (*http://asktom.oracle.com/*, created by Tom Kyte), Marco Stefanetti has proposed a solution that limits the scanning of tables to one scan each, but applies a group by over the union. The following query is the result of iterative and collaborative work between Marco and Tom:

```
select X.pk1, X.pk2, ..., X.pkn,
       count(X.src1) as cnt1,
       count(X.src2) as cnt2
from (select A.*,
             1 as src1,
             to_number(null) as src2
      from A
      union all
      select B.*,
             to_number(null) as src1,
             2 as src2
      from B) as X
group by X.pk1, X.pk2, ..., X.pkn
having count(X.src1) <> count(X.src2)
```

It is perhaps worth nothing that, although using union instead of union all didn't make much difference in the previous section where it was applied to the (probably very small) results of two differences, it matters here. In this case, we are applying the union to the two table scans; we can't have duplicates, and if the tables are big, there is no need to inflict the penalty of a sort.

The Stefanetti–Kyte method scales much better than the classical method. To test it, I ran both queries against two tables that were different by only one row. When the tables contain only 1,000 rows (1,000 and 999, to be precise), both versions run fast. However, as the number of rows increases, performance of the classic comparison method deteriorates quickly, as you can see in Figure 4-2.

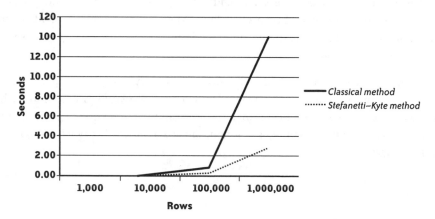

FIGURE 4-2. How two table comparison methods scale

By contrast, the Stefanetti–Kyte method behaves much better, even against a large number of rows.

Comparing checksums in SQL

Are those comparison algorithms appropriate in a refactoring assignment? I am afraid they are more useful for comparing data once rather than for iterative testing.

Suppose that you are in the process of rewriting a poorly performing query that returns many rows. If you want to apply the preceding methods to a result set, instead of a regular table, you may want to inject the query under study as a subquery in the from clause. Unless you are very, very gifted (and definitely more gifted than I), it is unlikely that you'll hit the right way to write the query in your very first attempt. And if you have to reexecute the slow "reference" query each time, it will definitely affect the time you need to reach a satisfying result. Therefore, it may be a good idea to create a result_ref table that stores the target result set:

```
create table result_ref
as (slow query)
```

Alternatively, and particularly if the expected result set is very large and storage is a concern, you may want to checksum this result set—from within SQL. MySQL provides a checksum table command, but this is a command for checking data integrity that applies to tables, not queries, and anyway, it provides no option to exclude some columns. All products do, however, provide a function to checksum data: MySQL has an md5( ) function, Oracle has dbms_crypto.hash( ), and SQL Server provides hashbytes( ), the latter two of which let us use either the MD5 or the SHA1 algorithm.* Actually, some products provide several functions for generating hash values (SQL Server also provides checksum( ) and Oracle provides dbms_utility.get_hash_value( )), but you must be careful about the function you use. Different hashing functions have different properties: a function such as checksum( ) is mainly designed to help build hash tables, whereas collisions, which mean several strings hashing into the same value, are acceptable to some extent. When you build hash tables, what matters most is the speed of the function. If we want to compare data, though, the odds of having different data hashing into the same value must be so small as to be negligible, which means that we must use a stronger algorithm such as MD5 or SHA1.

There is a snag: all those functions (except for SQL Server's checksum_aggr( ), which is rumored to be a simple binary *exclusive or* [XOR] operation) are scalar functions: they take a string to checksum as an argument, and they return a hash value. They don't operate on a set of rows, and you cannot pipe the result of a query into them as you can with md5sum, for instance. What would really be useful is a function that takes as an argument the text of an arbitrary query, and returns a checksum of the data set returned by this query—for instance, a function that would allow us to write the following:

```
set mychecksum = qrysum('select * from transactions');
```

---

* SHA1 is better for cryptography, but we are not trying to encrypt data, we just want to checksum it, and MD5 does the job perfectly well.

The result could be compared to a previous reference checksum, and a lengthy process could be aborted as soon as one difference is encountered. To reach this goal and write such a function, we need features that allow us to do the following:

- Execute an arbitrary query.
- Checksum a row returned by a query.
- Combine all row checksums into a global checksum.

The first bullet point refers to *dynamic SQL*. Oracle provides all required facilities through the `dbms_sql` package; SQL Server and MySQL are slightly less well equipped. SQL Server has `sp_executesql`, as well as stored procedures such as `sp_describe_cursor_columns` that operates on cursors, which are in practice handlers associated to queries. But as with MySQL, if we can prepare statements from an arbitrary string and execute them, unless we use temporary tables to store the query result, we cannot loop on the result set returned by a prepared statement; we can loop on a cursor, but cursors cannot directly be associated to an arbitrary statement passed as a string.

Therefore, I will show you how to write a stored procedure that checksums the result of an arbitrary query. Because I presume that you are interested in one or, at most, two of the products among the three I am focusing on, and because I am quickly bored by books with long snippets of a code for which I have no direct use, I will stick to the principles and stumbling blocks linked to each product. You can download the full commented code from O'Reilly's website for this book, and read a description of it in Appendix A.

Let's start writing a checksum function with Oracle, which provides all we need to dynamically execute a query. The sequence of operations will be as follows:

1. Create a cursor.
2. Associate the text of the query to the cursor and parse it.
3. Get into a structure a description of the columns or expressions returned by the query.
4. Allocate structures to store data returned by the query.

At this stage, we run into our first difficulty: PL/SQL isn't Java or C#, and dynamic memory allocation is performed through "collections" that are extended. It makes the code rather clumsy, at least for my taste. The data is returned as characters and is concatenated into a buffer. The second difficulty we run into is that PL/SQL strings are limited to 32 KB; past this limit, we must switch to LOBs. Dumping all the data to a gigantic LOB and then computing an MD5 checksum will cause storage issues as soon as the result set becomes big; the data has to be temporarily stored before being passed to the checksum function. Unfortunately, the choice of using a checksum rather than a copy of a table or of a result set is often motivated by worries about storage in the first place.

A more realistic option than the LOB is to dump data to a buffer by chunks of 32 KB and to compute a checksum for each buffer. But then, how will we combine checksums?

An MD5 checksum uses 128 bits (16 bytes). We can use another 32 KB buffer to concatenate all the checksums we compute, until we have about 2,000 of them, at which point the checksum buffer will be full. Then we can "compact" the checksum buffer by applying a new checksum to its content, and then rinse and repeat. When all the data is fetched, whatever the checksum buffer holds is minced through the MD5 algorithm a last time, which gives the return value for the function.

Computing checksums of checksums an arbitrary number of times raises questions about the validity of the final result; after all, compressing a file that has already been compressed sometimes makes the file bigger. As an example, I ran the following script, which computes a checksum of a Latin text by Ciccro and then loops 10,000 times as it checksums each time the result of the previous iteration. In a second stage, the script applies the same process to the same text from which I just removed the name of the man to whom the book is dedicated, Brutus.*

```
checksum=$(echo "Non eram nescius, Brute, cum, quae summis ingeniis
exquisitaque doctrina philosophi Graeco sermone tractavissent, ea
Latinis litteris mandaremus, fore ut hic noster labor in varias
reprehensiones incurreret. nam quibusdam, et iis quidem non admodum
indoctis, totum hoc displicet philosophari. quidam autem non tam id
reprehendunt, si remissius agatur, sed tantum studium tamque multam
operam ponendam in eo non arbitrantur. erunt etiam, et ii quidem eruditi
Graecis litteris, contemnentes Latinas, qui se dicant in Graecis legendis
operam malle consumere. postremo aliquos futuros suspicor, qui me ad alias
litteras vocent, genus hoc scribendi, etsi sit elegans, personae tamen et
dignitatis esse negent." | md5sum | cut -f1 -d' ')
echo "Initial checksum      : $checksum"
i=0
while [ $i -lt 10000 ]
do
  checksum=$(echo $checksum | md5sum | cut -f1 -d' ')
  i=$(( $i + 1 ))
done
echo "After 10000 iterations: $checksum"

checksum=$(echo "Non eram nescius, cum, quae summis ingeniis
exquisitaque doctrina philosophi Graeco sermone tractavissent, ea
Latinis litteris mandaremus, fore ut hic noster labor in varias
reprehensiones incurreret. nam quibusdam, et iis quidem non admodum
indoctis, totum hoc displicet philosophari. quidam autem non tam id
reprehendunt, si remissius agatur, sed tantum studium tamque multam
operam ponendam in eo non arbitrantur. erunt etiam, et ii quidem eruditi
Graecis litteris, contemnentes Latinas, qui se dicant in Graecis legendis
operam malle consumere. postremo aliquos futuros suspicor, qui me ad alias
litteras vocent, genus hoc scribendi, etsi sit elegans, personae tamen et
dignitatis esse negent." | md5sum | cut -f1 -d' ')
echo "Second checksum      : $checksum"
i=0
while [ $i -lt 10000 ]
```

* To all readers who remember vaguely either Roman history or Shakespeare's *Julius Caesar*: yes, that very same Brutus. It's a small world.

```
    do
      checksum=$(echo $checksum  | md5sum | cut -f1 -d' ')
      i=$(( $i + 1 ))
    done
    echo "After 10000 iterations: $checksum"
```

The result is encouraging:

```
$ ./test_md5
Initial checksum        : c89f630fd4727b595bf255a5ca762fed
After 10000 iterations: 1a6b606bb3cec62c0615c812e1f14c96
Second checksum         : 0394c011c73b47be36455a04daff5af9
After 10000 iterations: f0d61feebae415233fd7cebc1a412084
```

The first checksums are widely different, and so are the checksums of checksums, which is
exactly what we need.

You will find the code for this Oracle function described in Appendix A. I make it available
more as a curiosity (or perhaps as a monstrosity) and as a PL/SQL case study, for there is
one major worry with this function: although it displayed a result quickly when applied to
a query that returns a few thousand rows, it took one hour to checksum the following
when I was using the two-million-row table from Chapter 1:

```
select * from transactions
```

If I can admit that computing a checksum takes longer than performing a simpler operation, my goal is to be able to iterate tests of alternative rewrites fast enough. Therefore, I
have refactored the function and applied what will be one of my mantras in the next
chapter: it's usually much faster when performed, not only on the server, but also inside
the SQL engine.

One of the killer factors in my function is that I return the data inside my PL/SQL code
and then checksum it, because I am trying to fill a 32 KB buffer with data before computing the checksum. There is another possibility, which actually makes the code much simpler: to directly return a checksum applied to each row.

Remember that after parsing the query, I called a function to describe the various columns
returned by the query. Instead of using this description to prepare buffers to receive the
data and compute how many bytes may be returned by each row, I build a new query in
which I convert each column to a character string, concatenate their values, and apply the
checksumming function to the resultant string *inside the query*. For the from clause, all I
need to do is write the following:

```
... || ' from (' || original_query || ') as x'
```

At this stage, instead of painfully handling inside my function every column from each
and every row returned by my query, I have to deal with only one 16-byte checksum per
row.

But I can push the same logic even further: instead of aggregating checksums in my program, what about letting the aggregation process take place in the SQL query? Aggregating data is something that SQL does well. All I need to do is create my own aggregate

function to combine an arbitrary number of row checksums into an aggregate checksum. I could use the mechanism I just presented, concatenating checksums and compacting the resultant string every 2,000 rows. Inspired by what exists in both SQL Server and MySQL, I chose to use something simpler, by creating an aggregate function that performs an XOR on all the checksums it runs through. It's not a complicated function. It's not the best you can do in terms of ciphering, but because my goal is to quickly identify differences in result sets rather than encoding my credit card number, it's enough for my needs. Most importantly, it's reasonably fast, and it is insensitive to the order of the rows in the result set (but it is sensitive to the order of columns in the select list of the query).

When I applied this function to the same query:

```
select * from transactions
```

I obtained a checksum in about 100 seconds, a factor of 36 in improvement compared to the version that gets all the data and checksums it inside the program. This is another fine example of how a program that isn't blatantly wrong or badly written can be spectacularly improved by minimizing interaction with the SQL engine, even when this program is a stored procedure. It also shows that testing against small amounts of data can be misleading, because both versions return instantly when applied to a 5,000-row result set, with a slight advantage to the function that is actually the slowest one by far.

Enlightened by my Oracle experience, I can use the same principles with both SQL Server and MySQL, except that neither allows the same flexibility for the processing of dynamic queries inside a stored procedure as Oracle does with the dbms_sql package. The first difference is that both products have more principles than Oracle does regarding what a function can decently perform, and dynamic SQL isn't considered very proper. Instead of a function, I will therefore write procedures with an *out* parameter, which fits my purpose as well as a function would.

With SQL Server, first I must associate the text of the query to a cursor to be described. Unfortunately, when a cursor is declared, the text of the statement associated to the cursor cannot be passed as a variable. As a workaround, the declare cursor statement is itself built dynamically, which allows us to get the description of the various columns of the query passed in the @query variable.

```
--
-- First associate the query that is passed
-- to a cursor
--
set @cursor = N'declare c0 cursor for ' + @query;
execute sp_executesql @cursor;
--
-- Execute sp_describe_cursor_columns into the cursor variable.
--
execute sp_describe_cursor_columns
        @cursor_return = @desc output,
        @cursor_source = N'global',
        @cursor_identity = N'c0';
```

The next difficulty is with the (built-in) `checksum_agg()` function. This function operates on 4-byte integers; the `hashbytes()` function and its 16-byte result (with the choice of the MD5 algorithm) far exceed its capacity. Because the XOR operates bit by bit, I will change nothing in the result if I split the MD5 checksum computed for each row into four 4-byte chunks, apply `checksum_agg()` to each chunk, and finally concatenate the four aggregates. The operation requires some back-bending, but it does the trick.

With MySQL, as I have already pointed out, dynamic SQL possibilities are more limited than in Oracle or SQL Server. Nevertheless, writing a procedure that checksums an arbitrary query is less difficult than it might seem. We can work around the lack of support for the dynamic description of the columns returned by a query by creating a table that has the structure of the result set (I suppose that all computed columns have an alias):

```
create table some_unlikely_name as
select * from (original query)
limit 0
```

Note that it is `create table`, and not `create temporary table`. Because for MySQL the table is permanent, I can retrieve its description—that is, the description of the columns returned by the query—from `information_schema`. Of course, I would not advise drive-by table creation in a production database. But in a test or performance database, I usually lower my moral standards by a number of degrees.

Knowing the names of the columns, building a query that concatenates them and applies the `md5()` function to the result is a piece of cake. As with SQL Server, the 16-byte MD5 checksum is too big a mouthful for the built-in `bit_xor()` aggregate function: it takes as an argument, and returns, a 64-bit integer. As with SQL Server, splitting MD5 checksums (in two this time) and applying `bit_xor()` to each part separately before gluing everything back together in the end makes the checksums more palatable.

Limits of Comparison

As you have seen, there are several ways to check that a process rewrite gives the same result as the original version. Depending on whether you rewrite unitary queries or full processes, the volume of data you have to process, the speed with which you want to iterate, and the level of detail you need to help you correct potential differences, several options are possible; usually you will want to use a combination of methods, checking the number of rows there, checksumming here, and comparing data elsewhere.

Beware, though, that even the strictest comparison of data cannot replace a logical analysis of the code. Although you can prove that a proposition is false by finding one example for which it doesn't work, finding one example for which it works is no proof of truth. Because SQL is (loosely at times) based on logical concepts, exclusions, intersections, combinations of and and or conditions, plus the odd null that mischievously refuses to be either equal to or different from anything else, the proof of correctness is in the query itself. And there are even some very rare cases where correctness doesn't necessarily mean identical results.

A customer once asked me, after I presented a much faster rewrite of an initial query, whether I could prove that it gave the same result, and I was really annoyed: my query didn't return exactly the same results as the original one, on purpose. This query was the first stage in a two-stage process, and its purpose was to identify a small set of possible candidates in a fuzzy search. Because the second stage, which really identified the final result, was comparatively fast, I opted for a slightly laxer but much faster filtering in the first stage (while advocating a rethinking of the whole process). I would have gone nowhere with a strict identity of results in the first stage.

Now that we have test data and different ways to test whether rewrites apply equivalent processes to data, let's turn our attention back to the core topic of this book: improving existing SQL applications. First, let's consider the rewriting of slow queries, which we'll do in the following chapter.

## CHAPTER FIVE

Statement Refactoring

The problem for us was to move forward to a decisive victory,
or our cause was lost.

—Ulysses S. Grant (1822–1885)

Personal Memoirs, Chapter XXXVII

EVEN IF THERE IS OFTEN STILL ROOM FOR IMPROVEMENT WHEN ALL QUERIES HAVE BEEN "TUNED TO death," as you saw in Chapter 1 (and as I will further demonstrate in the next few chapters), when a big, bad query flagrantly kills performance, improving that query has a tremendous psychological effect. If you want to be viewed with awe, it is usually better to improve a killer query than to humbly ensure that the system will be able to scale up in the next few months.

Although optimizers are supposed to turn a poorly expressed statement into efficient data handling, sometimes things go wrong, even when the indexing is sane and all the relevant information is available to the optimizer. You know how it is: even if the optimizer does a good job 99 times out of 100, it is the botched attempt that everyone will notice. Assuming once again that proper statistics are available to the optimizer, failure to perform well usually results from one of the following:

- An optimizer bug (it happens!)

- A query that is so complex that the optimizer tried, in the limited time it grants itself, only a small number of rewrites compared to the large number of possible combinations, and failed to find the best path in the process

I'd like to point out that optimizer bugs are most commonly encountered in situations of almost inextricable complexity, and that properly writing the query is the most efficient workaround. Very often, writing a query in a simpler, more straightforward way requires much less work from the optimizer that will "hit" a good, efficient execution path faster. In fact, writing SQL well is a skill that you can compare to writing well: if you express yourself badly, chances are you will be misunderstood. Similarly, if you just patch together joins, where conditions, and subqueries, the optimizer may lose track of what is really critical in identifying the result set you ultimately want, and will embark on the wrong route.

Because what most people define as a "slow statement" is actually a statement that retrieves rows more slowly than expected, we could say that a slow statement is a statement with an "underperforming where clause." Several SQL statements can take a where clause. For most of this chapter, I will refer to select statements, with the understanding that the where clauses of update and delete statements, which also need to retrieve rows, follow the same rules.

Execution Plans and Optimizer Directives

First, a word of warning: many people link query rewriting to the analysis of execution plans. I don't. There will be no execution plan in what follows, which some people may find so strange that I feel the need to apologize about it. I can read an execution plan, but it doesn't say much to me. An execution plan just tells what has happened or will happen. It isn't bad or good in itself. What gives value to your understanding of an execution plan is an implicit comparison with what you think would be a better execution plan: for instance, "It would probably run faster if it were using this index; why is it doing a full table scan?" Perhaps some people just think in terms of execution plans. I find it much easier to think in terms of queries. The execution plan of a complex query can run for pages and pages; I have also seen the text of some queries running for pages and pages, but as a general rule a query is shorter than its execution plan, and for me it is far more understandable. In truth, whenever I read a query I more or less confusedly "see" what the SQL engine will probably try to do, which can be considered a very special sort of execution plan. But I have never learned anything really useful from the analysis of an execution plan that execution time, a careful reading of statements, and a couple of queries against the data dictionary didn't tell me as clearly.

I find that execution plans are as helpful as super-detailed driving instructions, such as "drive for 427 meters/yards/whatever, and then turn left into Route 96 and drive for 2.23 kilometers/miles/whatever…." If I don't know where I'm going, as soon as I miss an exit I will be lost. I'm much more comfortable with visual clues that I can identify easily, such as a gas station, a restaurant, or any other type of landmark, than with precise distances computed from maps, and road numbers or street names that are not always easy to read when you are driving. My approach to SQL is very similar; my landmarks are the knowledge of which tables are really big tables, which criteria are really selective, and where the reliable indexes are. An SQL statement tells a story, has a kind of plot; like a journey, you start from point A (the filtering conditions you find in your where clause), and you are going to point B (the result set you want). When you drive and find that it took far too long to get from point A to point B, a detailed analysis of the road you took will not necessarily help you to determine why the trip took so long. Counting traffic lights and timing how long you waited at each light may be more useful in explaining why it took so much time, but it will not tell you, the driver, what is the best route. A methodical study of traffic conditions is highly valuable to city planners, who look for places where congestion occurs and try to remove black spots. From my selfish point of view as a driver, in my quest for a faster way to get from point A to point B, I just need to know the places I'd rather avoid, study the map, and rethink my journey. Similarly, I find certain tuning approaches to be more appropriate for DBAs than for developers, simply because each group can pull different levers. You may or may not share my views; we have different sensibilities, and we may feel more comfortable with one approach than with another. Anyway, very often, different approaches converge toward the same point, although not always at the same speed. This chapter describes statement rewriting as I see and practice it.

If the way you approach a query and the way you achieve a faster query leaves much latitude to personal taste, I have many more qualms with optimizer directives (or hints), which some people consider the ultimate weapon in tuning efforts. Optimizer directives work; I have used them before and will probably use them again. Arguably, in some cases a directive makes for more maintainable code than an SQL trick to the same effect. Nevertheless, I consider the use of directives to be a questionable practice that is better avoided, and whenever I have to resort to them I feel like laying down my weapons and surrendering.

I will now explain with a few figures why I have such a dislike of optimizer directives. SQL is supposed to be a declarative language; in other words, you are supposed to state what you want and not how the database should get it. All the same, when you have a query you can consider that there is a "natural way" to execute it. This "natural way" is dictated by the way the query is written. For instance, if you have the following from clause:

```
from table1
     inner join table2
            on ...
     inner join table3
            on ...
```

you may consider that the natural way is to search table1 first for whatever is needed, then table2, then table3, using conditions expressed in the where clause to link the tables in a kind of chain. Of course, this would be a very naive approach to query execution. The task of the query optimizer is to check the various conditions and estimate how effectively they filter the data and how effectively they allow fast funneling on the final result. The optimizer will try to decide whether starting with table2, then proceeding to table3, then to table1 or any other combination would not be more efficient; similarly, it will decide whether using an index will be beneficial or detrimental. After pondering a number of possibilities, the optimizer will settle for an execution plan corresponding to the "natural way" of executing a functionally equivalent but different query. Figure 5-1 shows my representation of the work of the optimizer and how it transforms the original query into something different.

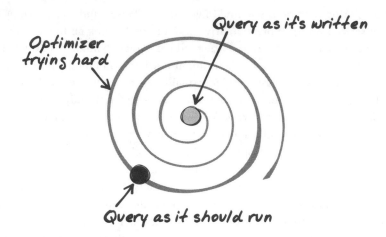

Query as it's written

Optimizer trying hard

Query as it should run

FIGURE 5-1. The query optimizer at work (allegory)

The difficulties of the optimizer are twofold. First, it is allotted a limited amount of time to perform its work, and in the case of a complex query, it cannot try all possible combinations or rewritings. For example, with Oracle, the `optimizer_max_permutations` parameter determines a maximum number of combinations to try. At some point, the optimizer will give up, and may decide to execute a deeply nested subquery as is, instead of trying to be smart, because it lacks the time to refine its analysis. Second, the more complex the query, the less precise the cost estimates that the optimizer compares. When the optimizer considers the different steps it might take, a crucial element is how much each step contributes to refining the result and how much it helps to focus on the final result set—that is, if I have that many rows in input, how many rows will I get as output? Even when you use a primary or unique key in a query to fetch data, there is a little uncertainty about the outcome: you may get one row, or none. Of course, the situation is worse when the criteria can match many rows. Every cost that the optimizer estimates is precisely that, an estimate. When the query is very complicated, errors in estimates cascade, sometimes canceling one another, sometimes accumulating. The optimizer increases the risk of having its estimates wrong.

As a result, when a complex query is very poorly written, the optimizer will often be unable to close the gap and find the best equivalent query. What will happen is a situation such as that shown in Figure 5-2: the optimizer will settle for an equivalent query that according to its estimates is better than the original one but perhaps only marginally so, and will miss an execution plan that would have been much faster.

In such a case, many people fall back on optimizer directives; having some idea about what the execution plan should be (possibly because they got it in a different environment, or prior to a software update, or because they stumbled upon it trying a number of directives), they add to the query DBMS-specific directives that orient the efforts of the optimizer in one direction, as shown in Figure 5-3.

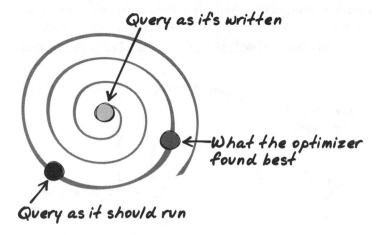

FIGURE 5-2. When the optimizer misses the best execution plan

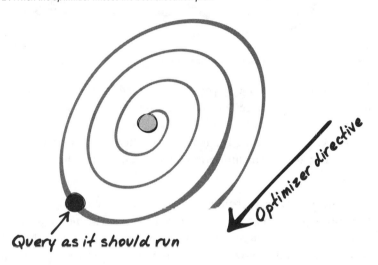

FIGURE 5-3. Orienting the efforts of the optimizer through the use of directives

The systematic use of directives is also applied when you try to achieve *plan stability*, the possibility offered by some products to record an execution plan that is deemed satisfactory and replay it whenever the same query is executed again.

My issue with directives and plan stability is that we are not living in a static world. As Heraclitus remarked 2,500 years ago, you never step into the same river twice: it's no longer the same water, nor the same human being. Put in a business perspective, the number of customers of your company may have changed a lot between last year and this year; last year's cash-cow product may be on the wane, while something hardly out of the labs may have been an instant success. One of the goals of optimizers is to adapt execution plans to changing conditions, whether it is in terms of volume of data, distribution of data, or even machine load. Going back to my driving analogy, you may take a different route to get to the same place depending on whether you left at rush hour or at a quieter time.

If you cast execution plans in stone, unless it is a temporary measure, sooner or later the situation shown in Figure 5-4 will occur: what once was the best execution plan no longer will be, and the straightjacketed optimizer will be unable to pull out the proper execution path.

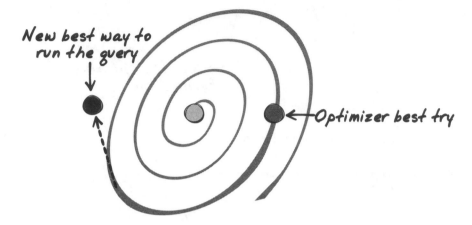

FIGURE 5-4. *When optimizer directives lead the optimizer astray*

Even in a stable business environment, you may have bad surprises: optimizers are a dynamic part of DBMS products, and even if you rarely see optimizers mentioned in marketing blurbs, they evolve significantly between versions to support new features and to correct quirks. Directives may be interpreted slightly differently. As a result, some major software upgrades may become nightmarish with applications that intensively use optimizer directives.

I hope you understand the reasons behind my uneasiness with optimizer directives; my goal when I rewrite a query is to turn the optimizer into my ally, not to prove that I am smarter than it is. My aim, therefore, is to rewrite a query in a simpler fashion that will not "lose" the optimizer, and to move, as in Figure 5-5, as closely as I can to what I estimate to be, under the present circumstances, the best writing of the query. For me, the best writing of the query is what best matches what the SQL engine should do. It may not be the "absolute best" writing, and over time the fastest execution plan may drift away from what I wrote. But then, the optimizer will be able to play its role and keep stable performance, not stable execution plans.

Now that I have expressed my goal, let's see how I can achieve it.

Analyzing a Slow Query

The first thing to do before analyzing a slow query is to bravely brace yourself against what may look like an extraordinarily complex statement. Very often, if you resist the temptation of running away screaming, you will have half won already. If indexing is reasonable, if statistics are up-to-date, and if the optimizer got lost, chances are that the statement is ugly (if it doesn't look ugly, its ugliness is probably hidden deep inside a view or

Closing the gap...

Query as it should run

FIGURE 5-5. Moving closer to what the SQL engine ought to do

user-written function). If the query refers to one or several views, it is probably best to find the text of the views and to reinject it inside the query as subqueries (this can be a recursive process). It will not make the query look better, but you will have a global view, and actually, it is often easier to analyze a daunting SQL statement than a mishmash of procedural calls. After all, like beauty, complexity is in the eye of the beholder. The case of functions is somewhat more difficult to handle than the case of views, as you saw in the previous chapter. If the functions refer to tables that don't appear in the query, it is probably better as a first stage to leave them in place, while keeping an eye on the number of times they may be called. If functions refer to tables already present in the query, and if their logic isn't too complicated, it's probably better to try to reinject them in the query, at least as an experiment.

Whenever I analyze a query, I always find that the most difficult part of the analysis is answering the question "what are the query writers trying to do?"

Getting help from someone who is both functionally knowledgeable and SQL-literate is immensely profitable, but there are many cases when you need to touch some very old part of the code that no one understands any longer, and you are on your own. If you want to understand something that is really complex, there aren't tons of ways to do it: basically, you must break the query into more manageable chunks. The first step in this direction is to identify what really matters in the query.

Identifying the Query Core

When you are working on a complex query, it is important to try to pare the query down to its core. The core query involves the minimum number of columns and tables required to identify the final result set. Think of it as the skeleton of the query. The number of rows the core query returns must be identical to the number of rows returned by the query you are trying to improve; the number of columns the core query returns will probably be much smaller.

Often, you can classify the columns you need to handle into two distinct categories: core columns that are vital for identifying your result set (or the rows you want to act on), and "cosmetic" columns that return information directly derivable from the core columns. Core columns are to your query what primary key columns are to a table, but primary key columns are not necessarily core columns. Within a table, a column that is a core column for one query can become a cosmetic column in another query. For instance, if you want to display a customer name when you enter the customer code, the name is cosmetic and the code is the core column. But if you run a query in which the name is a selection criterion, the name becomes a core column and the customer code may be cosmetic if it isn't involved in a join that further limits the result set. So, in summary, core columns are:

- The columns to which filtering applies to define the result set

- Plus the key columns (as in primary/foreign key) that allow you to join together tables to which the previous columns belong

Sometimes no column from the table from which you return data is a core column. For instance, look at the following query, where the finclsref column is the primary key of the tdsfincbhcls table:

```
select count(*),
       coalesce(sum(t1.boughtamount)
              - sum(t1.soldamount), 0)
from tdsfincbhcls t1,
     fincbhcls t2,
     finrdvcls t3
where t1.finclsref = t2.finclsref
  and t2.finstatus = 'MA'
  and t2.finpayable = 'Y'
  and t2.rdvcode = t3.rdvcode
  and t3.valdate = ?
  and t3.ratecode = ?
```

Although the query returns information from only the tdsfincbhcls table, also known as t1, what truly determines the result set is what happens on the t2/t3 front, because you need only t2 and t3 to get all the primary keys (from t1) that determine the result set. Indeed, if in the following query the subquery returns unique values (if it doesn't, there is probably a bug in the original query anyway), we could alternatively write:

```
select count(*),
       coalesce(sum(t1.boughtamount)
              - sum(t1.soldamount), 0)
from tdsfincbhcls t1
where t1.finclsref in
      (select t2.finclsref
        from fincbhcls t2,
             finrdvcls t3
       where t2.finstatus = 'MA'
         and t2.finpayable = 'Y'
         and t2.rdvcode = t3.rdvcode
         and t3.valdate = ?
         and t3.ratecode = ?
         and t2.finclsref is not null)
```

The first step we must take when improving the query is to ensure that the subquery, which really is the core of the initial query, runs fast. We will need to consider the join afterward, but the speed of the subquery is a prerequisite to good performance.

Cleaning Up the from Clause

As the previous example shows, you should check the role of tables that appear in the `from` clause when you identify what really matters for shaping the result set. There are primarily three types of tables:

- Tables from which data is returned, and to the columns of which some conditions (search criteria) may or may not be applied

- Tables from which no data is returned, but to which conditions are applied; the criteria applied to tables of the second type become indirect conditions for the tables of the first type

- Tables that appear only as "glue" between the two other types of tables, allowing us to link the tables that matter through joins

Figure 5-6 shows how a typical query might look with respect to the various types of tables involved. Tables are represented by rectangles, and the joins are shown as arrows. The data that is returned comes from tables A and D, but a condition is also applied to columns from table E. Finally, we have two tables, B and C, from which nothing is returned; their columns appear only in join conditions.

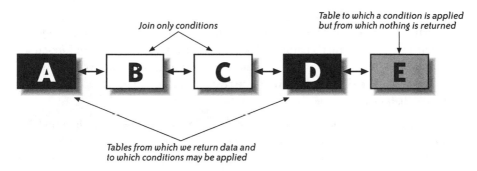

FIGURE 5-6. How tables can be classified in a typical query

Therefore, we obtain a kind of chain of tables, linked to one another through joins. In some cases, we might have different branches. The tables to watch are those at the end of the branches. Let's start with the easiest one, table E. Table E belongs to the query core, because a condition is applied to it (unless the condition is *always* true, which can happen sometimes). However, it doesn't really belong to the `from` clause, because no data directly comes "from" table E. The purpose of table E is to provide an existence (or nonexistence) condition: the reference to table E expresses "…and we want those rows for which there exists a matching row in E that satisfies this condition." The logical place to find a reference to table E is in a subquery.

There are several ways to write subqueries, and later in this chapter I will discuss the best way. We can also inject subqueries at various points in the main query, the select list, the from clause, and the where clause. At this stage, let's keep the writing simple. Let me emphasize the fact that I am just trying to make the query more legible before speeding it up. I can take table E out of the from clause and instead write something like this:

```
and D.join_column in (select join_column from E where <conditions>)
```

For table A, if the query both returns data from the table and applies search criteria to its columns, there is no doubt that it belongs to the query core.

However, we must study harder if some data is returned from table A but no particular search criterion is applied to it except join conditions. The fate of table A in such a case depends on the answer to two questions:

Can the column from table B that is used for the join be null?
> Null columns, the value of which is unknown, cannot be said to be equal to anything, not even another null column. If you remove the join between tables A and B, a row from table B will belong to the result set if all other conditions are satisfied but the column involved in the join is null; if you keep the join, it will not belong to the result set. In other words, if the column from table B can be null, the join with table A will contribute to shape the result set and will be part of the query core.

If the column from table B that is used for the join is mandatory, is the join an implicit existence test?
> To answer that question, you need to understand that a join may have one of two purposes:

> - To return associated data from another table, such as a join on a customer identifier to retrieve the customer's name and address. This is typically a case of foreign key relationship. A name is always associated to a customer identifier. We just want to know which one (we want to know the cosmetic information). This type of join doesn't belong to the query core.

> - To return data, but also to check that there is a matching row, with the implicit statement that in some cases no matching row will be found. An example could be to return order information for orders that are ready to be shipped. Such a join contributes to define the result set. In that case, we must keep the join inside the query core.

Distinguishing between joins that only provide data to adorn an already defined result set and joins that contribute to reducing that result set is one of the key steps in identifying what matters. In the process, you should take a hard look at any distinct clause that you encounter and challenge its usefulness; once you have consigned to subqueries tables that are present to implement existence conditions, you will realize that many distinct clauses can go, without any impact on the query result. Getting rid of a distinct clause isn't simply a matter of having eight fewer characters to type: if I empty my purse in front of you and ask you how many distinct coins I have, the first thing you'll do is to sort the coins, which will take some time. If I give you only distinct coins, you'll be able to answer immediately.

Like you, an SQL engine needs to sort to eliminate duplicates; it takes CPU, memory, and time to do that.

Sometimes you may notice that during this cleaning process some of the joins are perfectly useless.* While writing this book, I was asked to audit the performance of an application that had already been audited twice for poor performance. Both previous audits had pointed at queries built on the following pattern that uses the Oracle-specific syntax (+) to indicate an outer join (the table that is outer-joined is the one on the (+) side). All of these queries were taking more than 30 seconds to run.

```
select count(paymentdetail.paymentdetailid)
from paymentdetail,
     payment,
     paymentgrp
where paymentdetail.paymentid = payment.paymentid (+)
and payment.paymentgrpid = paymentgrp.paymentgrpid (+)
and paymentdetail.alive = 'Y'
and paymentdetail.errorid = 0
and paymentdetail.mode in ('CARD', 'CHECK', 'TRANSFER')
and paymentdetail.payed_by like 'something%'
```

Recommendations included the usual mix of index creation and haphazard database parameter changes, plus, because all three "tables" in the from clause were actually views (simple unions), the advice to use materialized views instead. I was apparently the first one to spot that all criteria were applied to paymentdetail, and that the removal of both payment and paymentgrp from the query changed nothing to the result, except that the query was now running in three seconds (without any other change). I hurried to add that I didn't believe that this counting of identifiers was of any real use anyway (more about this in Chapter 6).

At this early stage of query refactoring, I am just trying to simplify the query as much as I can, and return the most concise result I can; if I could, I'd return only primary key values. Working on a very lean query is particularly important when you have aggregates in your query—or when the shape of the query suggests that an aggregate such as the computation of minimum values would provide an elegant solution. The reason is that most aggregates imply sorts. If you sort on only the minimum number of columns required, the volume of data will be much smaller than if you sort on rows that are rich with information; you will be able to do much more in memory and use fewer resources, which will result in much faster processing.

After we have identified the skeleton and scraped off rococo embellishments, we can work on structural modifications.

---

* It happens more often than it should, particularly when a query has been derived from another existing query rather than written from scratch.

Refactoring the Query Core

You must consider the query core that you have obtained as the focus of your efforts. However, a query that returns minimum information isn't necessarily fast. This query is easier to work with, but you must rewrite it if it's still too slow. Let's study the various improvements you can bring to the query core to try to make it faster.

Unitary Analysis

A complex query is usually made of a combination of simpler queries: various select statements combined by set operators such as union, or subqueries. There may also be an implicit flow of these various simpler queries: some parts may need to be evaluated before others because of dependencies. It is worth noting that the optimizer may copyedit the SQL code, and in fact change or even reverse the order of dependencies. In some cases, the DBMS may even be able to split a query and execute some independent sections in parallel. But whatever happens, one thing is true: a big, slow query generally is a combination of smaller queries. Needless to say, the time required to execute the full query can never be shorter than the time that is required to execute the longest step.

You will often reach a good solution faster if you "profile" your query by checking the "strength" of the various criteria you provide. That will tell you precisely where you must act, and moreover, in the process it may indicate how much improvement you can expect.

Eliminating Repeated Patterns

It is now time to hunt down tables that are referenced several times. We can find a reference to the same table in numerous places:

- In different sections of a query that uses set operators such as union

- In subqueries at various places, such as the select list, from clause, where clause, and so forth

- Under various other guises in the from clause:
  - As a self-join—that is, a table directly linked to itself through different columns belonging to the same functional domain. An example could be a query that displays the manager's name alongside the employee's name when the employee ID of the manager is an attribute of the row that describes an employee.
  - Through an intermediate table that establishes a link between two different rows of a given table; for instance, in a genealogical database the marriages table would establish a link between two different rows from the persons table.

When you have spotted a table that seems to appear with some insistence in a query, you need to ask yourself two questions, in this order:

1. Can I fetch all the data I need from this table in a single access to the table?

2. If I can get all the data in a single pass, is it worthwhile to do so?

To give you an example, I once encountered in a query the following condition, where x is an alias for a table in the from clause (not shown):

```
...    and ((select min(o.hierlevel)
             from projvisibility p,
                  org o
            where p.projversion = x.version
              and p.id = x.id
              and p.accessid = o.parentid
              and o.id = ?)
             = (select min(o.hierlevel)
                  from projvisibility p,
                       org o
                 where p.projversion = x.version
                   and p.id = x.id
                   and p.accessid = o.parentid
                   and o.id = ?
                   and p.readallowed = 'Y'))
```

Here we have an obvious case of a repeated pattern, because after having verified that the two values that are substituted with the two ? place markers are indeed identical, we see that the only difference between the two subqueries is the last line in the preceding code snippet. What is this part of the query operating on? Basically, we are processing a set of values that is determined by three values, two of them inherited from the outer query (x.version and x.id), and the third one passed as a parameter. I will call this set of values S.

We are comparing a minimum value for S to the minimum value for a subset of S defined by the value Y for the readallowed column of the projvisibility table; let's call the subset S_R. When the SQL engine is going to examine S, looking for the minimum value, it will necessarily examine the values of S_R at the same time. Therefore, the second subquery clearly appears as redundant work.

The magical SQL construct for comparing subsets within a set is often case. Collecting the two minimum values at once isn't too difficult. All I have to do is to write:

```
select min(o.hierlevel)  absolute_min,
       min(case p.readallowed
              when 'Y' then o.hierlevel
              else null
           end) relative_min
  from ...
```

null is ignored by a function such as min( ), and I get my two values in a single pass. I just have to slightly modify the original query into the following:

```
... and exists (select null
                  from projvisibility p,
                       org o
                 where p.projversion = x.version
                   and p.id = x.id
                   and p.accessid = o.parentid
                   and o.id = ?
```

```
having min(o.hierlevel) =  min(case p.readallowed
                                   when 'Y' then o.hierlevel
                                   else null
                              end))
```

and the repeated pattern is eliminated with the redundant work (note that I have
removed the two aggregates from the select clause because I need them only in the having
clause). I could even add that the query is simplified and, to me at least, more legible.

Let's take a second, more complicated example:

```
select distinct
       cons.id,
       coalesce(cons.definite_code, cons.provisional_code) dc,
       cons.name,
       cons.supplier_code,
       cons.registration_date,
       col.rco_name
from weighing w
     inner join production prod
          on prod.id = w.id
        inner join process_status prst
             on prst.prst_id = prod.prst_id
     left outer join composition comp
          on comp.formula_id = w.formula_id
     inner join constituent cons
          on cons.id = w.id
     left outer join cons_color col
          on col.rcolor_id = cons.rcolor_id
where prod.usr_id = :userid
  and prst.prst_code = 'PENDING'
union
select distinct
       cons.id,
       coalesce(cons.definite_code, cons.provisional) dc,
       cons.name,
       cons.supplier_code,
       cons.registration_date,
       cons.flash_point,
       col.rco_name
from weighing w
     inner join production prod
          on prod.id = w.id
        inner join process_status prst
             on prst.prst_id = prod.prst_id
     left outer join composition comp
             on comp.formula_id = w.formula_id
        inner join constituent cons
             on cons.id = comp.cons_id
          left outer join cons_color col
                  on col.rcolor_id = cons.rcolor_id
where prod.usr_id = :userid
  and prst.prst_code = 'PENDING'
```

Here we have a lot of repeated patterns. The tables involved in the query are the same ones in both parts of the union, and the select lists and where clauses are identical; the only differences are in the joins, with cons being directly linked to w in the first part of the query, and linked to comp, which is itself outer-joined to w, in the second part of the query.

Interestingly, the data that is returned comes from only two tables: cons and col.

I will start with a schematic representation of the two parts of the query, to identify its core. I am using the same shade-coding as in Figure 5-6; that is, the tables from which some data is ultimately returned are shown as black boxes, and tables to which filtering conditions are applied but from which nothing is returned are shown as gray boxes. "Glue" tables are in white, joins are represented by arrows, and outer joins are represented by dotted arrows. Figure 5-7 shows the first part of the union.

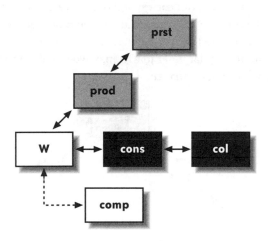

FIGURE 5-7. A representation of the first part of the union

There are two interesting facts in this part of the query: first, prod and prst logically belong to a subquery, and because w is nothing but a glue table, it can go with them.

The second interesting fact is that comp is externally joined, but nothing is returned from it and there is no condition whatsoever (besides the join condition) on its columns. That means that not only does comp not belong to the core query (it doesn't contribute to shaping the result set), but in fact it doesn't belong to the query at all. Very often, this type of error comes from an enthusiastic application of the cut 'n' paste programming technique. The join with comp is totally useless in this part of the query. The only thing it might have contributed to is to multiply the number of rows returned, a fact artfully* hidden by the use of distinct, which is not necessary because union does away with duplicate rows, too.

---

* As in "Oops, I have duplicate rows—oh, it's much better with distinct...."

The second part of the union, which I have represented in Figure 5-8, tells a different story. As in the first part of the union, prst, prod, and w can go to a subquery. In this case, though, comp is necessary because I can say that it links what is returned (data from cons and col) to the tables that allow us to define exactly which rows from cons and col we want. But there is something weird in the join: the outer join between comp and w tells the SQL engine "complete what you return from w with null values in lieu of the columns from comp if you cannot find a match in comp." So far, so good, except that comp is also linked—and with a regular, inner join—to cons on the other side. It is a sound practice to challenge any construct that doesn't fall in the "plain and basic" category, and outer joins are neither plain nor basic. Let's suppose that for one row provided by w we don't find a match in comp. Then a null value is returned for comp.cons_id, which is used for the join with cons. A null value is never equal to anything else, and no row from cons will ever match it. Rows that will be returned in this part of the query can correspond only to cases when there is a match between w and comp. The conclusion is immediate: the join between w and comp should be an inner join, not an outer one. The outer join adds no value, but as it is a potentially more tolerant join than the regular inner join, it may well send a wrong signal to the optimizer and contribute to poor performance.

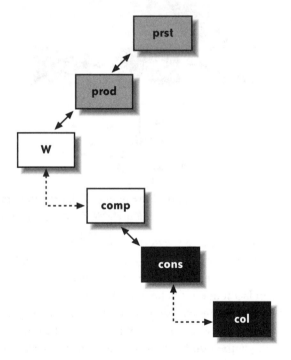

FIGURE 5-8. A representation of the second part of the union

Now, prst, prod, w, and comp can all be moved to a subquery, as in the first part of the union. I can rewrite the query as follows:

```
select cons.id,
       coalesce(cons.definite_code, cons.provisional_code) dc,
       cons.name,
       cons.supplier_code,
       cons.registration_date,
       col.rco_name
from constituent cons
     left outer join cons_color col
             on col.rcolor_id = cons.rcolor_id
where cons.id in (select w.id
                  from weighing w
                       inner join production prod
                               on prod.id = w.id
                       inner join process_status prst
                               on prst.prst_id = prod.prst_id
                  where prod.usr_id = :userid
                    and prst.prst_code = 'PENDING')
union
select  cons.id,
       coalesce(cons.definite_code, cons.provisional) dc,
       cons.name,
       cons.supplier_code,
       cons.registration_date,
       cons.flash_point,
       col.rco_name
from constituent cons
     left outer join cons_color col
             on col.rcolor_id = cons.rcolor_id
where cons.id in (select comp.cons_id
                  from composition comp
                       inner join weighing w
                               on w.formula_id = comp.formula_id
                          inner join production prod
                                  on prod.id = w.id
                          inner join process_status prst
                                  on prst.prst_id = prod.prst_id
                  where prod.usr_id = :userid
                  and prst.prst_code = 'PENDING')
```

If I now consider the subquery as a whole, instead of having the union of two mighty joins,
I can relegate the union to a subquery in a kind of factorization:

```
select cons.id,
       coalesce(cons.definite_code, cons.provisional_code) dc,
       cons.name,
       cons.supplier_code,
       cons.registration_date,
       col.rco_name
from constituent cons
     left outer join cons_color col
             on col.rcolor_id = cons.rcolor_id
where cons.id in (select w.id
                  from weighing w
                       inner join production prod
                               on prod.id = w.id
                       inner join process_status prst
                               on prst.prst_id = prod.prst_id
```

```
where prod.usr_id = :userid
 and prst.prst_code = 'PENDING
union
select comp.cons_id
from composition comp
      inner join weighing w
            on w.formula_id = comp.formula_id
         inner join production prod
               on prod.id = w.id
         inner join process_status prst
               on prst.prst_id = prod.prst_id
   where prod.usr_id = :userid
 and prst.prst_code = 'PENDING')
```

In the real case from which I derived this example, I had excellent performance at this point (runtime had dropped from more than a minute to about 0.4 seconds) and I stopped here. I still have a repeating pattern, though: the repeated pattern is the join between w, prod, and prst. In the first part of the new union, the id column from w is returned, whereas in the second part, the formula_id column from the same table is used to join to comp.

If performance had still been unsatisfactory, I might have tried, with Oracle or SQL Server, to use the with clause to factorize the repeated query:

```
with q as (select w.id, w.formula_id
          from weighing w
          inner join production prod
               on prod.id = w.id
          inner join process_status prst
               on prst.prst_id = prod.prst_id
        where prod.usr_id = :userid
          and prst.prst_code = 'PENDING')
```

In that case, the union would have become:

```
select q.id
from q
union
select comp.cond_id
from composition comp
      inner join q
            on q.formula_id = comp.formula_id
```

I'd like to point out that at this stage all of the modifications I applied to the query were of a purely logical nature: I gave no consideration to the size of tables, their structures, or the indexes on them. Sometimes a logical analysis is enough. Often, though, once the logical structure of the query has been properly identified and you have a clean, straight frame, it is time to look more closely at the data to reconstruct the query. The problem with SQL is that many constructs are logically equivalent (or almost logically equivalent, as you will see). Choosing the right one may be critical, and all DBMS products don't necessarily handle all constructs identically. Nowhere is this as flagrant as with subqueries.

Playing with Subqueries

You can use subqueries in many places, and it is important to fully understand the implications of all alternative writings to use them correctly and to avoid bugs. In this section, I will review the most important places where you can use subqueries and discuss potential implications.

Subqueries in the select list

The first place you can have subqueries is the select list; for instance, something such as the following:

```
select a.c1, a.c2, (select some_col from b where b.id = a.c3) as sub
from a ...
```

Such a subquery has a constraint: it cannot return more than one row (this type of subquery is sometimes called a *scalar subquery*). However, it can return no row at all, in which case the sub column will appear as a null value in the result. As a general rule, subqueries in the select list are correlated to the outer query: they refer to the current row of the main query, through the equality with a.c3 in the previous example.

If the optimizer doesn't try to rewrite the whole query or to cache intermediate results, the subquery will be fired for every row that is returned. This means that it can be a good solution for a query that returns a few hundred rows or less, but that it can become lethal on a query that returns millions of rows.

Even when the number of rows returned by the query isn't gigantic, finding several subqueries hitting the same table is an unpleasant pattern. For instance (case 1):

```
select a.c1, a.c2,
       (select some_col from b where b.id = a.c3) as sub1,
       (select some_other_col from b where b.id = a.c3) as sub2,
       ...
from a ...
```

In such a case, the two queries can often be replaced by a single outer join:

```
select a.c1, a.c2,
       b.some_col as sub1,
       b.some_other_col as sub2,
       ...
from a
     left outer join b
                 on b.id = c.c3
```

The join has to be an outer join to get null values when no row from b matches the current row from a.

In some rare cases, though, adding a new outer join to the from clause is forbidden, because a single table would be outer-joined to two other different tables; in such a case, all other considerations vanish and the only way out is to use similar subqueries in the select list.

Case 1 was easy, because both subqueries address the same row from b. Case 2 that follows is a little more interesting:

```
select a.c1, a.c2,
       (select some_col
        from b
        where b.id = a.c3
          and b.attr = 'ATTR1') as sub1,
       (select some_other_col
        from b
        where b.id = a.c3
          and b.attr = 'ATTR2') as sub2,
       ...
from a ...
```

In contrast to case 1, in case 2 the subqueries are hitting two different rows from table b; but these two rows must be joined to the same row from table a. We could naturally move both subqueries to the from clause, aliasing b to b1 and b2, and have two external joins. But there is something more interesting to do: merging the subqueries.

To transform the two subqueries into one, you must, as in the simple case with identical where conditions, return some_col and some_other_col simultaneously. But there is the additional twist that, because conditions are different, we will need an or or an in and we will get not one but two rows. If we want to get back to a single-row result, as in case 1, we must squash the two rows into one by using the technique of a case combined with an aggregate, which you saw earlier in this chapter:

```
select id,
       max(case attr
             when 'ATTR1' then some_col
             else null
           end) some_col,
       max(case attr
             when 'ATTR2' then some_other_col
             else null
           end) some_other_col
from b
where attr in ('ATTR1', 'ATTR2')
group by id
```

By reinjecting this query as a subquery, but in the from clause this time, you get a query that is equivalent to the original one:

```
select a.c1, a.c2,
       b2.some_col,
       b2.some_other_col,
       ...
from a
     left outer join (select id,
                             max(case attr
                                   when 'ATTR1' then some_col
                                   else null
                                 end) some_col,
                             max(case attr
```

```
                    when 'ATTR2' then some_other_col
                    else null
                  end) some_other_col
          from b
          where attr in ('ATTR1', 'ATTR2')
          group by id) b2
     on b2.id = a.c3
```

As with case 1, the outer join is necessary to handle the absence of any matching value. If in the original query one of the values can be null but not both values at the same time, a regular inner join would do.

Which writing is likely to be closer to the most efficient execution of the query? It depends on volumes, and on existing indexes.

The first step when tuning the original query with the two scalar subqueries will probably be to ensure that table b is properly indexed. In such a case, an index on (id, attr) is what I would expect. But when I replace the two scalar subqueries with an aggregate, the join between a.c3 and b.id is suddenly relegated to a later stage: I expect the aggregate to take place first, and then the join to occur. If I consider the aggregate alone, an index on (id, attr) will be of little or no help, although an index on (attr, id) might be more useful, because it would make the computation of the aggregate more efficient.

The question at this point is one of relative cardinality of id versus attr. If there are many values for attr relative to id, an index in which attr appears in the first position makes sense. Otherwise, we have to consider the performance of a full scan of b combined with an aggregate executed only once, versus the performance of a fast indexed query executed (on this example) twice by row that is returned. If table b is very big and the number of rows returned by the global query is very small, scalar subqueries may be faster; in all other cases, the query that uses scalar subqueries will probably be outperformed by the query that uses the from clause subquery.

Subqueries in the from clause

Contrary to subqueries in the select list, subqueries in the from clause are never correlated. They can execute independently from the rest. Subqueries in the from clause serve two purposes:

- Performing an operation that requires a sort, such as a distinct or a group by on a lesser volume than everything that is returned by the outer query (which is what I did in the previous example)

- Sending the signal "this is a fairly independent piece of work" to the optimizer

Subqueries in the from clause are very well defined as *inline views* in the Oracle literature: they behave, and are often executed, as views whose lifespan is no longer than the execution of the query.

Subqueries in the where clause

Contrary to subqueries in the select list or in the from clause, subqueries in the where clause can be either correlated to the outer query or uncorrelated. In the first case, they reference the "current row" of the outer query (a typical example of a correlated subquery is and exists ( )). In the second case, the subqueries can execute independently from the outer query (a typical example is and column_name in ( )*). From a logical point of view, they are exchangeable; if, for instance, you want to identify all the registered users from a website who have contributed to a forum recently, you can write something like this:

```
select m.member_name, ...
from members m
where exists (select null
              from forum f
              where f.post_date >= ...
                and f.posted_by = m.member_id)
```

or like this:

```
select m.member_name, ...
from members m
where m.member_id in (select f.posted_by
                      from forum f
                      where f.post_date >= ...)
```

But there are two main differences between the two preceding code snippets:

- A correlated subquery must be fired each time the value from the outer query changes, whereas the uncorrelated subquery needs to be fired only once.

- Possibly more important is the fact that when the query is correlated, the outer query drives execution. When the query is uncorrelated, it can drive the outer query (depending on other criteria).

Because of these differences, an uncorrelated subquery can be moved almost as is to the from clause. *Almost*, because in ( ) performs an implicit distinct, which must become explicit in the from clause. Thus, we also can write the preceding example as follows:

```
select m.member_name ...
from members m
     inner join (select distinct f.posted_by
                 from forum f
                 where f.post_date >= ...) q
          on q.posted_by = m.member_id
```

As you may remember from Chapter 1, various DBMS products exhibit a different affinity to alternative writings. As a result, we can kick a table out of the from clause during the first stage of our analysis because it implements only an existence test, and we can bring it back to the from clause if the DBMS likes joining inline views better than in ( ).

---

* I once encountered a correlated in ( ) statement, but unsurprisingly, it drove the optimizer bananas.

But you must fully understand the differences between the two writings. In the previous query, the distinct applies to the list of member identifiers found in the forum table, not to all the data that is returned from members. We have, first and foremost, a subquery.

The choice between correlated and uncorrelated subqueries isn't very difficult to make, and some optimizers will do it for you; however, the fact is often forgotten that assumptions about indexing are different when you use a correlated and an uncorrelated subquery, because it's no longer the same part of the query that pulls the rest. An optimizer will try its best with available indexes, and will not create indexes (although a "tuning wizard," such as the tuning assistants available with some products, might suggest them).

It all boils down to volume. If your query returns few rows, and the subquery is used as an additional and somewhat ancillary condition, a correlated subquery is a good choice. It may be a good choice too if the equivalent in ( ) subquery would return hundreds of thousands of rows, because writing something such as the following would make little sense:

```
and my_primary_key in (subquery that returns plenty of rows)
```

If you really want to access many rows, you don't want to use an index, even a unique index. In such a case, you have two possibilities:

- The expected result set is really big, and the best way to obtain the result set is through methods such as hash joins (more about joins later); in such a case, I'd move the subquery to the from clause.

- The expected result set is small, and you are courting disaster. Suppose that for some reason the optimizer fails to get a proper estimate about the number of rows returned by the subquery, and expects this number of rows to be small. It will be very tempted to ignore the other conditions (some of which must be very selective) and focus on the reference to the primary key, and it will have everything wrong. In such a case, you are much better off with a correlated subquery.

I came across a very interesting case while writing this book. The query that was causing worry was from a software package, and there was no immediate way to modify the code. However, by monitoring SQL statements that were executed, I traced the reason for slowness to a condition that involved an uncorrelated subquery:

```
...
and workset.worksetid in
                (select tasks.worksetid
                 from tasks
                 where tasks.projectversion = ?)
...
```

The tasks table was a solid, 200,000-row table. Indexing a column named projectversion was obviously the wrong idea, because the cardinality of the column was necessarily low, and the rest of the query made it clear that we were not interested in rare project version numbers. Although I didn't expect to be able to modify the query, I rewrote it the way I would have written it originally, and replaced the preceding condition with the following:

```
and exists (select null
          from tasks
          where tasks.worksetid = workset.worksetid
            and tasks.projectversion = ?)
```

That was enough to make me realize something I had missed: there was no index on the worksetid column of the tasks table. Under the current indexing scheme, a correlated subquery would have been very slow, much worse than the uncorrelated subquery, because the SQL engine would have to scan the tasks table each time the value of worksetid in the outer query changed. The database administrator rushed to create an index on columns (worksetid, projectversion) of the tasks table on the test database and, *without changing the text of the query*, the running time suddenly fell from close to 30 seconds down to a few hundredths of a second. What happened is that the optimizer did the same transformation as I had; however, now that indexing had been adjusted to make the correlated subquery efficient, it was able to settle for this type of subquery, which happened to be the right way to execute the query. This proves that even when you are not allowed to modify a query, rewriting it may help you better understand why it is slow and find a solution.

Activating Filters Early

Another important principle, filtering, must be brought into the process as soon as possible. This means you should eliminate rows before joining, sorting, or aggregating, and not after. I already mentioned the classic where versus having case, in which it sometimes makes a tremendous difference (particularly if the optimizer doesn't fix your mistakes behind your back) to eliminate rows before aggregation when conditions don't bear on the result of aggregation. But there are other common cases. Take, for instance, a schema that looks like the one in Figure 5-9, where a master table contains some basic information about a number of items, and peripheral tables contain attributes for these items that may or may not be present. All tables contain the item's identifier as well as two columns that specify when the row was created (mandatory column) or last modified (which can be null if the row was never modified since creation). The task was to provide a list of all items that had been modified as of a given date.

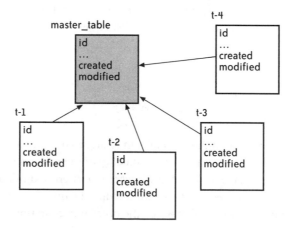

FIGURE 5-9. *Listing objects for which one attribute was recently modified*

I once found this task performed by the following code:*

```
select ...
from master_table m
     left outer join t1
                    on t1.id = master_table.id
     left outer join t2
                    on t2.id = master_table.id
     left outer join t3
                    on t3.id = master_table.id
     left outer join t4
                    on t4.id = master_table.id
where (case
         when coalesce(m.modified, m.created) > some_date then 1
         when coalesce(t1.modified, t1.created) > some_date then 1
         when coalesce(t2.modified, t2.created) > some_date then 1
         when coalesce(t3.modified, t3.created) > some_date then 1
         when coalesce(t4.modified, t4.created) > some_date then 1
         else 0
      end) = 1
```

The tables involved were not huge; all of them stored between thousands and tens of thousands of rows. But the query was very slow and ultimately returned few rows. The small result set meant that few records were modified during the period under scrutiny, and that the condition on the date was very selective. But to be able to deal with all the created and modified dates within a single expression, the SQL engine must first perform all joins—which is a lot of work on five tables of this size when no efficient filtering condition is applied before the join.

The answer in such a case is to identify the core query as the (small) set of identifiers that relate to rows recently modified. As such, we can rewrite the core query as follows:

```
select id
from master_table
where  coalesce(m.modified, m.created) > some_date
union
select id
from t1
where  coalesce(t1.modified, t1.created) > some_date
union
select id
from t2
where  coalesce(t2.modified, t2.created) > some_date
union
select id
from t3
where  coalesce(t3.modified, t3.created) > some_date
union
select id
from t4
where  coalesce(t4.modified, t4.created) > some_date
```

---

* The actual query was using the greatest( ) function that exists in both MySQL and Oracle, but not in SQL Server. I have rewritten the query in a more portable way.

Even when each select translates to a table scan, we end up scanning a volume that comprises hundreds of thousands of rows—in other words, not very much compared to filtering after the join. The implicit distinct and the resultant sort called for by union will operate on a small number of identifiers, and you quickly get a very short list of identifiers. As a result, you have managed to perform screening *before* the joins, and you can proceed from here to retrieve and join the few rows of interest, which will be an almost instantaneous process.

Simplifying Conditions

Once you have checked that no function is applied to a column that prevents using an efficient index on that column, there isn't much you can do to improve regular equality or inequality conditions. But we aren't done with subqueries. Even when we have chosen whether a subquery should be correlated or uncorrelated, we may realize that we have many conditions that are now expressed as subqueries (possibly as a result of our cleaning up the from clause).

Therefore, the next step is to minimize the number of subqueries. One of your guiding principles must be to visit each table as few times as possible (if you have studied operational research, think of the traveling salesman problem*). You can encounter a number of patterns where hitting each table only once is easy:

- If several subqueries refer to the same table, check whether all the information cannot be collected in a single pass. This type of rewriting is usually easier with uncorrelated subqueries. So, when you have something such as this:

  ```
  and c1 in (select col1 from t1 where ...)
  and c2 in (select col2 from t1 where ...)
  ```

  where c1 and c2 don't necessarily refer to columns from the same table in the outer query, it is sometimes possible, depending on the "compatibility" of the two where clauses, to have a single query that returns both col1 and col2. Then, you can move the subquery up in the from clause as an inline view (not forgetting to add distinct if necessary), and join with it.

- Conversely, when the same column from the outer query is related to various subqueries that hit different tables, as shown here:

  ```
  and c1 in (select col1 from t1 where ...)
  and c1 in (select col2 from t2 where ...)
  ```

  it may be interesting to combine the two subqueries with the intersect set operator if available, or with a simple join:

  ```
  and c1 in (select col1
                 from t1
                     inner join t2
                         on t2.col1 = t1.col1
                 where ...)
  ```

---

* Given a number of cities and the distances between them, what is the shortest round-trip route that visits each city exactly once before returning to the starting city?

- Another relatively common pattern is subqueries that implement a sort on two keys—namely, "I want the text associated to an identifier for the most recent date for which I have text for this identifier, and within that date I want the highest version number if I find several matching rows." You will often find such a condition coded as follows:

```
select t.text
from t
where t.textdate = (select max(x.textdate)
                        from t as x
                        where  x.id = t.id)
   and t.versionnumber = (select max(y.versionnumber)
                        from t as y
                        where y.id = t.id
                          and y.textdate = t.textdate)
order by t.id
```

Two such subqueries can actually be merged with the outer query. With Oracle or SQL Server, I would use a ranking function:

```
select x.text
from (select id,
             text,
             rank( ) over (partition by id
                        order by textdate desc,
                                 versionnumber desc) as rnk
        from t) x
where x.rnk = 1
order by x.id
```

With MySQL, I would sort by id and, as in the previous case, by descending textdate and versionnumber. To display only the most recent version of the text for each id, I would make tricky use of a local variable named @id to "remember" the previous id value and show only those rows for which id isn't equal to the previous value. Because of the descending sort keys, it will necessarily be the most recent one.

The really tricky part is the fact that I must at once compare the current id value to @id and assign this current value to the variable for the next row. I do this by using greatest( ), which needs to evaluate all of its arguments before returning, and evaluates them from left to right. The first argument of greatest( )—the logical function if( ), which compares the column value to the variable—returns 0 if they are equal (in which case the DBMS mustn't return the row) and 1 if they are different. The second argument of greatest( ) is a call to least( ) to which I pass first 0, which will be returned and will have no impact on the result of greatest( ), plus an expression that assigns the current value of id to @id. When the call to least( ) has been evaluated, the correct value has been assigned to the variable and I am ready to process the next row. As a finishing touch, a dummy select initializes the variable. Here is what it gives when I paste all the components together:

```
select x.text
from (select a.text,
             greatest(if(@id = id, 0, 1), least(0, @id := id)) must_show
        from t a,
             (select @id := null) b
```

```
        order by a.id,
                 a.textdate desc,
                 a.versionnumber desc) x
   where x.must_show = 1
```

Naturally, this is a case where you can legitimately question the assertion that SQL allows you to state what you want without stating how to obtain it, and where you can wonder whether the word *simplifying* in the title of this section isn't far-fetched. Nevertheless, there are cases when this single query allows substantial speed gains over a query that multiplies subqueries.

Other Optimizations

Many other optimizations are often possible. Don't misunderstand my clumping them together as their being minor improvements to try if you have time; there are cases where they can really save a poorly performing query. But they are variations on other ideas and principles exposed elsewhere in this chapter.

Simplifying aggregates

As you saw earlier, aggregates that are computed on the same table in different subqueries can often be transformed in a single-pass operation. You need to run a query on the union of the result sets returned by the various subqueries and carefully use the case construct to compute the various sums, counts, or whatever applied to each subset.

Using with

Both Oracle and SQL Server know of with, which allows you to assign a name to a query that may be run only once if it is referred to several times in the main query. It is common, in a big union statement, to find exactly the same subquery in different select statements in the union. If you assign a name to this subquery at the beginning of the statement, as shown here:

```
with my_subquery as (select distinct blah from ...)
```

you can replace this:

```
where somecol in (select blah from ...)
```

with this:

```
where somecol = my_subquery.blah
```

The SQL engine may decide (it will not necessarily do it) to execute my_subquery separately, keep its result set in some temporary storage, and reuse that result set wherever it is referenced.

Because it can work with only uncorrelated subqueries, using with may mean turning some correlated subqueries into uncorrelated subqueries first.

Combining set operators

The statements that most often repeat SQL patterns are usually statements that use set operators such as union. Whenever you encounter something that resembles the following:

```
select ...
from a, b, t1
where ...
union
select ...
from a, b, t2
where ...
```

you should wonder whether you couldn't visit tables a and b, which appear in both parts of the statement, fewer times. You can contemplate a construct such as this one:

```
select ...
from a, b,
     (select ...
      from t1
      where ...
      union
      select ...
      from t2
      where ...)
where ...
```

The previous rewrite may not always be possible—for instance, if table b is joined on one column to t1 in the first part of the statement, and on a different column to t2 in the second part. But you mustn't forget that there may be other intermediate possibilities, such as this:

```
select ...
from a,
     (select ...
      from b, t1
      where ...
      union
      select
      from b, t2
      where ...)
where ...
```

Without carefully studying the various criteria that comprise a query, table indexing, and the size of the intermediate result sets, there is no way you can predict which alternative rewrite will give the best results. Sometimes the query that repeats patterns and visits the various tables several times delivers superior performance, because there is a kind of reinforcement of the various criteria on the different tables that makes each select in the statement very selective and very fast. But if you find these repeated patterns while investigating the cause of a slow query, don't forget to contemplate other combinations.

Rebuilding the Initial Query

Once the query core has been improved, all you have to do is to bring back into the query all the tables that, because they didn't contribute to the identification of the result set, had been scraped off in our first stage. In technical terms, this means *joins*.

There are basically two methods for an SQL engine to perform joins.* Joins are essentially a matching operation on the value of a common column (or several columns in some cases). Consider the following example:

```
select a.c2, b.col2
from a, b
where a.c3 = <some value>
  and a.c1 = b.col1
  and b.col3 = <some other value>
```

Nested Loops

The method that probably comes most naturally to mind is the nested loop: scanning the first table (or the result set defined by restrictive conditions on this table), and then for each row getting the value of the join column, looking into the second table for rows that match this value, and optionally checking that these rows satisfy some other conditions. In the previous example, the SQL engine might:

- Scan table a for rows that satisfy the condition on c3.

- Check the value of c1.

- Search the col1 column in the b table for rows that match this value.

- Verify that col3 satisfies the other condition before returning the columns in the select list.

Note that the SQL optimizer has a number of options, which depend on indexing and what it knows of the selectivity of the various conditions: if b.col1 isn't indexed but a.c1 is, it will be much more efficient to start from table b rather than table a because it has to scan the first table anyway. The respective "quality" of the conditions on c3 and col3 may also favor one table over the other, and the optimizer may also, for instance, choose to screen on c3 or col3 before or after the matching operation on c1 and col1.

Merge/Hash Joins

But there is another method, which consists of processing, or preparing, the two tables involved in the join *before* matching them.

---

* I am voluntarily ignoring some specific storage tricks that allow us to store as one physical entity two logically different tables; these implementations have so many drawbacks in general usage that they are suitable for only very specific cases.

Suppose that you have coins to store into a cash drawer, where each type of coin goes into one particular area of the insert tray. You can get each coin in turn, look for its correct position, and put it in its proper place. This is a fine method if you have few coins, and it's very close to the nesting loop because you check coins one by one as you would scan rows one by one. But if you have many coins to process, you can also sort your coins first, prepare stacks by face value, and insert all your coins at once. This is sort of how a merge join works. However, if you lack a workspace where you can spread your coins to sort them easily, you may settle for something intermediate: sorting coins by color rather than face value, then doing the final sort when you put the coins into the tray. This is vaguely how a hash join works.

With the previous example, joining using this method would mean for the SQL engine:

- Dealing with, say, table a first, running filtering on column c3
- Then either sorting on column c1, or building a hash table that associates to a computation on the value of c1 pointers to the rows that gave that particular result
- Then (or in parallel) processing table b, filtering it on col3
- Then sorting the resultant set of rows on col1 or computing hash values on this column
- And finally, matching the two columns by either merging the two sorted result sets or using the hash table

Sometimes nested loops outperform hash joins; sometimes hash joins outperform nested loops. It depends on the circumstances. There is a very strong affinity between the nested loop and the correlated subquery, and between the hash or merge join and the uncorrelated subquery. If you execute a correlated subquery as it is written, you do nothing but a nested loop. Nested loops and correlated subqueries shine when volumes are low and indexes are selective. Hash joins and uncorrelated subqueries stand out when volumes are very big and indexes are either inefficient or nonexistent.

You must realize that whenever you use inline views in the from clause, for instance, you are sending a very strong "hash join" signal to the optimizer. Unless the optimizer rewrites the query, whenever the SQL engine executes an inline view, it ends up with an intermediate result set that it has to store somewhere, in memory or in temporary storage. If this intermediate result set is small, and if it has to be joined to well-indexed tables, a nested loop is an option. If the intermediate result is large or if it has to be joined to another intermediate result for which there can be no index, a merge or hash join is the only possible route. You can therefore (re)write your queries without using heavy-handed "directives," and yet express rather strongly your views on how the optimizer should run the query (while leaving it free to disagree).

## CHAPTER SIX

Task Refactoring

**No, it isn't strange, after changes upon changes, we are more
or less the same**

After changes we are more or less the same.

—Paul Simon (b. 1941)

The Boxer

REWRITING QUERIES IS OFTEN CONSIDERED TO BE THE ULTIMATE WAY TO IMPROVE A PROGRAM THAT
accesses a database. Even so, it is neither the most interesting nor the most efficient way to
refactor a program. You will certainly encounter from time to time a query that severe
editing will speed up beyond recognition. But increasingly, as optimizers become more
sophisticated and as statistics collection becomes more automated and more accurate,
query tuning grows into the kind of skill you exhibit on social occasions to show that you
have other qualities besides being a handsome, witty, and cultivated individual.

In real life, the tuning of single SQL statements is no longer as vital as it used to be. What
is increasingly important isn't to master the SQL skills that allow you to improve existing
statements, but rather to master those that allow you to perform in very few data accesses
what somebody less enlightened could write in only a convoluted procedural fashion.
Indeed, both skill sets are very close in spirit; as you saw in Chapter 5, efficiently rewriting
a statement is about hitting the tables fewer times, and so is efficiently designing an SQL
application. But you must take a high-level view and consider not only what you feed into
a query and what it returns, but also where the filtering criteria are coming from and what
you are ultimately going to do with the data you've just retrieved. Once you have all of
this clear in your mind, perhaps you'll be able to perform a complicated process in much

fewer steps, simplifying your program and taking full advantage of the power of the DBMS. Almost anyone can design a succession of relatively efficient (and untunable) unitary SQL statements. It's (re)thinking the whole task that is difficult and thrilling—something that the optimizer will never do for you.

At this point, it is probably worth mentioning that I regularly meet advocates of "ease of maintenance" who, although admitting that some SQL code could bear improvement, claim that it is worth trading better code for simpler code that will be easier to maintain. Somehow, I have always felt that the argument was spoiled by the obvious interest of my interlocutors (project managers with the IT company that wrote the application) in defending the work done so far and in assigning less expensive beginners to maintenance (you can always blame poor performance on the DBMS, the administrators, and the hardware).

I'm probably biased, but I am unconvinced that a lot of calls, nested loops, and branching all over the place are a real improvement over a sophisticated SQL query in the middle of an otherwise rather plain program (it isn't forbidden to add comments to the query), especially when I see the difference in performance. The learning curve is probably much steeper with SQL than with a procedural language, which young developers have usually practiced more at university labs, but I cannot believe that lowering programming standards generates good returns in the long term. I just want to demonstrate you what you can do, show what benefits you can expect, compare procedural complexity to SQL complexity, and let you decide what to do.

The SQL Mindset

Every SQL specialist will tell you that whenever you write SQL statements, you mustn't think the same way you think when you write a procedural or object-oriented program. You don't operate against variables: you operate against rows, millions of them sometimes. If, like many people do, you envision an SQL table as a kind of array of records or a sublimated file, chances are that you will want to process it like you would process an array or a file in a procedural program. Referring to an SQL "statement" is, in fact, misleading when you are a programmer experienced in another language. SQL statements are statements to the extent that they state what data you want to be returned or modified, but they are not statements in the same sense as procedural statements, which are simple steps in a program. In fact, an SQL statement is a program of its own that generates many low-level operations, as I hope Chapter 5 amply demonstrated. The difficulty that besets us is that SQL statements (and in particular, select statements) don't interface too well with procedural languages: you have to loop on a result set to retrieve the data, and therefore, cursors and loops are a natural feature of the vast majority of SQL applications.

Using SQL Where SQL Works Better

If loops in SQL programs are probably unavoidable at some point, I usually find in programs many flow constructs that are unnecessary. Tons of them. Seeing at the beginning of a procedure the declaration of dozens of variables to hold results returned from a database is often a bad omen. The *question* is, when you loop on a result set, what do you do with what you return from the database? If you display the data to the user, or write it to a file, or send it over a network, there is nothing to say against the loop and you are beyond criticism. But if the data that is retrieved is just fed into a series of cascading statements, or if it is further processed in the application to get results that the DBMS could have returned directly, chances are that SQL is poorly used.

Here is another way to ask the same question: how much value does your code add to the processing of data? I once encountered a case that fortunately is not too typical but exemplifies SQL misuse extremely well. The pseudocode looked something like this:

```
open a cursor associated to a query
loop
  fetch data from the cursor
  exit loop if no data is found
  if (some data returned by the query equals a constant) then
      ...
      do things
      ...
  end if
end loop
```

There was no else to the if construct. If we want to process only a subset of what the cursor returns, why return it? It would have been much simpler to add the condition to the where clause of the query. The if construct adds no value; fetching more rows than necessary means more data transiting across the network and fetch operations for naught.

In a similar vein, I once was called to the rescue on a program written about 8,000 miles away from the previous example, not so much because it was executing slowly, but rather because it was regularly crashing after having exhausted all available memory. What I found is a loop on the result of a query (as usual), fetching data into a structure called accrFacNotPaid_Struct, and inside that loop the following piece of code:*

```
    // check to see if entry based upon cycle rid and expense code exists
    TripleKey tripleKey = new TripleKey(accrFacNotPaid_Struct.pid_deal,
                                        accrFacNotPaid_Struct.cycle_rid,
                                        accrFacNotPaid_Struct.expense_code);
    if (tripleKeyValues.containsKey(tripleKey)) {
      MapFacIntAccrNotPaidCache.FacIntStr
          existFacNotPaid_Struct =
            (MapFacIntAccrNotPaidCache.FacIntStr)tripleKeyValues.get(tripleKey);
      existFacNotPaid_Struct.accrual_amount += accrFacNotPaid_Struct.accrual_amount;
    }
    else
      {
      tripleKeyValues.put(tripleKey, accrFacNotPaid_Struct);
      mapFacIntAccrNotPaidCache.addAccrNotPaid(accrFacNotPaid_Struct);
      mapFacIntAccrNotPaidCache.addOutstdngAccrNotPaid(accrFacNotPaid_Struct);
      }
```

---

* As usual, identifiers have been tampered with.

To me, duplicating the data returned from database tables into dynamically allocated structures didn't seem like the brightest of ideas. The final blow, though, was the understanding that with just the following bit of code, I could have accomplished what the developer was trying to achieve:

```
select pid_deal, cycle_rid, expense_code, sum(accrual_amount)
from ...
group by pid_deal, cycle_rid, expense_code
```

So much for the virtuoso use of Java collections.

If SQL can do it easily, there is no need to do it in the code. SQL will process data faster. That's what it was designed to do.

Assuming Success

Another cultural gap between the procedural and the SQL mindsets is the handling of errors and exceptional cases. When you write a procedural program, good practice dictates that you check, *before* doing anything, that the variables to be handled make sense in the context in which they're being used. Whenever you encounter a procedural program that does the same thing when it interacts with a database, you can be sure that it can be greatly improved.

Many developers assume that the only costly interactions with the database are those that result in physical input/output (I/O) operations on the database server. In fact, *any* interaction with the database is costly: the fastest of SQL statements executes many, many machine instructions, and I am not even considering communications between the program and database server.

If paranoia is almost a virtue in C++, for instance, it becomes a vice if every single check is implemented by an SQL query. When you are programming in SQL, you mustn't think "control," you must think "data integrity" or, if you like it better, "safe operation." An SQL statement must do only what it is supposed to do and nothing more; but, instead of protecting the execution of your statement by roadblocks, moats, and barbed wire, you must build safeguards into the statement.

Let's take an example. Suppose your project specs read as follows:

> We have a number of member accounts that have been locked because members have failed to pay their membership fee. The procedure must take an account identifier and check that the sum of payments received for this account in the past week results in a positive balance. If this is the case and if the account was locked, then it must be unlocked.
>
> A specific error message must be issued if the account doesn't exist, if the payments received during the past week are insufficient, or if the account isn't locked.

Most of the time, the logic of the code will look like this:

```
// Check that the account exists
select count(*)
from accounts
where accountid = :id
 if count = 0 => "Account doesn't exist"
// Check that payments are sufficient
//(group by because there may be several transactions)
select count(x.*)
from (select a.accountid
       from accounts a, payment b
      where b.payment_date >= <today minus seven days>
        and a.accountid = b.accountid
      group by a.accountid
      having sum(b.amount) + a.balance >= 0) as x
 if count = 0 => "Insufficient payment"
// Check whether account is locked
select count(*)
from accounts
where accountid = :id
  and locked = 'Y'
  if count = 0 => "Account isn't locked"
// Unlock account
update accounts
set locked = 'N'
where accountid = :id
```

This is a straight implementation of specs, and a poor one in an SQL context. In such a case, the correct course to take is to ensure that the update shall do nothing if we aren't in the specified conditions. We are unlikely to wreck much if the account doesn't exist. The only things we really need to care about are whether the member's account is in the black and whether it is currently locked.

Therefore, we can write a safe update statement as follows:

```
update accounts a
set a.locked = 'N'
where a.accountid = :id
  and a.locked = 'Y'
  and exists (select null
               from payments p
              where p.accountid = a.accountid
                and p.paymentdate >= <today minus seven days>
              group by p.accountid
              having sum(p.amount) >= a.balance)
```

This statement will do no more harm to the database than the super-protected statement. Of course, in the process of rewriting the statement, we have lost any way to check error conditions. Or have we? All database interfaces provide either a function or an environment variable that tells us how many rows were updated by the last statement. So, let's say we're talking about the $$PROCESSED variable. We can replace preemptive screening with forensic analysis:

```
if ($$PROCESSED = 0) then
  /* Oops, not what was expected */
  select locked
  from accounts
  where a.accountid = :id
  if no data found => account doesn't exist
  else if locked = 'N' then account wasn't locked
  else insufficient payment
```

Those two algorithms were coded as Visual Basic functions (the full code is downloadable from the book site and described in Appendix A). The unlocked_1 function implements the inefficient algorithm within the application, which checks conditions first and does the update when it gets the "all clear" signal; the unlocked_2 function implements a correct SQL algorithm that executes first and then checks whether the execution didn't work as expected. Figure 6-1 shows the result when both procedures were run on about 40,000 accounts, with a variable percentage of rows ending in error.

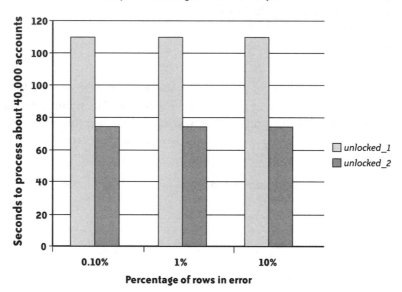

FIGURE 6-1. A function that checks and does, compared to a function that does and checks (SQL Server/Visual Basic)

It's clear which method is most efficient: we could expect convergence if processing were to fail in most cases, but with a reasonable percentage of errors the "optimistic" version implemented by unlocked_2 outperforms the "pessimistic" version of unlocked_1 by a factor of two.

Every test that accesses the database and precedes the statement that really matters has a heavy cost compared to the rest of the code. If you check first, then do, you penalize everyone. If you do first, then check (if necessary) the overhead will be applied only to operations that failed in the first place. Even if a check runs very fast, taking, say, 0.001 second of CPU time, if you repeat it two million times it consumes 33 minutes of CPU time, which can hurt badly at peak hours when the CPU becomes a critical resource.

Restructuring the Code

You saw in Chapter 5 that one of the guiding principles of statement refactoring is to try to reduce the number of "visits" to each table, and in particular, to each row. To refactor tasks, you must apply the same principles: if the same table is touched by two successive statements, you must question whether what you do in the program between the two statements truly justifies the return trip to the database server. It is relatively easy to decide whether statements that follow each other sequentially can be combined into a single foray in the database. Programs in which the logical path is winding can be much harder to beat into a handful of efficient statements. But SQL allows much logic to be grafted upon data access, as you will see next.

Combining Statements

Very often, one finds in programs successions of statements that are not really justified as "standalone" statements. For instance, I have seen several cases of scripts in which a number of successive updates were applied to the same table when several of them could have easily been performed as a single statement, or data that was inserted by one statement to be updated by the next statement, when the final result could have been inserted at once. This slicing up of operations seems pretty common in scripts that build a decision support system or that migrate data before an upgrade; the process is thought of as a sequence of successive operations, which is good, but is coded in the same way, which is bad. An or in the where clause and a clever use of case is often all that is needed to divide runtimes by two, three, or more depending on the number of statements you can combine.

Pushing Control Structures into SQL

A number of successive queries applied to the same table should attract your attention, even when they are embedded in if ... then ... else constructs. Look at the following example, which contains three queries, but where only two tables are referenced (identifiers starting with p_ denote parameters that are passed to the queries):

```
select  count(*)
into    nAny
from    t1
where   chaid = p_chaid
  and   tneid = p_tneid
  and   levelname = 'LEVEL1';
if nAny > 0 then
  [ assignments 1 ]
else
  select  count(*)
  into    nAny
  from    t1
  where   chaid = p_chaid
    and   tneid = p_tneid
    and   levelname = 'LEVEL2';
  if nAny > 0 then
    [ assignments 2 ]
  else
```

```
         [ assignment 3 ]
         if p_taccode = 'SOME VALUE' then
            select count (*)
            into   nAny
            from   t2
            where  taccode = p_taccode
              and  tpicode = p_tpicode
              and  tneid = p_tneid
              and  ttelevelname = 'LEVEL2';
            if nAny > 0
              [ assignment 4 ]
            else
              [ assignment 5 ]
            end if;
         else
            [ assignment 6 ]
         end if;
      end if;
   end if;
```

The first two queries are hitting the same table; worse, they are applying the same conditions except for the value of one constant. Indeed, we might have histograms, an index on column levelname, and very different distributions of values LEVEL1 and LEVEL2; these are possibilities that should be checked before stating that there is a huge performance gain waiting to be achieved. The fact that two columns out of three in the where clause are suffixed by id causes me to think that they belong to a composite primary key. If my hypothesis is true, the speed of execution of the two queries will be about the same, and if we manage to combine them, the resultant query should run significantly faster.

Using aggregates

Aggregates are often convenient for simplifying if ... then ... else constructs. Instead of checking various conditions successively, they allow you to collect in a single pass a number of results that can be tested later, without any further access to the database. The previous example would be a good ground for this technique. If I replace the first two statements with the following:

```
select sum(case levelname
             when 'LEVEL1' then 1
             else 0
           end) as count1,
       sum(case levelname
             when 'LEVEL2' then 1
             else 0
           end) as count2
into nAny1, nAny2
from t1
where  chaid = p_chaid
  and  tneid = p_tneid
  and  levelname in ('LEVEL1', 'LEVEL2');
```

I probably won't make the first query measurably longer, and I'll no longer have to run the second one: I'll just need to successively test the values of nAny1 and nAny2. My improvement factor will naturally depend on the number of times I get 0 in nAny1 and in nAny2. A query or two should help us get a quick estimate.

Using coalesce( ) instead of if … is null

Some tests may call for certain replacements. The following snippet is shorter than the previous example, but is actually more challenging. Its purpose is to determine the value to assign to variable s_phacode:

```
select  max(dphorder)
into    n_dphorder
from    filphase
where   filid = p_filid
 and    phacode || stepcode != 'RTERROR'
 and    phacode || substr(stepcode,1,3) != 'RTSUS'
 and    dphdteffect <= p_date;
if n_dphorder is null then
   s_phacode := 'N/A'
else
   select  max(phacode)
   into    s_phacode
   from    filphase
   where   filid = p_filid
     and dphorder = n_dphorder;
end if;
```

In the first query, I cannot say that the comparison of concatenated columns to constants enraptures me, but the fact that conditions are inequalities means that indexes, which prefer affirmation, are unlikely to be much help here. I would have preferred seeing this:

```
where (phacode != 'RT'
       or (stepcode != 'ERROR' and stepcode not like 'SUS%'))
```

But we are talking detail here, and this shouldn't impair performance because negative conditions are unlikely to be selective.

Since the only purpose of the n_dphorder variable is to fetch a value that is to be re-injected, the first step consists of replacing the variable with the first query in the second query:

```
select coalesce(max(phacode), 'N/A')
into s_phacode
from filphase
where filid = p_filid
  and dphorder = (select max(dphorder)
                  from filphase
                  where filid = p_filid
                    and phacode || stepcode != 'RTERROR'
                    and phacode || substr(stepcode,1,3) != 'RTSUS'
                    and dphdteffect <= p_date);
```

If the subquery returns null, the main query will return null too, because there may not be any case where the condition on dphorder is satisfied. I use coalesce( ) rather than a test in the calling code so that whatever happens, I get what I want in a single query.

I still have two references to the filphase table, but they are inside a single query. Because I expect the first original query to return a defined value in most cases, I'll execute only one round trip to the SQL engine where I would otherwise have generally executed two. More importantly, the SQL engine gets a query that gives the optimizer more opportunities for improvement than two separate queries. Of course, we can also try to rewrite the query further and ease the work of the optimizer, as we saw in the previous chapter. As the query is written here, we would have to check a number of things. If (filid, dphorder) happens to be the primary key, as it may well be, limiting the following query to the first row returned offers some possibilities, if you are ready to deal with the case when no data is found:

```
select phacode
from filphase
where filid = p_filid
  and dphdteffect <= p_date
  and (phacode != 'RT'
       or (stepcode != 'ERROR' and stepcode not like 'SUS%'))
order by dphorder desc, phacode desc
```

Using exceptions

Sometimes statements cannot be efficiently combined or rewritten, but digging a little will usually reveal many procedural processes that can be written better, particularly in stored functions and procedures. "Utility" functions, which are usually called over and over, are an excellent ground for refactoring. When you monitor statements that are issued against a database and you search the origin of relatively short statements that are executed so often that they load the server heavily, they usually come from utility functions: lookup functions, transcoding functions, and so forth.

Whenever you can get rid of a user-defined function that executes calls to the database and replace this function (if you really need it) with a view, you should not hesitate to do so. And you should not be impressed by the apparent complexity of the function—very often, complexity is merely the product of poor SQL handling.

Here is another real example. In an Oracle application, there are a number of distinct series of codes. All code series are identified by their name and are listed in a table named codes. To each series is associated a number of codes, and since this is an internationalized application, a message is associated to each (code, supported language) combination. Translated messages are stored in the code_values table. Here is the code for the function:

```
/* Function getCodeValue
Desc : Returns, in the language specified, the value of a code provided
       in a code series provided.
```

```
Parameters : 1. p_code_series        - Name of the code series
             2. p_code               - Code to be searched for
             3. p_language           - Language to be used for searching
             4. p_ret_desc (boolean) - True, if function should return
                                       the decoded text
                                       False, if function should return
                                       the no. of records returned from
                                       the code_values table
                                      (mostly this helps to verify, if
                                       it returns 1 or 0 rows)
*/
function getCodeValue( p_code_series in codes.code_series%type
                     , p_code        in code_values.code%type
                     , p_language    in code_values.language%type
                     , p_ret_desc    in boolean :=true
                               -- true = Description ,  false=count
                     ) return varchar2 is

   cursor c_GetCodeText ( v_code_series in codes.code_series%type
                        , v_code        in code_values.code%type
                        , v_language    in code_values.language%type
                        ) is
       select cv.text
       from code_values cv,
            codes c
       where c.code_series = cv.code_series
         and c.code_series = v_code_series
         and cv.code = v_code
         and cv.language = v_language;

   v_retvalue     code_values.code_value_text%type;
   v_temp         number;
begin
  select count(1)
  into v_temp
  from code_values cv,
       codes c
  where c.code_series = cv.code_series
    and c.code_series = p_code_series
    and cv.code = p_code
    and cv.language = p_language;

  if p_ret_desc then  -- return the Decoded text
    /* check if it returns multiple values */
    if coalesce(v_temp,0) = 0 then
      /* no value returned */
      v_RetValue :='';
    elsif coalesce(v_temp,0) = 1 then
      /* if it returns one record, then find the decoded text and
         return */
      open  c_GetCodeText(p_code_series, p_code, p_language);
      fetch c_GetCodeText into v_retvalue;
      close c_GetCodeText;
    else
```

```
       /* if it returns multiple values, then also return only first
          value. We can modify the code here to return NULL or process
          it differently if needed.
       */
       open  c_GetCodeText(p_code_series, p_code, p_language);
       fetch c_GetCodeText into v_retvalue;
       close c_GetCodeText;

    end if;
  else  --  return only the count for the code
    v_retvalue := v_temp;
  end if;

  return v_retvalue;
end getCodeValue;
```

All right. Here we have two queries that are basically the same, one that checks whether there is a match and one (the cursor query) that actually does the job. Let's take a closer look at the query:

```
select cv.text
from code_values cv,
     codes c
where c.code_series = cv.code_series
  and c.code_series = v_code_series
  and cv.code = v_code
  and cv.language = v_language;
```

The v_code_series parameter is used to specify the "code family," and the code_series value that matches the parameter is used in turn to access the proper row in code_values. As you saw in the preceding chapter, the only justification for doing this would be the need to check that we really have a matching row in code. Developer, my friend, do the words *foreign key* ring a bell? Oracle is perfectly able to ensure that there will be no inconsistency between codes and code_values. A useless access to codes using its primary key will certainly not add much to the cost of the query; but, as I would expect the triplet (code_series, code, language) to be the primary key of code_values, if I execute two primary key accesses where one is enough, I am doubling the cost. There may be times when this function is intensely used, and when it will matter.

Now, let's look at the function. The same mistake is made twice, in the query that counts and in the query that really returns the value. But why count when we really want the data? Let's analyze what is done after the number of matching values is counted:

1. First, coalesce(v_temp, 0) is checked. There is no need to be paranoid. When you count, you get either 0 or a value greater than 0. Getting null is impossible. It could have been worse, and we have at least avoided coalesce(abs(v_temp), 0). Of course, it's a really minor mistake, with no real performance implication. But seeing this type of construct sends bad signals, and it should incite you to look for more serious mistakes in the code. As David Noor, one of the early reviewers of this book, pleasantly put it: dumb, insignificant errors are often found near dumb, highly significant errors.

2. Second, we check whether we find one, zero, or more than one code. Dealing with zero or one code doesn't require any prior count: all you have to do is fetch the value and check for the error condition that is generated when there is nothing to fetch (in PL/SQL, it will be implemented by an exception block that will catch the predefined no_data_found exception). For the other error condition, what do we do when we find several codes? Well, there is another predefined exception, too_many_rows. But I just said that I would expect (code_series, code, language) to be the primary key of code_values. If primary keys are correctly defined, and I don't think that is asking much, it simply cannot happen any more often than count(*) returning null. The lengthy comment about how to properly handle that case would lead us to believe that the developer carefully thought about it. Actually, he simply didn't think in SQL terms.

The way the code is written, with the use of if ... elsif ... else ... end if instead of multiple if ... end if blocks, and the ratio of comment to code prove that we have a developer with some experience and probably a decent mastery of procedural languages. But he gave several signs that his understanding of SQL and relational databases is rather hazy.

The core of this function should be:

```
begin
    select text
    into v_text
    from code_values
    where code_series = p_code_series
      and code = p_code
      and language = p_language;
    if p_ret_desc then
        return v_text;
    else
        return 1;
    end if;
exception
    when no_data_found then
        if p_ret_desc then
            return '';
        else
            return 0;
        end if;
end;
```

All the other tests in the code are made useless by:

```
alter table codes
add constraint codes_pk primary key(code_series);
alter table code_values
add constraint code_values_pk primary key(code_series, code, language);
alter table code_values
add constraint code_values_fk foreign key (code_series)
references codes(code_series);
```

If I want to assess how much my work has improved the original function, I can estimate that getting rid of a useless join in a query that was executed twice improved performance by a factor of two. Realizing that the query had to be executed only once in all cases improves by another factor of two when I actually want the text associated with the code. I can only hope that it is by far the most common case.

For hairsplitters, we could argue that we could make the function as I rewrote it earlier slightly more efficient when we just want to check for the existence of a message. If I ask for the text to be returned, the SQL engine will search the primary key index, and will find there the address of the matching row (unless my index is a clustering index, but we are in an Oracle context, so it shouldn't be). Getting the row itself will require one extra access to another block in memory, which is useless if I just want to check the existence of an index entry. Therefore, if checking for the existence of a message is something critical (which is unlikely), we could improve the function by executing `select 1` when the text is not wanted. But the necessity of the option that only counts isn't very clear to me; testing what is returned is more than enough.

The lesson to learn from such an example is that if you really want an efficient program, one of the keys is to find the divide between what belongs to the database side and what belongs to the "wrapping language" side. Nearly all developers tilt the scale to the side they master best, which is natural; doing too much on the procedural side is by far the most common approach, but I have also seen the opposite case of people wanting to perform all the processes from inside the database, which is often just as absurd. If you want to be efficient, your only tool mustn't be a hammer.

Naturally, when a function becomes something that simple, its *raison d'être* becomes questionable. If it is called from within an SQL statement, an outer join (to cater to the case of the missing message) with code_values would be far more efficient.

Fetching all you need at once

As a general rule, whenever you need something from the database, it is much more efficient to write the query so that it always returns what you ultimately want without requiring a subsequent query. This rule is even more important when there are high odds that several queries will be issued. For example, consider the handling of messages in various languages that are stored in a database. Very often, when you want to return some text in a given language, you are not sure whether all the strings have been translated. But there is usually at least one language in which all the messages are up-to-date, and this language is defined as the default language: if a message cannot be found in the user's favorite language, it is returned in the default language (if the user cannot make sense of it, at least the technical support team will be able to).

For our purposes, let's say the default language is Volapück (code *vo*).

You can code something like this:

```
select message_string
from text_table
where msgnum = ?
  and lang = ?
```

And if the query returns no rows, you can issue this to get the Volapück message:

```
select message_string
from text_table
where msgnum = ?
  and lang = 'vo'
```

Alternatively, you can issue a single query:

```
select message_string
from (select message_string,
             case lang
                  when 'vo' then 2
                  else 1
             end k
      from text_table
      where msgnum = ?
        and lang in (?, 'vo')
      union all
      select '???' message_string,
             3 k
      from dual
      order by 2) as msg
```

and limit the output to the first row returned using the syntax of your SQL dialect (top 1, limit 1, or where rownum = 1). The ordering clause ensures that this first row will be the message in the preferred language, if available. This query is slightly more complicated than the basic query, particularly if you are right out of "SQL 101" (fresh, enthusiastic, and eager to learn). But the calling program will be much simpler, because it no longer has to worry about the query returning no rows. Will it be faster? It depends. If you have an energetic team of translators that misses a message only once in a while, performance will probably be a tad slower with the more complex query (the difference will probably be hardly noticeable). However, if some translations are not up-to-date, my guess is that the single query will pay dividends before long.

But as in the example with code_values, the real prize isn't always having one query instead of sometimes having one and occasionally having two: the real prize is that now that we have one statement, we can turn this statement into a subquery and directly graft it into another query. This, in turn, may allow us to get rid of loops, and have straight SQL processes.

Shifting the logic

To conclude our discussion of variations on the injection of control logic flow inside SQL statements, there are also cases when, even if you cannot have a single statement, a little remodeling can bring significant improvements.

Suppose you have the following:

```
select from A where ...
test on result of the query
    if some condition
        update table B
    else
        update table C
```

If the second case—that is, the update of table C—is by far the most common occurrence, something such as the following is likely to be faster on average, if executing the update that includes the first query is faster than executing the query and then the update:

```
update table C where (includes condition on A)
if nothing is updated then
    update table B
```

Getting Rid of count( )

In the previous examples you saw some samples of useless calls to count( ). Developers who abuse count( ) are almost…countless. Needless to say, when you need to publish an inventory report that tells how many items are in stock, a count( ) is blameless. Generally speaking, a count( ) associated to a group by clause has a good business-related reason to be issued. The occurrences of count( ) I have an issue with are those that are plain tallies. In most cases, they are issued, as in one of the previous examples, as tests of existence.

Again, we are in the situation of paranoid programming that procedural developers with little exposure to SQL are so fond of. There is no need to check beforehand whether data exists. If you want to fetch data, just do it, and handle the case when nothing is found. If you want to update or delete data, just do it, and check afterward whether the number of rows that were affected is what you expected; if it isn't, it is time for emergency measures. But for the 99% of cases that will work smoothly, there is no need to execute two queries when only one is needed. If you execute two queries for each transaction, you will be able to execute on the same hardware only half the number of transactions you could with only one query.

So far, I have encountered only one case for which a prior count has the appearance of solid justification: the requirement to display the total number of rows found in searches that can return pages and pages of results. If the number of rows is too high, the user may want to refine his search—or the program may cancel the search. This legitimate require-ment is usually implemented in the worst possible way: a count(*) is substituted with the list of columns that follows the select in the real query, without paying attention to the core query. But even a tightly tailored initial count is, in most cases, one query too many.

I mentioned in Chapter 5 the case of a count( ) that could run 10 times faster if we simply removed two external joins that were useless for restricting the result set; I also mentioned that the query was pointless in the first place. Here is the whole story: the problem was that from time to time, a user was issuing a (slow) query that was returning around 200,000 rows, causing the application server to time out and all sorts of unpleasant conse-quences to ensue. The early tally of the number of rows was introduced to be able to pre-vent queries from executing if the result set contained more than 5,000 rows. In that case, the user had to refine the search criteria to get a more manageable result.

My recommendation was to limit, in all cases, the result set to 5,001 rows. The only diffi-culty was in getting the number of rows at the same time as the rows were retrieved, without issuing any additional query. MySQL, Oracle, and SQL Server all allow it, in one way or another.

With MySQL, for instance, the solution would have been to issue this:

```
select ...
limit 5001;
```

followed by this:

```
select found_rows();
```

Both Oracle and SQL Server allow us to return the total number of rows in the result set on each row, thanks to the count(*) over ( ) construct, which gets the data and the tally in one operation. You might think that, apart from reducing the number of round trips to the database, the benefit is light and a regular count distinct from a regular fetch takes place on the server. Actually, very often the SQL engine needn't execute an additional count: when the data that you return is sorted, which is rather common, you mustn't forget that before returning to you the very first row in the result set, the SQL engine has to compare it to every other row in the result set. The full result set, and therefore its number of rows, is known when you get the first row of a sorted result set.

With that said, in the case of MySQL, found_rows( ) cannot be called before you fetch the data from the result set you want to evaluate, which can seem of little value. After all, you can fetch the result set, count the lines along the way, and know the result without having to call found_rows( ) afterward. Using the transactions table introduced in Chapter 1 and a limit set to 500 rows, I attempted to cheat. I executed a select statement, then called found_rows( ) before fetching the result from my query in *sample_bad.php* that follows:

```php
<?php

require('config.php');

/* Use prepared statements */
$mycnt = 0;
$stmt  = $db->stmt_init();
$stmt2 = $db->stmt_init();
if ($stmt->prepare("select accountid, txdate, amount"
                   . " from (select accountid, txdate, amount"
                   . " from transactions"
                   . " where curr = 'GBP'"
                   . " limit 501) x"
                   . " order by accountid, txdate")
    && $stmt2->prepare("select found_rows()")) {
    $stmt->execute();
    $stmt->bind_result($accountid, $txdate, $amount);
    $stmt2->execute();
    $stmt2->bind_result($cnt);
    if ($stmt2->fetch()) {
        printf("cnt : %d\n", $cnt);
    } else {
        printf("cnt not found\n");
    }
    while ($stmt->fetch()) {
        $mycnt++;
    }
```

```
        $stmt->close();
        $stmt2->close();
    } else {
        echo $stmt->error;
    }
    $db->close();
?>
```

It didn't work, and when I ran it I got the following result:

```
$ php sample_bad.php
cnt not found
```

You really have to fetch the data (even with the SQL_CALC_FOUND_ROWS modifier) to have
found_rows() return something. If you want to know how many rows you get when you
put an immutable cap over the number of rows retrieved *before* you have fetched everything, you must cheat a little harder. This is what I did in *sample_ok.php*:

```
<?php

require('config.php');

/* create a prepared statement */
$stmt = $db->stmt_init();
if ($stmt->prepare("select counter, accountid, txdate, amount"
                . " from ((select 1 k, counter, accountid, txdate, amount"
                . "          from (select 502 counter,"
                . "                       accountid,"
                . "                       txdate,"
                . "                       amount "
                . "                  from (select accountid, txdate, amount"
                . "                          from transactions"
                . "                         where curr = 'GBP'"
                . "                         limit 501) a"
                . "                order by accountid, txdate) c"
                . "          union all"
                . "          (select 2 k, found_rows(), null, null, null)"
                . "          order by k) x)"
                . " order by counter, accountid, txdate")) {
        $stmt->execute();
        $stmt->bind_result($counter, $accountid, $txdate, $amount);
        // Fetch the first row to see how many rows are in the result set
        if ($stmt->fetch()) {
            if ($counter == 501) {
                printf("Query returns more than 500 rows.\n");
            } else {
                while ($stmt->fetch()) {
                    printf("%6d %15s %10.2f\n", $accountid, $txdate, $amount);
                }
            }
        } else {
            echo $stmt->error;
        }
        $stmt->close();
    } else {
        echo $stmt->error;
```

```
    }
    $db->close();
?>
```

Through a union all, I concatenated the call to found_rows() to the execution of the query of which I wanted to count the rows; then I added the first order by to ensure that the result of found_rows() was displayed after the data, to ascertain that it would indeed count the number of rows in my result set. Then I sorted the result in reverse order, having written my query so that the number of rows would always be returned first and the remainder sorted according to my will.

Naturally, the full result set was fetched on the server; as my maximum number of rows was rather small, the double sort was not an issue. The big advantage was that I knew immediately, after having fetched only one row, whether it was worthwhile to fetch the rest of the data. It simplified my program enormously on the client side.

I'd like to call your attention to an optimization. When displaying the result of a search, it is customary to have an order by clause. For example, if you write:

```
select ...
order by ...
limit 501
```

at most 501 rows will be returned, but the full result set of the query (as it would be returned without the limiting clause) has to be walked for the sort. If you write:

```
select *
from (select ...
      limit 501) as x
order by ...
```

you will get the first 501 rows returned by the query, and then you will sort them, which may be considerably faster. If the limitation clause fires—that is, if the query returns more than 501 rows—both queries will return a different result, and the second one will be pretty meaningless. But if your goal is to discard any result set that contains more than 500 rows, it matters very little whether the 501 rows that are returned are the first ones or not. If the result set contains 500 rows or less, both writings will be equivalent in terms of result set and speed.

I gladly admit that the MySQL query errs on the wild side. The task is much easier with SQL Server or Oracle, for which you can use count() with the over () clause and return the total number of rows in the result set on each line. With SQL Server, the query will read as follows:

```
select accountid, txdate, amount, count(*) over () counter
from (select top 501
             accountid, txdate, amount
      from transactions
      where curr = 'GBP') as tx
order by accountid, txdate
```

If this query finds, say, 432 rows, it will repeat 432 in the last column of every row it returns.

Note once again that I am careful to limit the number of rows returned, and then to sort. Because I know I will discard the result when I get 501 rows, I don't mind getting a meaningless result in that case.

The question, though, is whether replacing something as simple as a count(*) with a single expression as complicated as the MySQL one is worthwhile. Most people are persuaded that simple SQL is faster. The answer, as always, must be qualified.

To explain this point, I wrote three simple PHP programs derived from the previous MySQL example. I looped on all 170 currencies in my currencies table. For each one, I fetched the transactions if there were fewer than 500 of them; otherwise, I just displayed a message that read "more than 500 transactions". To ensure optimal test conditions, I indexed the transactions table on the curr column that contains the currency code.

In the first program that follows, I have two statements—$stmt and $stmt2, which respectively count the number of transactions and actually fetch the data when there are fewer than 500 transactions for the currency in my two-million-row table:

```php
<?php

require('config.php');

/* create two prepared statements */
$stmt  = $db->stmt_init();
$stmt2 = $db->stmt_init();

if ($stmt->prepare("select count(*) from transactions where curr = ?")
    && $stmt2->prepare("select accountid, txdate, amount"
                    . " from transactions"
                    . " where curr = ?"
                    . " order by accountid, txdate")) {
    if ($result = $db->query("select iso from currencies")) {
        while ($row = $result->fetch_row()) {
            /* Bind to the count statement */
            $curr = $row[0];
            $counter = 0;
            $stmt->bind_param('s', $curr);
            $stmt->execute();
            $stmt->bind_result($counter);
            while ($stmt->fetch()) {
            }
            if ($counter > 500) {
                printf("%s : more than 500 rows\n", $curr);
            } else {
                if ($counter > 0) {
                    /* Fetch */
                    $stmt2->bind_param('s', $curr);
                    $stmt2->execute();
                    $stmt2->bind_result($accountid, $txdate, $amount);
                    /* We could display - we just count */
                    $counter2 = 0;
```

```
            while ($stmt2->fetch()) {
                $counter2++;
            }
            printf("%s : %d rows\n", $curr, $counter2);
        } else {
            printf("%s : no transaction\n", $curr);
        }
      }
    }
    $result->close();
  }
}
$stmt->close();
$stmt2->close();
$db->close();
?>
```

In the second program, I made just one improvement: I want to count whether I have less than or more than 500 transactions. From the standpoint of my program, having 501 transactions is exactly the same as having 1,345,789 transactions. However, in its innocence, the SQL engine doesn't know this. You tell it to count, and it counts—down to the very last transaction. My improvement, therefore, was to replace this:

```
select count(*)
from transactions
where curr = ?
```

with this:

```
select count(*)
from (select 1
      from transactions
      where curr = ?
      limit 501) x
```

In the third program, I have only the following "complicated" statement:

```
<?php

  require('config.php');
  require('sqlerror.php');

  $stmt = $db->stmt_init();

  if ($stmt->prepare("select counter, accountid, txdate, amount"
                   . " from ((select 1 k, counter, accountid, txdate, amount"
                   . "        from (select 502 counter,"
                   . "                     accountid,"
                   . "                     txdate,"
                   . "                     amount "
                   . "              from (select accountid, txdate, amount"
                   . "                    from transactions"
                   . "                    where curr = ?"
                   . "                    limit 501) a"
                   . "        order by accountid, txdate) c"
                   . "      union all"
                   . "      (select 2 k, found_rows(), null, null, null)"
```

```
                        . "          order by k) x)"
                        . " order by counter, accountid, txdate")) {
        if ($result = $db->query("select iso from currencies")) {
            while ($row = $result->fetch_row()) {
                /* Bind to the count statement */
                $curr = $row[0];
                $counter = 0;
                $stmt->bind_param('s', $curr);
                $stmt->execute();
                $stmt->bind_result($counter, $accountid, $txdate, $amount);
                if ($stmt->fetch()) {
                    if ($counter > 500) {
                        printf("%s : more than 500 rows\n", $curr);
                        $stmt->reset();
                    } else {
                        $counter2 = 0;
                        while ($stmt->fetch()) {
                            $counter2++;
                        }
                        printf("%s : %d rows\n", $curr, $counter2);
                    }
                } else {
                    printf("%s : no transaction\n", $curr);
                }
            }
            $result->close();
        }
    }
    $stmt->close();
    $db->close();
?>
```

I ran and timed each program several times in succession. The result is shown in
Figure 6-2. On my machine, the average time to process my 170 currencies with the first
program and a full count was 7.38 seconds. When I limited my count to what I really
needed, it took 6.09 seconds. And with the single query, it took 6.28 seconds.

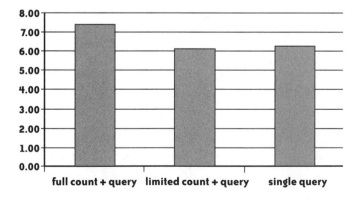

Checking the Number of Rows Returned

FIGURE 6-2. Comparing different strategies to check the number of rows returned before fetching the data (MySQL/PHP)

A difference of one fat second in processing only 170 entries is a gain I find impressive. You can imagine what kind of difference you would see if you had to repeat these operations tens of thousands of times—and think about the price of a machine 15% faster than what you currently have. Although the SQL expression in the third program is complicated, sorts twice, and does all kinds of ugly things, it behaves rather honorably, even if it's not as fast as the second program.

In this case, identification of the result set was pretty fast. To check what happens when it takes longer to get the result set, I ran tests with Oracle this time, using the analytical version of count( )* to return the total number of rows in the result set on each row. I ran the query with an index on currencies which gave me a "fast where clause," and without an index on currencies which gave me a "slow where clause." As you can imagine, the difference in processing time was not on the same order of magnitude. To ease comparison, I have assigned time 100 to the basic version of the program (full count, then query) and expressed the other results relative to this one. The full picture is shown in Figure 6-3. With the fast where clause, the result mirrors what I obtained with MySQL: basically, the query is so fast that the overhead induced by the analytical function offsets the advantage of having a single round trip to the database. But with the slow where clause the balance is shifted. Because it now takes time to identify the rows, finding them and counting them in a single operation brings a very significant benefit.

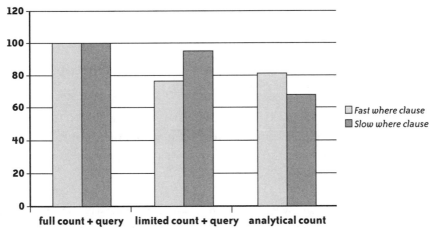

FIGURE 6-3. Comparison of different methods, depending on the speed to identify the result set (Oracle, PL/SQL)

The lesson to learn from this is that removing a prior count by re-injecting the tally into the query that actually returns data, whether it is with the relatively elegant use of count( ) over ( ) or with something slightly more clunky, brings more benefits, as the identification of the result set is slow and painful. Therefore, it is a technique that can bring a very significant improvement when used properly.

* That is, count(*) over ( ), as in the previous SQL Server example.

The case when we are not ready to discard search results that return a very large number of rows is not very different, except that you cannot use the optimization methods that consist of reducing the result set before sorting. In that case, you cannot afford a meaningless sort. But otherwise, even if you operate by batches, using the common technique of returning successive "pages" of data, the basic ideas are very similar.

Avoiding Excesses

I insisted in the preceding paragraphs on the importance of reducing the number of SQL statements and trying to get as much as possible in a single statement. An important point to keep in mind is that the goal isn't to have a single, monstrous, singing and dancing SQL statement; the goal is to have as few statements as possible along one execution path, which isn't exactly the same thing. I sometimes encounter statements with conditions such as the following:

```
where 1 = ?
  and ...
```

There is no point in sending the statement to the SQL engine, having it analyzed, and letting the DBMS decide, upon the value of the parameter, whether it should execute the statement or not. The decision of executing or not executing a statement belongs to the calling program. The more interesting cases are those where branching depends on the result of queries, constructs that are similar to the following one:

```
select c1, ...
into var1, ...
from T
where ...
if (var1 = ...)
then
  New operations against the database
[else]
end if;
```

In such a case, depending on the nature of the conditions, you can use the different techniques I described earlier.

Getting Rid of Loops

Getting rid of some statements by letting SQL deal with conditions will improve a number of cases, but the real El Dorado of refactoring lies in the removal of loops that contain SQL statements. In the majority of cases, these are themselves loops on the result set of a query (cursor loops). The removal of loops not only improves performance, but also improves code readability, which is a desirable software engineering objective for maintenance.

When you execute statements in a loop, you send in quick succession identical statements (except for a few parameters that may vary) to the DBMS. You multiply context switches between your wrapping program and the SQL engine, you give the optimizer very small morsels to work on, and you end up with programs that are often slower than what they ought to be—orders of magnitude slower.

Here is a very simple example: I used emp and dept, the sample tables describing employees and departments traditionally used by Oracle, to return the names of employees and the names of the departments where they work. First I used a loop on emp, using the returned department number to fetch the name of the department. Then I used a straight join. I used the regular 14-row and 4-row sample tables; my only improvement was to respectively declare that empno is the primary key of emp and deptno is the primary key of dept, and gathering statistics on both tables. To magnify the differences, I ran my test 20,000 times, and this is the last result of two successive runs:

```
ORACLE-SQL> declare
  2     v_ename    emp.ename%type;
  3     v_dname    dept.dname%type;
  4     n_deptno   dept.deptno%type;
  5     cursor c is select ename, deptno
  6                   from emp;
  7  begin
  8    for i in 1 .. 20000
  9    loop
 10      open c;
 11      loop
 12        fetch c into v_ename, n_deptno;
 13        exit when c%notfound;
 14        select dname
 15        into v_dname
 16        from dept
 17        where deptno = n_deptno;
 18      end loop;
 19      close c;
 20    end loop;
 21  end;
 22  /

PL/SQL procedure successfully completed.

Elapsed: 00:00:27.46

ORACLE-SQL> declare
  2     v_ename    emp.ename%type;
  3     v_dname    dept.dname%type;
  4     cursor c is select e.ename, d.dname
  5                   from emp e
  6                     inner join dept d
  7                       on d.deptno = e.deptno;
  8  begin
  9    for i in 1 .. 20000
 10    loop
 11      open c;
 12      loop
 13        fetch c into v_ename, v_dname;
 14        exit when c%notfound;
 15      end loop;
 16      close c;
 17    end loop;
 18  end;
 19  /
```

```
PL/SQL procedure successfully completed.

Elapsed: 00:00:09.01
```

Without the cursor loop, my code runs three times faster. Yet, I am in the most favorable of cases: primary key search, everything in memory, running a procedure that isn't stored but behaves as though it were (a single PL/SQL block is passed to the DBMS). It doesn't seem far-fetched to imagine that in cases where tables are slightly more voluminous and operations are slightly less straightforward, this "modest" 3:1 ratio erupts into something considerably more impressive.

Many times, trying to think without a loop causes you to completely rethink the process and gain several orders of magnitude in performance. Consider, for instance, the following pattern, which is rather common when you are interested in the most recent event (in the widest acceptance of the word) linked to an item:

```
loop
   select ...
   where date_col = (select max(date_col)
                     from ...
                     where <condition on something returned by the loop>
                       and ....)
```

The subquery hits the same "history table" as the outer query and depends on what is returned by the loop. Very often, this subquery is also correlated and depends on the outer query as well. As a result, the number of times when it will be executed is likely to be enormous. If you replace the whole loop with something such as the following:

```
select ..
from t1
   inner join (select c1, max(date_col) date_col
               from ...
               where ...
               group by c1) x
      on x.c1 = t1....
      and x.date_col = t1.date_col
where ...
```

you compute once and for all the dates of interest, de-correlate everything, and end up with a much more efficient query that your friend, the optimizer, will process at lightning speed now that it can see the full picture.

There is only one snag with the removal of loops: sometimes cursor loops are justified. Before refactoring a program, you must therefore understand why the original developers used a loop in the first place. Very often, it is because they didn't know better; but there are cases where loops were the chosen technical answer to a legitimate concern.

Reasons behind loops

People execute statements in loops for one of several reasons:

If ... then ... else *logic*

As you just saw, it is often possible to push if ... then ... else logic inside queries. Having a single query inside a loop removes the need for the loop, and the whole block can generally be replaced with a join that glues together the query in the cursor and the query inside the block. Actually, here lies the real benefit of replacing procedural if ... then ... else logic with an SQL query.

To change operations that affect several tables in sequence

Sometimes some data is collected—for instance, it's read from a staging table loaded from an XML stream—and then it is inserted into several tables in the process of storing the hierarchical XML structure into a clean relational structure.

To make changes that the developer wants to be committed on a regular basis, inside the loop, to satisfy one or several goals

Releasing locks

Depending on the coarseness of locking, updates may severely impair concurrency. If any uncommitted change blocks either people who want to read the data being changed, or people who want to change some other data in the same table, locks should be released as quickly as possible. The only way to release locks is to end a transaction, either by committing or by rolling back the changes. If you execute a single, long-running update, there is no way to commit before it's over. By processing data in small batches inside a loop, you get better control of your locks.

Not generating too much "undo"

You are probably familiar with the fact that if you are operating in transactional mode, each time you change some data the DBMS will save the original value. This is how you can cancel your changes at any time and roll back to a state where you know the data is consistent. In practice, it means you need some storage for temporarily recording the "undo history" until you commit your changes and make them final. Depending on the product, undo information will go to the transaction log or to a dedicated storage area. In a massive update, storage requirements can run high: some long-running transactions have been known to fail for lack of undo space. Even worse, when a long-running transaction fails, the undoing takes roughly the same amount of time as the doing, making a bad situation worse. And after a system crash, it can also lengthen the period of unavailability, because when a database restarts after a crash, it must roll back all pending transactions before users can work normally. This is another case that provides a motive to operate on smaller slices that are regularly committed.

Error handling

If you massively update data (e.g., if you update data from temporary tables in a staging area), one wrong piece of data, such as data that violates an integrity constraint, is enough to make the whole update fail. In such a situation, you need to first identify the faulty piece of data, which is sometimes difficult, and then relaunch the full process after having fixed the data. Many developers choose to process by small chunks: what was successfully updated can be committed as soon as you are sure the data is correctly loaded, and incorrect data can be identified whenever it is found.

While we're on the topic of transactions, I must state that commit statements weigh more heavily on performance than many developers realize. When you return from a call that executes a commit, you implicitly get a guarantee that your changes have been recorded and will remain, regardless of what happens. For instance, if the system crashes, when the DBMS hands back control to your program after a successful commit, it solemnly pledges that your changes will still be there after the restart, even if the system crashes in the next 0.00001 second. There is not an infinite number of ways to ensure the persistence of updates: you must write them to disk. Commit statements bring to the flow of activity a sudden change of pace. Just imagine some hectic in-memory activity, with programs scanning pages, jumping from an index page to the corresponding table pages, changing data here and there, waiting sometimes for a page brought into memory to be scanned or modified. At the same time, some changed pages are asynchronously written to the database files in the background. Suddenly, your program commits. I/O operations become synchronous. For your program, everything freezes (not too long, fortunately, but allow me some poetic license) until everything is duly recorded into the journal file that guarantees the integrity of your database. Then the call returns, and your program breaks loose again.

In this scenario, you must walk a very fine line: if you commit too often, your program will just spend a lot of its elapsed time in an I/O wait state. If you don't commit often enough, your program may block several concurrent transactions (or end up being blocked by an equally selfish program in the fatal embrace of a deadlock). You must keep these points in mind when analyzing the contents of a loop.

Analysis of loops

Whenever you encounter SQL processing within a loop, you should ask yourself the following questions immediately, because you'll often find loops where none are necessary:

Do we have only select *statements in the loop, or do we also have* insert, update, *or* delete *statements?*
  If you have only select statements, you have much less to worry about in terms of the more serious locking and transaction issues unless the program is running with a high isolation level* (I talk about isolation levels in the next chapter). If many different tables are referenced inside the loop within a mishmash of if ... then ... else logic, it will probably be difficult to get rid of the loop; sometimes the database design falls into the "interesting" category and writing clean SQL is mission impossible. But if you can reduce the innards of the loop to a single statement, you can get rid of the loop.

If we have inserts, do we insert data into temporary tables or into final tables?
  Some developers have a love for temporary tables that I rarely find justified, even if they sometimes have their use. Many developers seem to ignore insert ... select .... I have regularly encountered cases where a complicated process with intermediate filling of temporary tables could be solved by writing more adult SQL and inserting the result of a query directly. In these cases, the gain in speed is always very impressive.

---

* This is more of an issue with SQL Server and MySQL than with Oracle.

If the database content is changed within the loop, are the changes committed inside or outside the loop?
Checking where changes are committed should be the first thing you do when reviewing code, because transaction management is the soundest of all justifications for executing SQL statements within loops. If there is no commit within the loop, the argument crumbles: instead of improving concurrency, you make contention worse because chances are your loop will be slower than a single statement, and therefore, your transactions will hold locks longer.

If you have no commit statement inside the loop, you can decide on two opposite courses: committing inside the loop or trying to get rid of the loop. If you encounter serious locking issues, you should probably commit inside the loop. Otherwise, you should try to get rid of the loop.

Challenging loops

As you saw in this chapter, in many cases you can simplify complicated procedural logic and graft it into SQL statements. When you have reached the stage where inside the cursor loop you have nothing but variable assignment and one query, you usually have won: replacing the whole loop with a single query is often just a small step away. But even when operations that change the contents of the database are involved, you can sometimes break the loop curse:

Successive change operations
The case of multiple change operations applied to several tables in sequence (e.g., inserting the data returned by a cursor loop into two different tables of data coming from a single data source) is more difficult. First, too few people seem to be aware that multitable operations are sometimes possible (Oracle introduced multitable insert in version 9). But even without them, you should explore whether you can replace the loop with successive statements—for instance, whether you can replace this:

```
loop on select from table A
    insert data into table B;
    insert data into table C;
```

with this:

```
insert into table B
select data from table A;
insert into table C
select data from table A;
```

Even if you have referential integrity constraints between tables B and C, in general this will work perfectly well (you can run into difficulties if referential constraints are exceedingly complex, as sometimes happens). Naturally, performance will depend on the speed of the query (or queries, because the queries need not be exactly identical) that returns data from table A. If it's hopelessly slow, the loop may be faster, all things considered. However, if you got any benefit from reading Chapter 5 and you managed to speed up the query, the two successive insert statements will probably be faster, and all the more so if the result set on which we loop contains many rows.

You no doubt have noticed that I am happily trampling on one of my core principles, which is to not access the same data repeatedly. However, I am trampling on it with another principle as moral warrant, which is that doing in my program what can be done within the SQL engine is pointless, even when my program is a stored procedure that runs on the server.

Undo generation

The case of undo generation is another legitimate concern, which is often answered a little lightly. I have rarely seen the rate at which changes are committed being decided after some kind of study about how much undo was generated, how long it took to roll back a transaction that failed just before the commit, or simply a comparison of the different rates. Too often, the number of operations between commits seems to be a random number between 100 and 5,000.

Actually, it's what you are doing that decides whether undo generation will be critical. When you insert data, the DBMS doesn't need to record petabytes of information to undo what you are doing in case of failure (even if you are inserting a lot of data). I have seen a DBMS swallow every day eight million rows injected by a single insert ... select ... without any hiccups, even though the statement was running for one hour (which was considerably faster than the alternative loop). How fast you will be able to undo in case of failure depends on whether you are inserting the data at the end of a table (in which case it will be easy to truncate everything that your process has added), or whether, in the process, the DBMS is using your data to fill up "holes" left over from prior deletions.

When you delete data, it's a different matter; you will probably have a lot of data to save as you delete, and undoing in case of failure will, in practice, mean inserting everything back. But if you really have to delete massive amounts of data, truncate is probably the command you want; if it isn't possible to truncate a full table or partition, you should consider saving what you want to keep to a temporary table (for once), truncating, and then re-injecting, which in some cases may make processes run much faster.

Updates sit somewhere in the middle. But in any case, don't take for granted that you absolutely need to commit on a regular basis. Try different commit rates. Ask the database administrators to monitor how much undo your transactions are generating. You may discover that finally no real technical constraint is forcing you to commit often, and that some loops may go away.

Transactions

The stronger arguments against some types of rewriting, such as using multiple insert ... select ... statements, are the handling of transactions and error management. In the previous loop example:

```
loop on select from table A
    insert data into table B;
    insert data into table C;
```

I can commit my changes after having inserted data into tables B and C, either after each iteration or after any arbitrary number of iterations. With the double insert ... select ...

approach it is likely that the only time I can commit changes is when both insert statements have completed.

I have no clear and easy answer to those arguments, which are important ones.* Opposite answers are defensible, and what is acceptable often depends on ancillary circumstances.

When batch processes are initiated by receipt of a file, for instance, my choice is usually to favor speed, remove all the loops I can remove, and commit changes as little as I can. If something breaks, we still have the original file and (assuming that we don't have multiple data sources) fixing and rerunning will mean nothing more than a delay. Because very often a loopless program will run far more quickly than a procedural program, the run/failure/fix/run sequence will take much less time than a program that loops and commits often. Taking a little risk on execution is acceptable if there is no risk on data.

When the data source is a network flow, everything depends on whether we are working in a cancel-and-replace mode or whether everything must be tracked. If everything must be tracked, very regular commit statements are a necessity. As always, it's a question of what you are ready to pay for in terms of time and infrastructure for what level of risk. The answers are operational and financial, not technical.

I am not convinced that the question of locks should be given prominence when choosing between a procedural and a more relational approach. Releasing locks on a regular basis isn't a very sound strategy when massive updates are involved. When you execute a commit statement in a loop, all you do is release locks to grab other locks in the next iteration. You can find yourself in one of two situations:

- Your program is supposed to run alone, in which case locking is a nonissue and you should aim to maximize throughput. There is no better way to maximize throughput than to remove as many procedural elements as possible.

- Your program runs concurrently with another program that tries to acquire the same lock. If your program briefly holds a lock and releases it, you have nothing to gain, but you allow the concurrent process to get the lock in the very small interval when you don't own it, and it can block you in turn. The concurrent process may not play as fair as you do, and it may keep the lock for a long time. The whole concept of concurrency is based on the idea that programs don't need the same resources at the same time. If your program is blocked while another program is running, you are better off locking the resources you need once and for all, doing what you can to minimize the global time when you hold the resources, and then, when you're done, handing it over to another program. Sometimes sequential execution is much faster than parallel execution.

The case of row locking is a little more compelling, and its success depends on how the various programs access the rows. But here we are touching on issues that relate to the flow of operations, which is the topic of the next chapter.

---

* I can nevertheless point out functionalities such as Oracle's batch error handling.

## CHAPTER SEVEN

Refactoring Flows and Databases

Diseases desperate grown
By desperate appliance are relieved,
Or not at all.

—William Shakespeare (1564–1616)

Hamlet, IV, 3

S O FAR, I HAVE FOCUSED ON IMPROVING CODE AND MAKING BETTER USE OF THE DBMS FROM A UNITARY standpoint. Not unitary as in "single row," but unitary as in "single instance of the program." With the possible exception of some critical batch programs, rarely does a program have exclusive access to a database; most often, multiple instances of the same program or different programs are querying and updating the data concurrently. Ensuring that programs are as efficient and as lean as time, budget, and the weight of history allow is a prerequisite to their working together efficiently. You will never get a great orchestra by assembling bad musicians, and very often one bad musician is enough to ruin the whole orchestra. Bringing together virtuosi is a good start, but it's not everything. I won't spoil much by saying that if you replace a complex game of ping-pong between a program and the DBMS with efficient operations, you are in a better position to gear up. Yet, scalability issues are complex, and there is more to orchestrating a harmonious production than improving the performance of processes that run alone, because more points of friction will appear. I briefly mentioned contention and locking in previous chapters, but I didn't say much about environments where there is intense competition among concurrent users. In these environments, laissez faire often makes bottlenecks turn to strangleholds, and you need to regulate flows when concurrency dramatically degrades performance.

In turn, diminishing contention often requires changes to either the physical or the logical structure of the database. It is true that good design is one of the main factors defining performance. But refactoring is an activity that operates in a sort of last-in, first-out fashion: you start with what came last in the development process, and end with what came first. Unfortunately, when you are called in for refactoring, databases have usually been in production for quite a while and are full of data. Reorganizing the databases isn't always a viable option, even when the logical structure is untouched, simply because you cannot afford the service interruption that results when transferring the data, rebuilding the indexes, and deactivating and reactivating integrity constraints (which can take days, literally), or simply because management feels rather chilly about the business risk involved. It's even worse when physical alterations come along with changes to the logical view that will require program changes, as is usually the case. It's always better to plan for the basement garage before you build the house; moreover, the costs of digging that basement garage after the building is complete aren't exactly the same for a one-story suburban house as they are for a skyscraper. Sometimes tearing everything down and rebuilding may be cheaper. With a database, an operation as simple as adding a new column with a default value to a big table can take hours, because data is organized as rows (at least with the best-known DBMS products) and appending data to each row requires an enormous amount of byte shifting.*

With that being said, when business imperatives don't leave much leeway for organizing processes, reviewing the organization of the database may be your last card to play. This chapter expands on the topics of concurrent access and physical reorganization.

Reorganizing Processing

In Chapter 1, I advised you to try to monitor queries that the DBMS executes. You may be surprised by what you find, and you may see that queries that are fairly innocent when considered alone may not be so innocent when considered as a herd. For instance, you may discover costly hardcoded queries that different sessions execute several times in a brief period and are unlikely to return a different result each time. Or you may discover that the application side of this time-tracking package happily loads (through a series of select * from ... without any where clause) the entire table that stores employees and the entire table that references tasks each time someone connects to report what he or she has been doing during the week.† It never hurts to ask innocently whether a query actually needs to be run that number of times, and if so, whether it is possible to store the result set to some temporary area so that only the first session runs the expensive query and the others just retrieve the result from a cache. Or whether, instead of loading all the necessary data at once, it would be a better idea to limit oneself to data that is always required

---

* Which is likely to wreak havoc.
† True story. It was cleverly improved in the next version of the program, which fixed some severe performance issues: not by adding a where clause (stop dreaming), but by using a local cache on the user's PC.

and to introduce some "load-on-demand" feature for whatever doesn't fall into the previous categories. People who write functional specs usually think "one program instance." By raising a number of questions and suggesting alternative possibilities to people who know the functional side very well, you will not necessarily find a suitable solution on your own, but very often you will trigger a discussion from which many ideas for improvement will emerge.

Competing for Resources

When dealing with databases and concurrency, the best model to keep in mind is one or several service providers, with a number of requesters trying to obtain the service, as shown in Figure 7-1. The issue is that whenever one requester is being serviced, others usually have to wait.

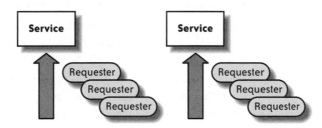

FIGURE 7-1. How you should see a DBMS

This model applies as well to the following:

- Low-level resources such as CPU usage, input/output (I/O) operations, or memory areas that need to be written or read

- High-level resources such as rows or tables that are locked

The model of the service providers serving requesters that line up (queue) and the ensuing "queuing theory" is very well known and is one of the pillars of software engineering. Beneath the mathematics, it describes situations that are common in real life. If you have to wait for the CPU because your machine is running flat out and if you are certain that you will require most of the CPU cycles, there is no question that you have to upgrade your machine. But often, while lines are accumulating with many requesters waiting for one resource, other service providers within the same system are just idle. For instance, this may happen when your machine is spending a lot of time waiting for I/O operations to complete. The difficulties lie in regulating flows and spreading the load among heterogeneous resources.

Service time and arrival rate

Let's first consider what happens with a single service provider. In a system based on service providers and requesters, the two values that really matter are how long it takes the service provider to perform its task (the service time) and how fast requesters pop in (the arrival rate). Most important of all is the relationship between these two values.

When the arrival rate, even for a short while, is too high for the service time, you get a lengthening line of requesters waiting to be serviced.

For instance, look at what happens in a currency exchange booth where you have only one employee. If people who want to change their money arrive slowly, and if there is enough time to service one person before someone else arrives, everything is relatively fine. But the real trouble starts when requesters arrive faster than they can be serviced, because they accumulate; imagine that the currency exchange booth is in an airport and that an A380 airplane has just landed....

There are only a few ways to improve throughput in such a system.

On the service provider side, you can do one of the following:

- Try to service the request faster by doing exactly the same thing at a faster pace.

- Add more employees to provide the same service. This method works great if there is no interaction among the employees—for instance, if each employee has a stack of banknotes in various currencies and can change money independently from the others. This method will work very poorly if all the employees need to get exclusive access to a shared resource—for instance, if they are instructed to take a photocopy of passports, and if there is only one photocopier for all employees. In that case, the bottleneck will be access to the photocopier; customers will feel that they wait for the employee, when in reality they are waiting for the photocopier. However, having more employees may only be beneficial when there is some overlap between the employees' activities: if while one employee photocopies passports another one is collecting them from new customers, while a third is counting banknotes and a fourth is filling a slip, global throughput will be far superior to the case when only one employee is active. Nevertheless, the increase in capacity will soon be limited, and before long, adding more employees will simply mean more employees waiting for the photocopier.

On the requester side, you can do one of the following:

- Express your requests better so as to get an answer faster.

- Try to organize yourself better so as to avoid long lines. For instance, if you take your children to a theme park and find the line at one attraction discouragingly long, you will go elsewhere and try to come back when the line is shorter.

If the request happens to be an SQL query, providing a faster response to the same request is the domain of tuning, and when tuning fails or isn't enough, faster hardware. Expressing requests better (and getting rid of unnecessary requests such as tallies) was the topic of the two previous chapters. The other two points—increasing parallelism and trying to distribute the load differently in time rather than in space—may present some refactoring opportunities. Unfortunately, you often have much less elbow room in these scenarios than when you are refactoring queries or even processes. It is rare that you cannot improve a slow query or process. But not every process lends itself to parallelism; for instance, nine women will not give birth to a baby after one month of pregnancy.

As such, the performance gain brought by parallelism doesn't come from one task being shared among several processes, but rather from many similar tasks overlapping. When they reached Spain in 1522 after having sailed around the globe, Magellan's companions reported that the ruler of Jailolo, one of the Moluccan Islands, had 600 children; it didn't take him 5,400 months (that's 450 years) to father them, but having 200 wives definitely helped.

Increasing parallelism

There are several ways to increase parallelism, directly or indirectly: when a program performs a simple process, starting more instances of this program can be a way to increase parallelism (an example follows); but, adding more processors inside the box that hosts the database server or the application server can also serve the same kind of purpose in a different way. If several levers can, under suitable circumstances, help you increase throughput, they achieve it by pulling different strings:

- If you start more instances of the same program on the same hardware, it's usually because no low-level resource (CPU, I/O operations) is saturated, and you hope to make better use of your hardware by distributing resources among the different instances of your program. If you discover that one of your programs spends a lot of time waiting for I/Os and nothing can be done to reduce this time, it can make sense to start one or several other instances that will use the CPU in the meantime and help with the work.

- If you add more processors or more I/O channels, it usually means (or should mean) that at least one of the low-level resources is saturated. Your aim is, first of all, to alleviate pain at one particular place.

You will need to be very careful about how the various instances access the tables and rows, and ensure that no single piece of work is performed several times by several concurrent instances that are ignorant of one another and that the necessary coordination of programs will not degenerate into something that looks like a chorus line with everyone lifting her leg in sync. If every instance of the program waits for I/O at the same time, parallelism will have succeeded only in making performance worse.

Among prerequisite conditions to efficient parallelism, one finds fast, efficient transactions that monopolize unsharable resources as little as possible. I mentioned in the preceding chapter the fact that replacing a procedural process with a single SQL query has an advantage other than limiting exchanges between the application side and the server side: it also delegates to the database optimizer the task of executing the process as quickly as possible. You saw in Chapter 5 that there were basically two ways to join two tables: via nested loops and via hash joins.* Nested loops are sequential in nature and resemble what you do when you use cursor loops; hash joins involve some preparatory steps that can sometimes be performed by parallel threads. Of course, what the optimizer ultimately chooses to do

---

* Merge joins are very close in spirit to hash joins.

will depend on many factors, including the current version of the DBMS. But by giving the optimizer some control over the process, you keep all options open and you authorize parallelism, whereas when your code is full of loops you prevent it.

Multiplying service providers at the application level

I created a simple test case to show how you can try to parallelize processing by adding more "service providers" within an application. I only used MySQL for this example (because it allows storage engines that have different grains for locking), and I created a MyISAM table. As row-level locking cannot be applied to MyISAM tables, I have a reasonable worst-case scenario.

In many systems, you find tables that are used primarily as a communication channel between processes: some "publisher" processes record into the table tasks to be performed, while some other "consumer" processes read the table, getting a "to-do" list on a first-in, first-out basis, perform the task, and usually write some ending status back into the table when the task is complete (or has failed). I have partly simulated such a mechanism by focusing exclusively on the "consumer" side. I created a table called `fifo` that looks like this:

```
mysql> desc fifo;
+--------------+---------------------+------+-----+---------+----------------+
| Field        | Type                | Null | Key | Default | Extra          |
+--------------+---------------------+------+-----+---------+----------------+
| seqnum       | bigint(20) unsigned | NO   | PRI | NULL    | auto_increment |
| producer_pid | bigint(20)          | NO   |     |         |                |
| produced     | time                | NO   |     |         |                |
| state        | char(1)             | NO   |     |         |                |
| consumed     | time                | YES  |     | NULL    |                |
| counter      | int(11)             | NO   |     |         |                |
+--------------+---------------------+------+-----+---------+----------------+
6 rows in set (0.00 sec)
```

I inserted into this table 300 rows with state R as in *Ready* and a value of 0 for counter. A consumer gets the value of seqnum for the oldest row in state R. If none is found, the program exits; in a real case, with permanently active publisher processes, it would sleep for a few seconds before polling again. Then the consumer updates the row and sets state to P as in *Processing*, using the value of seqnum just found; I would have preferred executing a single update, but because I need seqnum to update the row when the task is complete, I have to execute two queries.* Then I simulate some kind of processing by sending the program to sleep for a random number of seconds that is designed to average two seconds. Then the program updates the row, setting the state to D for *Done*, setting a completion timestamp, and incrementing counter by one.

---

* Note that it is possible with Oracle and some interfaces to execute an update and return a value at once.

I should add that there is no other index on fifo except for the primary key index on seqnum; in particular, there is no index on state, which means the search for the earliest unprocessed row will translate into a table scan. This indexing pattern is in no way surprising in such a case. Usually, a table that is used to exchange messages between processes contains very few rows at one point in time: if the system is properly tuned, publishers and consumers work at about the same rate, and some kind of garbage collection program removes processed lines on a regular basis. Indexing state would mean adding the cost of maintaining the index when publishers insert new rows, when consumers change the value of the column, and when rows are cleaned up; it might be worth the overhead, but it is very difficult without extensive testing to declare whether, on the whole, an index on state would help. In this case, there is none.

The first version of the program (*consumer_naive.c*) executes the following SQL statements in a loop:

```
select min(seqnum) from fifo
where state = 'R';

update fifo
set state = 'P'
where seqnum = ?; /* Uses the value returned by the first query */
```

...brief nap...

```
update fifo
set state = 'D', consumed = curtime(), counter = counter + 1
where seqnum = ?;
```

It uses the default "auto-commit" mode of the MySQL C API, which implicitly turns every update statement into a transaction that is committed as soon as it is executed.

Learning that with an average "processing" time of around two seconds it takes 10 minutes to process the 300 rows of my fifo table should surprise no one. But can I improve the speed by adding more consumers, which would process my input in parallel? This would be a way to solve a common issue in these types of architectures, which is that publishers rarely publish at a smooth and regular rate. There are bursts of activity, and if you don't have enough consumers, tasks have a tendency to accumulate. As this example shows, getting rid of the backlog may take some time.

When I start 2 consumers it takes five minutes to process all the tasks, with 5 consumers it takes two minutes, with 10 consumers only one minute, with 20 consumers about 35 seconds, and with 50 processes very close to 15 seconds. There is only one major snag: when I check the value of counter, there are a number of rows for which the value is greater than one, which means the row has been updated by more than one process (remember that a process increases counter when it's done). I ran my test five times with a varying number of parallel consumers. Figure 7-2 shows the average results that I obtained.

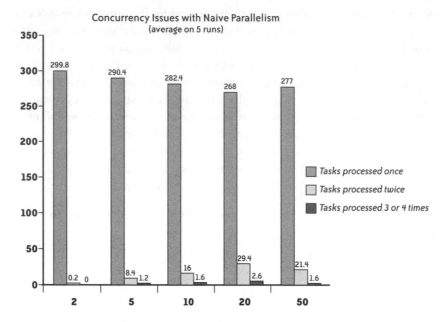

Concurrency Issues with Naive Parallelism
(average on 5 runs)

Tasks processed once
Tasks processed twice
Tasks processed 3 or 4 times

FIGURE 7-2. When concurrency gets you into trouble

Performing tasks several times isn't a desirable outcome. Seeing the same debit appear twice on a bank statement would probably not amuse me, no more than discovering that the ticket I bought for a concert or sports event was sold to two or three other people as well.

Parallelism requires synchronization of a sort, and with SQL two elements are involved:

* Isolation level
* Locking

Isolation level defines a session's awareness of what other concurrent sessions are doing. The ISO standard, which all products more or less support, defines four levels, of which two are of greater practical interest:

Read uncommitted

In this level, all sessions are instantly aware of what the others are doing. When one session modifies some data, all the other sessions see the change, whether it has been committed or not. This is an extremely dangerous situation, because a transaction can base its own computations on changes that will be rolled back later. You can very easily cause data inconsistencies that will be extremely hard to trace. The only case when you are safe is when you are using auto-commit mode. You can no longer read any uncommitted data, because changes are committed immediately. But auto-commit mode can accommodate only very simple processes.

Read committed

In this level, a session doesn't see the changes brought by another session before they are committed. This is similar to what happens when you are using version control software: when a file is checked out, and while someone else is modifying it, you can see only the latest version that was checked in—and you cannot modify it while it is locked. Only when it has been checked in (the equivalent of commit) will you see the new version. This isolation level is the default for SQL Server.

This can be considered a relatively safe isolation level, but it can get you into trouble when you have long-running queries on a table that execute concurrently with very fast updates to that table. Consider the following case: in a bank, you are running an end-of-month query summing up the balance of all of your customers' accounts. You have many customers, most customers own several accounts, and your accounts table contains tens of millions of rows. Summing up tens of millions of rows isn't an instant operation. While your report is running, business carries on as usual. Suppose that an old client, whose current account data is stored "at the beginning of the table" (whatever that means), has recently opened a savings account, the data for which resides toward the end of the table. When your report starts to execute, the current account contains 1,000, and the new savings account contains 200. The report sums up the values, reads 1,000, and proceeds. Soon after the program reads the current account balance, your customer decides to transfer 750 from the current account to the savings account. Accounts are accessed by account numbers (which are the primary keys), the transaction is very fast and is committed immediately, and the savings account is credited 750. But your report program, crunching numbers slowly, is still working on another customer's account, far away in the table. When the report program finally reaches this particular customer's savings account, as the transaction was committed many CPU cycles ago, it reads 950. As a result, the sum is wrong.

There is a way to avoid this type of issue, which is to require the DBMS to record, at the beginning of a query, some timestamp or functionally equivalent sequence number, and to revert to the version of the data that was current when the query started whenever that query encounters a row that was updated after the reference timestamp. This flashback to the time when the query started occurs whether the change has been committed or not. In the previous example, the program would still read the value 200 for the savings account, because it is the value that was current when the query started. This mechanism is what SQL Server calls *row versioning* and what it implements with the READ_COMMITTED_SNAPSHOT database option. This mode happens to be the default mode with Oracle, where it is called *read consistency*, and is considered to be a variant of the standard read committed isolation level; it is also how the InnoDB storage engine works with MySQL in the read committed isolation level (but it's not the default level for InnoDB).

Of course, there is no such thing as a free lunch, and using row versioning means that old data values must be kept as long as possible instead of being disposed of as soon as the transaction commits. In some environments that combine slow queries and numerous rapidly firing transactions, keeping a long history can lead to excessive usage of temporary storage and, sometimes, runtime errors. There is usually a cap on the amount of storage that is used for recording past values. Uncommitted values are kept until storage bursts at the seams. Committed values are kept as long as possible; then, when storage becomes scarce, they are overwritten by the previous values corresponding to recent changes. If a select statement requires a version of data that was overwritten to accommodate new changes, it will end in error (in Oracle, this is the infamous "snapshot too old" error). Rerunning the statement will reset the reference time and, usually, will lead to successful execution. But when this type of error occurs too often, the first thing to check is whether the statement cannot be made to run faster; if not, whether changes are not committed too often; and if not, whether more storage cannot be allocated for the task.

Repeatable read

The repeatable read isolation level is an extension of row versioning: instead of keeping a consistent view of data for the duration of a query, the scope is the whole transaction. This is the default level with the InnoDB engine for MySQL. With the previous account balance example, if you were to run the query a second time in the repeatable read level, the report program would still see 1,000 in the current account and 200 in the savings account (while in the read committed mode, the report program would read 250 and 950 the second time, assuming that no other transfer has taken place between those two accounts). As long as the session doesn't commit (or roll back), it will have the same vision of the data that it first read. As you can expect, issues linked to the amount of storage required to uphold past data history are even more likely to occur than in the read committed level.

What can happen, though, is that new rows that have been inserted since the first select will pop up. The read is repeatable with respect to the data that has been read, but not with respect to the table as a whole. If you want the table to look the same between successive select statements, regardless of what happens, you must switch to the next isolation level.

Serializable

This isolation level is a mode in which transactions ignore all the changes brought to the database by the other transactions. Only when the transaction ends does the session see the changes brought to the database by the other sessions since the beginning of the transaction. In a way, commit doubles as a refresh button.

In real life, read committed (with or without row versioning) and repeatable read are the only isolation levels that matter in the vast majority of cases. They are the two levels that offer a very consistent view of data without putting too much strain on the system in terms of locks and upkeep of change history.

I just mentioned locks in reference to the various synchronization mechanisms the system maintains on your behalf to keep data consistent. When you define an isolation level, you define, by default, a locking pattern. But you can also explicitly lock tables, to specify to the system that you want exclusive write or, sometimes, read access* to one or several tables,

---

* Oracle never blocks other readers.

and that anyone who will require an access that conflicts with yours after you have grabbed your lock will have to wait until you end your transaction. Conversely, if someone is already accessing the table in a mode that is incompatible with your request when you try to lock the table, your session will have to wait* until the other session commits or rolls back its changes.

But let's return to our MySQL/MyISAM program; we are operating in the default auto-commit mode, and MyISAM allows only one process to update one table at one time. The problem we have (that concurrent processes pounce on the same row) occurs in the phase when we try to grab a row to process—namely, when we execute the following:

```
select min(seqnum) from fifo
where state = 'R';

update fifo
set state = 'P'
where seqnum = ?;
```

What happens is that one process gets the identifier of the next row to process, and before it has time to update the table, one or several other processes get the very same identifier. We clearly need to ensure that once we have identified a row as a candidate for processing (i.e., once the select statement has returned an identifier), no other process will get hold of it. Remember that we cannot combine these two statements because we need the identifier to update the row when we are done. A single statement would have fit the bill, because the internal mechanisms of a DBMS ensure the so-called ACID (Atomicity, Consistency, Isolation, Durability) property of a single update statement. (In plain language, you don't have to worry about a single statement because the DBMS ensures data consistency.)

If we want to run multiple instances of the program and benefit from parallelism, we need to refactor the code once again. One way to do this is to turn off auto-commit mode to get better control of transactions, and then, in the main loop, to lock the table for our exclusive use *before* we look for the next row to process, update the table, and finally release the lock. At this point, we will be guaranteed to have an ID that we know no other parallel thread will get, and we can feel comfortable knowing that this ID will be processed only once. I used this strategy in my *consumer_lock.c* program.

Another way to proceed is as follows:

```
set the number of updated rows to zero
loop
   select min(seqnum) from fifo
   where state = 'R';
   /* Exit if nothing found */
   update fifo
   set state = 'P'
   where seqnum = ?
     and state = 'R';
until the number of updated rows is 1;
```

* Although Oracle allows you to specify that the lock command should return an error, if it cannot be satisfied immediately.

When the row is updated, the program checks that it still is in the state where it is expected to be; if the assumption that the row is still in the "Ready" state is not satisfied, it means that another process was quicker to grab it, and we just try to get another row. The algorithm is very close to the original program, except that the update statement is made safe and I have added a provision for failure. I called this program *consumer_not_so_naive.c*.

I also wrote another program that uses the "safe update" strategy but also assumes the underlying InnoDB storage engine and the availability of row-level locking. The third program adds the for update clause to the select statement that identifies the next row to process, thus locking the selected row. This program is called *consumer_inno.c*. I ran all three programs with a pseudobacklog of 200 rows to clear, an average sleep time of 0.4 seconds, and a varying number of concurrent processes between 1 and 50. The results are shown in Figure 7-3. The most outstanding feature of the figure is probably that all three curves overlap one another almost perfectly. All three solutions scale extremely well, and the time that it takes for *n* processes to clear the backlog is the time it takes one process to clear the backlog divided by *n*.

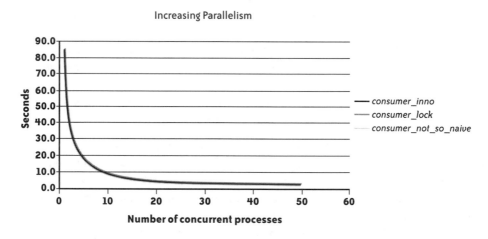

FIGURE 7-3. *Running parallel processes after adjustment*

You might wonder why it doesn't make any difference whether we are using table locking or row locking. You mustn't forget that "service providers" from the application viewpoint are requesters for the database. In this light, there are two very simple reasons why row locking doesn't perform better than table locking:

- The first reason is that all processes are chasing the same row, which is the oldest unprocessed row. For each process, only one row counts, and this row is the critical resource. Whether you are stuck waiting for that row or for the table makes no difference, and row locking brings no measurable benefit in such a case.

- The second reason is that even if we have to scan the fifo table, its modest number of rows makes the select statement almost instant. Even when you lock the table for the duration of the select and update statements, the lock is held for so little time in regard to the "rate of arrival" that waiting lines don't build up.

Contrary to what you might think, the grain of locks isn't necessarily the decisive factor in terms of performance on relatively small tables (i.e., up to thousands or tens of thousands of rows). If access to data is fast, concurrency is moderate, and locks are held for a fraction of a second, you'll probably have no performance issue. It's when you have thousands of concurrent processes that target different rows in big tables and updates that are not instant that row locking makes a difference by allowing some overlap when rows are modified.

Shortening critical sections

In concurrent programming, a critical section is a part of the code that only one process or thread can access. When the DBMS sets a lock, at your explicit request or implicitly, the code that executes up to the end of the transaction, whether it is SQL statements or the code from a host language that executes SQL calls, potentially becomes a critical section. It all depends on the odds of blocking another process. Beware that, even with row locking, locks that operate on ranges of rows can easily block other processes. Waits on locks can occur all the more easily as the DBMS escalates locks (like SQL Server or DB2), which means that when many unitary resources are locked by the same process, the numerous locks are automatically replaced by a single unitary lock that has a coarser grain. You may switch from, for instance, many locks on the rows in a page to one lock on the whole page, or worse.

If you want your various concurrent processes to coexist peacefully, you must do your best to shorten critical sections.

One important point to keep in mind is that whenever you are updating rows, deleting rows, or inserting the result of a query into a table, the identification of the rows to update, delete, or insert is a part of the response time of the SQL statement. In the case of an insert ... select ... statement, this is explicit. For the other cases, the implicit select statement is a result of the where clause. When this substatement is slow, it may be responsible for the greatest part of the response as a whole.

One efficient way to improve concurrency when using table locking is to refactor the code to proceed in two steps (it may look like I am contradicting what I preached in the previous chapter, but read on). If you are operating in table locking mode, as soon as the DBMS begins to execute update t set ..., table t is locked. Everything depends on the relative weight of the time required to find the rows versus the time required to update them. If locating the rows is a fast process, but the update takes a long time because you are updating a column that appears in many indexes, there isn't much you can do (apart from dropping some of the indexes that might be of dubious benefit). But if the identification of the result set takes a substantial fraction of the time, it is worth executing the two phases separately, because locating rows is far less lock-intensive than updating them. If you want to update a single row, you first get into one or several variables the best identifiers that you can get—either the columns that make the primary key, or even better (if available), an identifier similar to the rowid (the row address) that is available in Oracle (which doesn't need a two-step update because it implements row-level locking). If you want to update many rows, you can use a temporary table instead.* Then you apply your changes, which locks the full table, but by using these identifiers—and committing as soon as you are done—you minimize the lapse of time during which you hold a monopoly on the table.

Isolating Hot Spots

More parallelism usually means increased contention, and very often throughput is limited by a single point of friction. A typical case I have seen more than once is the table that holds "next identifier" values for one or several surrogate keys—that is, internal identifiers that are used as handy aliases for cumbersome, composite primary keys. A typical example would be the value of the orderid that will be assigned to the next order to be created. There is no reason to use such a table, because MySQL has auto-increment columns, SQL Server has identity columns, and Oracle (as Postgres or DB2) has sequences. Even if implementations vary, the functionality is the same, and the various mechanisms implemented have been optimized in relation to the DBMS that supports them. Moreover, all database products feature a simple means to get for use elsewhere the value that was last generated.

The kindest reason I can find for developers to manage their surrogate keys is the will to be independent from the underlying DBMS in a quixotic quest for portability. One reaches the limits of SQL portability very quickly: most commonly used functions, such as those used in date arithmetic, depend heavily on the DBMS. Even a function as exotic as the function that computes the length of a string is called length( ) in Oracle and MySQL, but len( ) in T-SQL. Unless you limit yourself to the most basic of queries (in which case this book will be of very little use to you), porting SQL code from one product to another will mean some rewriting—not necessarily difficult rewriting, but rewriting nevertheless (many of the examples in this book prove the point). Now, if your goal is to have an application that is consistently underperforming across a wide array of database products, managing the generation of your surrogate keys is fine. If you have any concern about performance, the soundest strategy consists of identifying and keeping all the parts of the code that are specific to one product in an abstraction layer or central place, and shamelessly using what a DBMS has to offer.

Getting rid of a table that holds counters often requires some serious rewriting, and even more serious testing, because you usually find queries and updates against such a table executed from many places in the code. The existence of a dedicated function changes nothing in regard to this effort because even with an Oracle sequence, there is no reason to run

```
select sequence_name.nextval
into my_next_id
from dual;
```

before an insert statement when you can directly insert sequence_name.nextval. Picking a value from a sequence or having it automatically generated instead of fetching it from a

---

* I am not a great fan of temporary tables. But, as with all features, they have their use.

table is a much deeper change than caching the values returned by a function. Nevertheless, contention issues on a table that holds "next numbers" can hamper performance very badly, and if monitoring shows you that a significant fraction of time is spent on this table, you should replace it with a DBMS-specific generator.

Many times there is no particularly bad design choice, but rather the logic of processing causes several processes to operate in the same "area" of a database, and therefore to interfere with one another. For instance, if several processes are concurrently inserting rows into the same table, you must be careful about how your table is physically stored. If you use default parameters, all processes will want to append to the table, and you will have a hot spot after the last row inserted: all processes cannot write to the same offset of the same page in memory at the same time, and even with very fine-grained locks some kind of serialization must take place.

Dealing with multiple queues

In the example where processes were removing tasks from the `fifo` table, I provided an example where parallelism was added to the application, and where the shared resource was the `fifo` table. But as I stated, the queuing model applies at many levels, from a high level to a low level. Let me drill down a little and take the simplest of examples: what happens when we insert one row into a table. As Figure 7-4 shows, we have several potential queues:

1. We may need to acquire a lock on the table, and if the table is already locked in an incompatible or exclusive mode, we'll have to wait.

2. Then we shall either find a free slot in the table to insert data, or append a row at the end of the table. If several processes attempt to perform data insertion at the same time, while one writes bytes in memory, others will necessarily have to wait; we may also have some recursive database activity required to extend the storage allocated to the table.

3. Then there will probably be one or more indexes to maintain: we shall have to insert the address of the newly inserted row associated with the key value. Storage allocation work is again possible, and if several processes are trying to update indexes for the same key value, or for very close key values, they will try to write the same area of the index, and as with the table, some serialization will be required.

4. Then, committing the change will mean a synchronous write to a logfile. Once again, several processes cannot simultaneously write to a logfile, and we'll have to wait for acknowledgment from the I/O subsystem to return to the program.

This list is in no way exhaustive; it is possible that some I/O operations will be needed to bring into memory pages relevant to the table or its indexes, or that foreign key constraints will have to be checked to ensure that data inserted actually matches correct values. Triggers may fire, and may execute more operations that will translate into a series of queues. Processes may also have to wait in a run queue for a processor if the machine is overloaded.

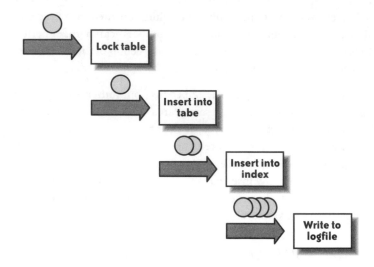

FIGURE 7-4. Multiple queues: where does it jam?

Nevertheless, the simple vision of Figure 7-4 is enough for you to understand that a single line where you spend too much time is enough to kill performance, and that when there are several places where you can wait you must be careful about not trying to optimize the wrong problem.* To illustrate that point I wrote and ran a simple example using a tool called Roughbench (freely available from *http://www.roughsea.com* and from the download area associated with this book, at *http://www.oreilly.com/catalog/9780596514976*). Roughbench is a simple JDBC wrapper that takes an SQL file and runs its contents repeatedly for either a fixed number of iterations or a fixed period of time. This tool can start a variable number of threads, all executing the same statement, and it can generate random data.

I therefore created the following test table:

```
create table concurrent_insert(id        bigint not null,
                     some_num     bigint,
                     some_string varchar(50));
```

In another series of runs, I made id an auto-increment column and declared it as the primary key (thus implicitly creating a unique index on it). Finally, in a last series of runs, I kept id as the primary key and partitioned the table on this column into five partitions.

I inserted rows into the table for one minute, using successively one to five threads, and checked how many rows I managed to insert.

I didn't pick the variants of my test table at random. The indexless table is a mere baseline; in a properly designed database, I would expect every table to have some primary key or at least a unique column. But it allows us to measure the impact, both with a single thread

---

* I cannot do better on this topic than redirect Oracle users to *Optimizing Oracle Performance* by Cary Millsap with Jeff Holt (O'Reilly), which explains in detail how to identify where time is really spent and the various traps to avoid. A chapter of the book is also dedicated to queuing theory for database practitioners.

and in a concurrent environment, of having a (nonclustered) primary key based on an auto-increment column. What I expect is, logically, lower performance with an index than without, straight from the case when I have a single thread, because index management adds up to table management. When I run more than one thread, I am interested in checking the slope of the curve as I add more processes: if the slope doesn't change, my index adds no friction. If the slope is gentler, the index is bad for concurrency and scalability. As far as partitioning is concerned, the DBMS has to compute for each row in which partition it must go, which is done (in this case) by hashing the value of id. Partitioning should therefore make a single thread slightly less efficient than no partitioning. But I also expect processes to impede one another as concurrency increases; I have created as many partitions as my maximum number of processes with the idea of spreading concurrent inserts across the table and the index—which should not help if the whole table is locked during an insertion.

Table 7-1 shows the relative results I got committing after each insert for the MyISAM and InnoDB storage engines.* They don't really match what we could have expected.

TABLE 7-1. Relative insertion rate, commit after every row

		Threads				
	Engine	**1**	**2**	**3**	**4**	**5**
No index	MyISAM	1.00	1.39	1.45	1.59	1.50
Auto-increment PK	MyISAM	0.78	1.19	1.21	1.36	1.31
Partitioning	MyISAM	0.75	1.12	1.13	1.26	1.23
No index	InnoDB	0.31	0.49	0.58	0.63	0.68
Auto-increment PK	InnoDB	0.32	0.47	0.59	0.63	0.67
Partitioning	InnoDB	0.30	0.46	0.56	0.61	0.65

Table 7-1 requires a few explanations:

- First, scalability is very poor. Of course, multiplying by five the number of rows inserted by running five times more processes is the stuff of fairytales and marketing data sheets. But even so, as the machine was coming close to CPU saturation with five active threads, but not quite, I should have done better.

- There is a very significant drop in performance with the InnoDB storage engine, which isn't, in itself, shocking. You must remember that InnoDB implements many mechanisms that are unavailable with MyISAM, of which referential integrity isn't the least. Engine built-in mechanisms will avoid additional statements and round trips; if the performance when inserting looks poor compared to MyISAM, some of the difference will probably be recouped elsewhere, and on the whole, the gap may be much smaller.

---

* Because results obtained on my relatively modest dual-core biprocessor test machine have little universal value, I have expressed all results in relation to the number of rows I managed to insert with one thread into the unindexed MyISAM table. For the record, it was about 1,500 rows per second.

By the way, if you really want impressive throughput, there is the aptly named BLACKHOLE storage engine (the equivalent of the Unix /dev/null file…).

- Results peak at four threads with MyISAM (on a machine with the equivalent of four processors). InnoDB starts from a much lower base, but the total number of rows inserted grows steadily, and even if scalability is far from impressive it is much better than what MyISAM displays. With InnoDB, the number of rows inserted in one minute is about 2.2 times greater with five threads than with one.

- The most remarkable feature is probably that, if with MyISAM the primary key degrades performance, and if partitioning brings no improvement when concurrency increases as expected, there is no difference between the different variants with InnoDB. The uniform InnoDB performance is more striking when you plot the figures in Table 7-1 side by side as I did in Figure 7-5 (only one thing doesn't appear clearly in Figure 7-5, which is that the ratio between best insertion rate and worst insertion rate is much better with InnoDB than with MyISAM in my test).

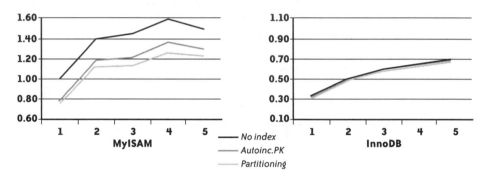

FIGURE 7-5. Plotting the results of Table 7-1

The reason the InnoDB tables show no difference is simple: the queue that blocks everything is the queue that writes to the logfile. Actually, identifying the point that slows down the whole chain would have been easier with SQL Server or Oracle than with the MySQL engine version against which I carried out my tests; in that version information_schema.global_status was rather terse on the topic of waits, and the copious output of show engine innodb status isn't very easy to interpret when you don't know exactly what you are looking for.

Nevertheless, the difference is obvious when I commit changes with every 5,000 rows inserted. My choice of 5,000 is arbitrary. I kept the same reference as in Table 7-1, which is the number of rows inserted in auto-commit mode into an unindexed MyISAM table.

Table 7-2 tells quite a different story from Table 7-1: with a single thread, if adding an index seems, somewhat surprisingly, to make no difference for InnoDB, partitioning still slightly degrades performance. But when you check the evolution as I added more threads, you can notice that if committing much less often has merely pushed up the MyISAM curves, removing the log bottleneck has let a new pattern emerge for InnoDB.

The difference in behavior with InnoDB appears perhaps more clearly in Figure 7-6: first, if we ignore the unrealistic case of the indexless table from three threads onward, performance with partitioning is better on InnoDB. Second, we can also check that contention is worse in the primary key index than in the table, since performance grows much more slowly with than without an index. Third, partitioning removes contention on both the table and the index and, combined with row locking, allows us to get the same insertion rate as when there is no index.

TABLE 7-2. Relative insertion rate, commit after 5,000 rows

		Threads				
	Engine	1	2	3	4	5
No index	MyISAM	1.49	2.21	2.15	2.40	2.47
Auto-increment PK	MyISAM	1.26	1.80	1.74	1.97	1.78
Partitioning	MyISAM	1.19	1.86	1.60	1.74	1.58
No index	InnoDB	1.18	1.83	1.95	2.17	2.01
Auto-increment PK	InnoDB	1.19	1.69	1.76	1.85	1.72
Partitioning	InnoDB	1.11	1.68	1.86	2.11	2.01

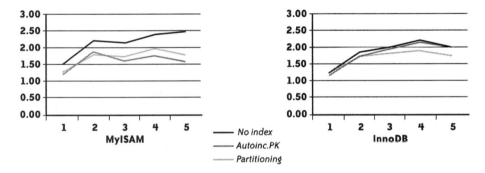

FIGURE 7-6. When you no longer block on logfiles

My modest machine prevented me from pushing my tests further by adding even more threads, and performance actually peaked with four threads. There are a number of lessons to learn from this simple example:

You mustn't start by trying to improve the wrong queue

The primary issue in the example was initially the commit rate. With a commit after each insert, it was pointless to partition the table to improve performance. Remember that partitioning a table that already contains tens of millions of rows is an operation that requires planning and time, and it isn't totally devoid of risk. If you wrongly identify the main bottleneck, you may mobilize the energies of many people for nothing and feed expectations that will be disappointed—even if the new physical structure can be a good choice under the right circumstances.

Bottlenecks shift

Depending on concurrency, indexing, commit rate, volume of data, and other factors, the queue where arrival rate and service time are going to collide isn't always the same one. Ideally, you should try to anticipate; building on past experience is probably the best way to do this.

Removing bottlenecks is an iterative process

Whenever you improve a point of friction, a queue where lines are lengthening, you more quickly release a number of requesters that are going to move to the next queue, thereby increasing the arrival rate for this next queue and possibly making it unsustainable for the service provider. You mustn't be surprised if one performance improvement suddenly brings to light a new problem that was previously hiding in the shadow of the problem you just solved.

You must pay attention to raw performance, but also to scalability

Raw performance and scalability aren't always exactly the same, and it can make sense to settle for a solution that isn't the most efficient today, but which will ensure a smooth and more predictable growth path. This is particularly true if, say, some hardware upgrade has already been scheduled for the next quarter or the quarter after the next, and you want to get as much benefit as possible from the upgrade. It may be efficient storage, or more processors, or faster processors—an improvement that may unlock one bottleneck and bring no benefit to others. Therefore, you have to juggle with the improvement paths that you have identified and choose the one that is likely to bear the most fruit.

To underline the fact that raw performance under one set of circumstances and scalability aren't exactly the same thing, consider Figure 7-7, where I charted side by side both the performance measure I got with four threads in the various configurations, as well as the ratio in performance I got by going from one thread to four (this ratio is indicated as "Scalability" in the figure). In this very limited example, you can see that the combination of partitioning with the InnoDB engine combines good performance (the best performance when you consider only the cases where a primary key is defined) and decent scalability. If you expect long-term growth, it looks like the best bet in this example. On the other hand, if the only variation in load that you expect is a sudden burst from time to time, opting for the simple MyISAM solution isn't necessarily bad. But MyISAM plus partitioning is a solution that, once again in this example, does more harm than good (I say "in this example" because you may have concerns other than alleviating contention to use a partitioned table; simplifying archival and purges is a good reason that has nothing to do with contention and locks).

Parallelizing Your Program and the DBMS

Multiplying requesters and service providers, and trying to make everything work in harmony by minimizing locking and contention while ensuring data consistency, are techniques that aren't always perfectly mastered but at least come easily to mind. I have much more rarely seen (outside of transaction monitors, perhaps) people trying to parallelize their program and the activity of the DBMS. Although even a modest machine can nowadays

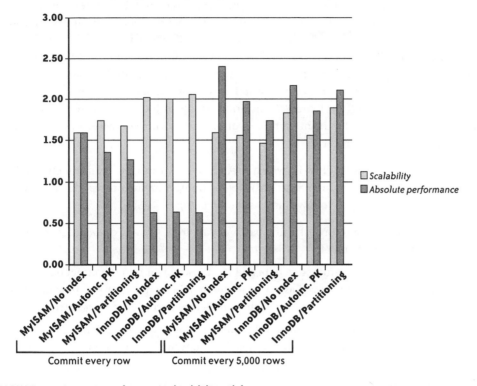

Benefit of Running Four Concurrent Processes

FIGURE 7-7. Comparing performance and scalability with four processes

process several tasks in a truly parallel fashion, we are still using programming languages that can trace their ancestry back to FORTRAN, COBOL, and the time when a single processor was sequentially executing instructions one by one. Add to this the fact that multitasking isn't natural to mankind (to me, at least), and it is no surprise to discover that processes are often designed to be very linear in nature.

When you execute select statements within a program, the sequence of operations is always the same, regardless of the DBMS and the language that calls it:

1. You get a handler to execute a statement.

2. You execute a call to parse the statement.

3. Optionally, you attach ("bind") some input parameters to your statement.

4. You define memory areas where you want to retrieve the data returned from the database.

5. You execute the query.

6. As long as the return code indicates success, you fetch rows.

Sometimes some kind of compound API bundles several of the steps I just described into a single function call. But even if you ultimately get an array of values, all the steps are here.

What most people fail to realize is that almost all database calls are synchronous—that is, whenever you execute a database call, your program is idle until the call returns. This is a nonissue in a transactional environment with heavy concurrency because unless all concurrent processes are stuck on the database side in a waiting line, while your session is idle another session will put the CPU to good use. However, in some environments you can increase throughput by putting the client side to work while the DBMS is working too. A good case in point is the loading of data warehouses, a batch operation that is often known as an ETL process for Extract/Transform/Load. If, as is often the case, you extract from one database to load into another one, your program will wait twice: when you fetch the data and when you insert it.

If the DBMS API functions allow it (which isn't always the case), you can sometimes significantly improve throughput, particularly if your transformation process needs some CPU time, by proceeding as follows (and as shown in Figure 7-8):

- The extraction phase returns the first batch of data from the source database. Meanwhile, you cannot do much.

- Instead of sequentially processing data and then inserting it into the target database, you copy the data just received as is to another area in memory, or you bind another area of your memory to your select statement before fetching the next batch.

- While the second batch is fetched, another thread transforms what batch #1 returned and writes it to a third memory area. When done, it waits for extraction #2 to complete.

- At the same time, a third thread takes the transformed set in the third buffer, copies it to a fourth buffer, and loads the contents of this fourth buffer into the target database.

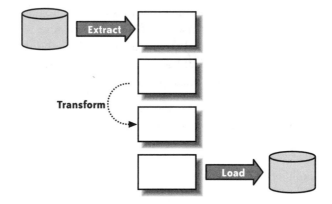

FIGURE 7-8. Parallelizing ETL processes

In cruise mode, you have three threads working in parallel, one fetching the nth batch of data while the second one transforms batch $n - 1$ and the third one loads batch $n - 2$.

Needless to say, synchronization may be tricky because no thread must overwrite a memory area that hasn't yet been fully processed by the next thread in line, nor must it start to read its input if the previous thread isn't done yet. I wouldn't advise getting into this type of mechanism, if you don't have a mastery of semaphores and multithreading.

You can apply the same idea to the context of applications that have to run over a wide area network (WAN). I have seen a number of applications that were accessing databases located on another continent. As long as the speed of light doesn't get upgraded, there isn't much you can do to avoid about 500 milliseconds of network latency between New York and Hong Kong, so using a memory cache for locally storing read-only data makes sense. Usually, what hurts is loading the cache, which is done either when you start (or restart) an application server, or when you connect if the cache is private to a session. A computer can perform a lot during a half second of network latency. If, instead of fetching data, populating the cache, fetching the next batch of data, populating the cache, and so on, you have one thread that populates the cache, allocates memory, and links data structures while another thread fetches the remaining data, you can sometimes significantly improve startup or connection times.

Shaking Foundations

In this chapter, I have shown that sometimes table partitioning is an efficient way to limit contention when several concurrent processes are hitting the database. I don't know to what extent modifying the physical design of the database really belongs to refactoring, but because the underlying layout can have a significant impact on performance, I will now present a number of changes to consider, and explain briefly when and why they could be beneficial. Unfortunately, physical changes are rarely a boon to all operations, which makes it difficult to recommend a particular solution without a profusion of small-print warnings. You must thoroughly test the changes you want to bring, establish some kind of profit and loss statement, and weigh each increase and decrease in performance against its importance to the business. As I stated earlier, partitioning a big table that hasn't been partitioned from the start can be a mighty undertaking that, as with any mighty undertaking, involves operational hazards. I have never seen physical design changes being contemplated for small databases. Reorganizing a big database is a highly disruptive operation that requires weeks of careful planning, impeccable organization, and faultless execution (I could add that nobody will appreciate the effort if it works as it should, but that you are sure to gain unwanted notoriety if it doesn't); don't be surprised if your database administrators exhibit some lack of enthusiasm for the idea. You must therefore be positively certain that the changes are a real solution, rather than a displacement of problems.

Partitioning is only one, and possibly the most commendable, of several types of physical changes you can make to a table. You can also contemplate changes that affect both the logical and the physical structure of the database—changes that may be as simple as adding a column to a table to favor a particular process, more difficult like changing the data type, or as complex as restructuring tables or displacing some part of the data to a distant database.

Altering the physical structure of the database in view of performance improvement is an approach that is immensely popular with some people (but not database administrators) who see physical reorganization as a way to give a boost to applications without having to question too many implementation choices in these applications.

It must be clear in your mind that physical reorganization of any kind is not magic, and that gains will rarely be on the same order of magnitude as gains obtained by modifying database accesses, as you saw in Chapters 5 and 6. Any alteration to the database demands solid reasons:

- If you poorly identify the reason for slowness, you may waste a lot of effort. The previous example with the concurrent insertions is a case in point: with a commit after each insert, partitioning brought no measurable benefit because the bottleneck was contention when writing to the journal file, not contention when writing to the table or to the primary key index. Only after having solved the logfile issue does the bottleneck shift to competing insertions into the table and (mostly) the index, and does partitioning help to improve performance.

- Another important point is that the benefits you can gain from physical reorganization usually stem from two opposite ends of the spectrum: either you try to cluster data so as to find all the data you need when you request it in a few pages, minimizing the amount of memory you have to scan as well as the number of I/O operations, or you try to disseminate data so as to decrease contention and direct various "requesters" to different "queues." It is likely that any partitioning will adversely affect some parts of the code. If you improve a critical section and worsen an ancillary part, that's fine. If you replace a problem with another problem, it may not be worth the trouble.

With that being said, let's now see how we can speed up processing.

Marshaling Rows

As we just saw, partitioning is the best way to decrease contention, by making concurrent processes hit different physical areas of a single logical table. But another reorganization that matters is to do whatever is needed to cluster together rows that usually belong to the same result set. Such an organization is more important for rows that are retrieved through a range scan on an index—that is, a condition such as the following:

```
and some_indexed_column between <min value> and <max value>
```

I mentioned in Chapter 2 the relationship between the order of the keys in the index and the order of the corresponding rows; nowhere does this relationship matter as much as in a range scan. In the worst case, what can happen is something that looks like Figure 7-9: when you scan your index, the successive keys that you meet all refer to rows that are stored in different pages of the table.* Such a query is likely to result in many I/O operations because only some of the pages will already be in memory when they're needed.

---

* That's *blocks* for you Oracle folks.

To this you can add CPU waste because each page will need to be accessed in memory to retrieve only one row.

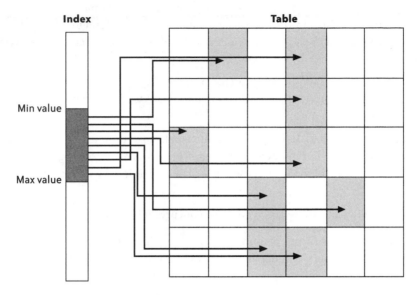

FIGURE 7-9. An unfortunate index range scan

Of course, the ideal case would be to find all the rows addressed by the set of keys gathered in a single page, or in as few pages as possible: this would minimize I/O operations, and scanning the pages would really be profitable. If we want such an ideal situation for all possible ranges of keys, we have only one solution: we must find the rows in the table in the same order as the keys in the index. To achieve this goal, either we re-create the table and reinsert the rows after sorting by the index key (with the risk of having to perform the same operation at regular intervals if rows are regularly inserted, updated, and deleted), or we define the table to have a self-organizing structure that suits our needs. We can reach our goal by defining the index as a clustering index with SQL Server or MySQL and the InnoDB engine, or defining the table as an index-organized table (the Oracle equivalent).[*]

We must be aware of a number of conditions:

- Rows are ordered with respect to index idx1 or with respect to index idx2, but not with respect to both, unless there is a very strong relationship between the column(s) indexed by idx1 and the column(s) indexed by idx2—for instance, an auto-incrementing sequence number and an insertion date. One index, and therefore one category of range searches, will be unfairly favored over all others.

---

[*] There are other possibilities, such as adding more columns to the index so as to find all the information in the index, which avoids the indirect access to the table.

- The index that structures the table usually has to be the primary key index. It may happen that, if the primary key is made of several columns, the order of the columns in the primary key won't quite match the order we want. That would mean we must redefine the primary key, which in turns means we must redefine all foreign keys that point to that primary key, and perhaps some indexes as well—all things that can take you pretty far.

- Insertions will be costlier, because instead of carelessly appending a new row, you will have to insert it at the right place. No, you don't want to update a primary key, and therefore, updates aren't an issue.

- Tables that are wide (i.e., have many columns) make insertions much more painful and such an organization doesn't benefit them much: if rows are very long, very few rows will fit into one page anyway, and their being suitably ordered will not make much of a difference.

- Contention will really be severe if we have concurrent inserts.

When some of these conditions cannot be satisfied, partitioning once again can come to the rescue. If you partition by range over the key, data will not be as strictly ordered as in the previous case, but it will be somewhat herded: you will be sure that your entire result set will be contained in the partition that contains the minimum value and all the following partitions, up to the partition that contains the maximum value for your scan. Depending on the various conditions provided in the query, it is even possible that an index will not be necessary and that directly scanning the relevant partitions will be enough.

As with clustering indexes, this will be a use of partitions that may increase rather than decrease contention. The typical case is a date partitioning by week on the row creation date in a table that keeps one year of data online: at any given moment, the most active part of the table will be the partition that corresponds to the current week, where everyone will want to insert at once. If data insertion is a heavily concurrent process, you must carefully choose between using partitioning that spreads data all over the place, and partitioning that clusters data. Or you can try to have your cake and eat it too by using subpartitioning: suppose the table contains purchase orders. You can partition by range of ordering dates, and within each partition divide again on, say, the customer identifier. Concurrent processes that insert purchase orders will indeed hit the same partition, but because presumably each process will deal with a different customer, they will hit different subpartitions if the customer identifiers don't hash to the same value.

Subpartitioning (which I have rarely seen used) can be a good way to keep a delicate balance between conflicting goals. With that said, it will not help you much if you run many queries where you want to retrieve all the orders from one customer over the course of a year, because then these orders will be spread over 52 subpartitions. I hope you see my point: partitioning and subpartitioning are great solutions for organizing your data, but you must really exhaustively study all the implications to ensure that the overall benefit is worth the trouble. In a refactoring environment, you will not be given a second chance, and you really need to muster the support of all people involved—database administrators in particular. Whenever I encounter a table with more than one million rows, partitioning automatically appears on my checklist with a question mark. But whether I recommend the partitioning always depends. I'm usually very suspicious when I encounter a table that contains several hundred millions of rows and isn't partitioned; however, some tables in the range of one million to tens of millions of rows are sometimes better left unpartitioned.

Splitting Tables

Whether you use a clustering index, turn your table into an index-organized table, or slice and dice it into partitions and subpartitions, you "merely" affect the physical structure of the database. For your programs, the table will remain the same, and even if the reorganization that you decide upon will make you hated intensely by several people who would have rather spent their weekend doing something else, you can at least pretend that it will be transparent for programs (if you remember Chapter 5, you may nevertheless have to review a few queries). Some other physical alterations to the database may bring significant benefits, but require (slight) adjustments to queries.

A frequent case for poor performance is the existence of tables with very wide rows, for a reason similar to the example shown in Figure 7-9: index range scans hit mostly different blocks. In that case, the cause isn't row ordering, and reorganizing the table as we saw previously will not help. The cause is that because rows are wide, each page or block stores very few rows. This situation frequently occurs when a table contains multiple long varchar columns, text columns,* or large objects (LOBs)—especially when they are updated often, causing fragmentation in the data blocks. When LOBs are very big, they are stored in special pages, and rows contain only a pointer to these pages (the pointer is sometimes known as the *locator*). But because the use of indirections can severely impact performance, smaller LOBs are often stored in-row (up to 4,000 bytes with Oracle and 8,000 bytes with SQL Server; with MySQL it depends on the storage engine). You don't need many 2,000- or 4,000-character columns in a row to be filled to have a very low density of rows per table page and ruin range scans.

One solution may be to split a wide table t into two tables, as I show in Figure 7-10 (the circles represent the primary key columns). The case is based on the fact that long columns rarely participate in queries that return many rows, and that joins and extra fetches add a negligible overhead to small result sets. In such a case, you can try to isolate into a table that I have renamed t_head, which contains all (narrow) columns that are indexed, plus a few other columns that may be critical when identifying result sets. As a result of the column selection, rows in t_head are short, density is high, and we can even use a clustering index or partition the table and ensure that index range scans (or full table scans, for that matter) will hit a small number of pages, full of information.

---

* Clob columns in Oracle.

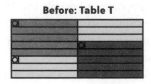

Before: Table T

After:
Table T_head

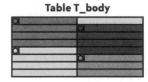

Table T_body

FIGURE 7-10. Splitting tables

All the long columns, plus the primary key columns that are duplicated, are moved to a second table called t_body. This second table behaves as a kind of secondary storage, "indexed" by the same primary key as t_head.

In such a case, because the initial table disappears, a number of changes must be brought to the programs:

- All select and some update statements that hit only columns that now belong to t_head or t_body must reference the new table to take advantage of the new structure. For update statements it may be tricky. It depends on how the table is initially populated. It may happen that when you insert a new row you set values only for columns that now belong to t_head. In that case, there is no reason to insert into t_body a matching row that is empty except for the primary key columns. But then, the very first update applied to a column of t_body must translate to an insert statement—by catching an exception, not by checking beforehand whether the row exists!

- All select statements that refer to columns now split between t_head and t_body must refer to a view that joins t_head to t_body so as to look like the original table. The join may need to be an outer join, because t_body may not yet contain a matching row for each row in t_head.

- As previously explained, insert statements into t may become either successive inserts into t_head and t_body, or inserts into t_head followed much later by inserts into t_body.

- For delete statements, the case is simpler: you merely have to delete from the two tables in a single transaction.

Altering Columns

You can make several changes to columns: you can play on their contents, split them, or add new columns. Like all physical changes, none of these changes is to be undertaken lightly, and because the logical structure of the tables is modified there must be parallel changes in the programs.

Changing the contents

One particularly effective change that you can experiment with, even if it looks pretty insignificant, is to play on the null/not null attribute of a column. As a general rule, any column that always contains data should be declared as not null (null is the default with Oracle). It can make a significant difference for the optimizer to know that there is always a defined value in the column, because it affects join strategies as well as subqueries and cardinality estimates. Even when the column may not be populated, it can make sense to use a default value. If you have an index on a single column that can contain null values, a product such as Oracle doesn't index null values, and a condition such as the following will necessarily translate (if there is no other condition) into a full scan, even if the majority of rows contain values:

```
and column_name is null
```

Using a default value would allow a straight and efficient index search.[*]

An opposite strategy is sometimes successful: if a column contains nothing more than a Y/N flag and the only rows you are interested in are the ones for which the value is Y (a minority), replacing a value that isn't much loaded with significance, such as N, with null may make indexes and rows more compact (some products don't store nulls) and searches slightly more efficient (because there are fewer blocks to read). But in most cases, the difference will be so modest that it will not really be worth the effort; besides, some database engines now implement compression mechanisms that render this optimization moot.

Splitting columns

Many performance issues stem directly from the lack of normalization of databases—particularly not abiding by *first normal form*, which states that columns contain atomic values with regard to searches, and that conditions should apply to a full column, not to a substring or to any similar subdivision of a column. Of course, partial attempts at normalization smack of despair: too often, proper normalization would mean a total overhaul of the database design. Such a grand redesign may be badly necessary, but it is likely to be a hard sell to the powers that hold the purse. Unfortunately, half-baked attempts at fixing glaring inadequacies don't often make a bad situation much better. Suppose you have a column called name which contains first names, middle initials, and last names. This type of column turns even simple searches into operations from hell. Forget about sorts by family name (and if the family name comes first, you may be sure to find in the list some names of foreign origin for which the first name will have been mistaken for the family name), and searches are likely to end up in pathetic conditions for which indexes are utterly useless, such as the following:

```
where upper(name) like '%DOE%'
```

---

[*] With dates, and, as a general rule, all columns on which range searches are performed, dummy values that replace null columns may give the optimizer the wrong idea about the scope of values, and therefore the wrong idea about what percentage of a table a range scan is going to sweep through.

In such a case, it doesn't take long to realize that the column content should be split into manageable, atomic pieces of information, and perhaps that forcing data to uppercase or lowercase on input might be a good idea, even if the rendition means new transformations. But the question, then, is whether information should be duplicated, with the old column kept as is to minimize disturbances to existing programs, or whether you should be more radical and get rid of it after its replacement. The big issue with keeping the old column is data maintenance. If you don't want to modify the existing insert statements, either you populate the new columns through a trigger or you define them (with SQL Server) as persisted computed columns that you can index. Whether you call the function that chops the string from within a trigger or in the definition of the computed column doesn't make much of a difference. The function call will make inserts and updates (relatively) slow, and automated normalization of strings is likely to be very bug-prone as long as names don't follow very simple patterns. As a result, you'll probably end up spending much more time trying to fix the transmogrifying function than modifying the insert and update statements in the first place. It may not look so initially, but it may be safer to take the jump, burn your vessels, and not try to maintain a "compatibility mode" with what you reckon to be a poor choice of implementation.

Adding columns

The opposite of trying to normalize data is the more popular course of action, which is to denormalize it. Most often, the rationale behind denormalization is either the avoidance of joins (by propagating, through a series of tables, keys that allow shortcuts), or the avoidance of aggregates by computing values for reporting purposes on the fly. For instance, you can add to an orders table an order_amount column, which will be updated with the amount of each row referring to the order in the order_details table, where all articles pertaining to the order are listed one by one.

Denormalization poses a threat to data integrity. Sooner or later, keys that are repeated to avoid joins usually land you in a quagmire, because referential integrity becomes nearly impossible to maintain, and you end up with rows that you are unable to relate to anything. Computations made on the fly are safer, but there is the question of maintenance: keeping an aggregate up-to-date throughout inserts, updates, and deletes isn't easy and errors in aggregates are more difficult to debug than elsewhere. Moreover, if the case was sometimes rather good for this type of denormalization in the early days of SQL databases, extensions such as the addition of the over ( ) clause to the standard aggregate functions make it much less useful.

The most convincing uses I have seen for denormalization of late were actually linked to partitioning: some redundant column was maintained in big tables where it was used as a partition key. This represented an interesting cross between two techniques to make data storage more suitable to existing queries.

Very often, denormalization denotes an attempt at overlaying two normalized schemas. Normalization, and in particular the very idea of data atomicity that underlies the first normal form, is relative to the use we have for data. Just consider the case when, for performance reasons, you want to store aggregates alongside details. If you were interested in details *and* aggregates, there would be no reason to maintain the aggregates: you could compute them at almost no extra cost when retrieving the details. If you want to store the aggregates, it is because you have identified a full class of queries where only the aggregates matter; in other words, a class of queries where the atom is the aggregate. This isn't always true (e.g., a precomputed aggregate may prove handy in replacing a having clause that would be very heavy to compute on the fly), but in many cases denormalization is a symptom of a collision between operational and reporting requirements. It is often better to acknowledge it, and even if a dedicated decision support database* is overkill, to create a dedicated schema based on materialized views rather than painfully maintaining denormalized columns in a transactional database.

Materializing views

Materialized views are, at their core, nothing more than data replication: usually, a view stores the text of a query, which is reexecuted each time the view is queried. The creation of a materialized view is, in practice, equivalent to the following:

```
create table materialized_view_name
as
select ....
```

With SQL Server, a view is materialized when you create a unique clustered index on it. Afterward, all modifications to base tables are propagated to the copy. With Oracle, there is a special create materialized view statement, in which you specify, among other things, how the view must be refreshed: automatically each time a transaction on the base tables commits, or asynchronously through a "refresh" job that is scheduled by the DBMS. In this latter case, the materialized view can be either completely refreshed (a kind of cancel and replace mode) or incrementally refreshed, which requires the creation of log tables associated to the base tables. A refresh that occurs when a transaction commits requires a log. MySQL up to and including version 6.0 doesn't support materialized views, but mechanisms such as those implemented by Oracle can be developed with triggers (the triggers that Oracle uses to manage materialized views have been incorporated into the kernel in Oracle 8*i*, but previous releases were using regular triggers); you can automatically generate these triggers by querying the information_schema views.

Everything has a price, and the existence of a materialized view means that all operations that change the base tables will cost more and take longer, because of the operations needed to record and to apply the changes to the materialized view on commit—unless you have opted for a full refresh, which could be a viable solution if there may be some lag between data in the materialized view and data in the base tables, and if refreshes are part of nightly batch processes.

---

* Which might use a different technology, such as an OLAP cube, or column-based processing such as Sybase's IQ product.

There are basically two uses for materialized views:

- The first use, which I just suggested, is as a kind of light ETL process. If the overhead on the base tables is bearable—and if you manage to isolate a part of your application that is more about reporting or decision support—materialized views, which can be indexed so as to get the best performance, will be your powerful allies. Oracle and SQL Server are even able to recognize the query that was used to create the materialized view, and hit the prebuilt result set rather than execute the query when they encounter it.

- The second use is when one or several of your queries refer to distant tables on another server. If you do not need a synchronous vision of data, getting a local copy will give the optimizer more freedom to choose a good path. When you hit a distant table, nested loops usually aren't an option, because each iteration would require a round trip over the network. Very often, the SQL engine will lap up the data over the network, store it locally (unindexed), and do its best to run the query. By using a materialized view, you can have your local copy, you can index it as you want, and you can have nested loops if they happen to be the most efficient way to run the query.

Much too often, developers consider materialized views as a panacea. I once attended a meeting with a handful of seasoned DBAs where some developers suggested creating, for multidimensional analysis, 13 materialized views on a table that was to store around one billion rows. The DBAs almost fainted. More recently, I saw a developer using materialized views to solve performance issues with queries that were referring to the most recent date in a table destined to hold two years' worth of data. It contained a series of materialized views that followed this pattern:

```
select *
from t
where date_column = (select max(date_column) from t)
```

On closer inspection, the (big) tables weren't partitioned, and the only indexes were primary key indexes—on surrogate keys.

As I hope this book has demonstrated, creating materialized views, in spite of their undeniable usefulness in some cases, isn't the first step to take when trying to improve performance.

## CHAPTER EIGHT

How It Works: Refactoring in Practice

Riguarda bene omai s ì com'io vado
Per questo loco al vero che disiri,
Sì che poi sappi sol tener o guado.
Observe me well, how through this place I come
Unto the truth thou wishest, that hereafter
Thou mayst alone know how to keep the ford.

—Dante Alighieri (1265–1321)

Paradiso, II, 124–126

(trans. Henry W. Longfellow)

IN THIS BOOK, I'VE TRIED TO EXPLAIN THE VARIOUS PATHS YOU CAN EXPLORE TO REFACTOR UNDERPERFORMING SQL applications. In this short chapter, I will briefly describe how I usually proceed when I am asked to look at a database application that doesn't live up to expectations. I'll try to be both concrete and abstract: concrete because I want to show refactoring in practice and abstract because I want to describe mental processes, not give a mock demonstration. Needless to say, you will find justifications and detailed explanations in the previous chapters, but not in this one.

Can You Look at the Database?

Very often, there is a vague rumor that something is wrong with an application, but you are asked to fix whatever you can without knowing exactly what the problem is.

- If you are lucky, the most critical performance issues have already been narrowed to one process or task, and the behavior is the same on a test database as on the main production database. If you are very lucky, someone who knows the functional side of the application well has volunteered to help you.

In such a case, the best course to take is probably to turn tracing on, and let someone else run the task that is too slow. Secure the benevolence of the database administrator; you will need privileges to query the application tables, but also the data dictionary tables, dynamic performance views, and possibly some system stored procedures. Check where trace files are generated and make sure you can access them easily. Try to gather as much data as you can: SQL statements that are issued, elapsed time, CPU time, number of executions, number of rows processed, and, if available, information about wait times. Try to get hold of the application code as well. Even if it's written in a language you have never used, the program logic will tell you how the various SQL statements that you are going to trace are combined.

- If the information that something is wrong has rippled to you through several people up and down the management ladder, and if the problem cannot easily be reproduced on a test database, you must query the production database. Once again, the first thing to negotiate is a number of privileges that are the preserve of a happy few. Don't ask for full DBA privileges; that may be politically difficult to negotiate. But do come with a prepared list of privileges:

Mandatory privileges
> The right to query dynamic performance views and the subset of the data dictionary that describes the objects used by the application

Highly desirable privileges
> The right to query the application tables

You don't need the right to update application tables or to delete rows from them, even if it's update or delete statements that are slow. You can study these statements by replacing them with select statements. Very often, you can diagnose a lot without even querying the application tables; you may even be able to suggest some possible solutions for improving performance. Of course, if you want to provide a solution, that is a different matter. But even if data is confidential, it is likely that statistical information regarding distributions will be willingly communicated to you (all the more willingly if the problem is acute). It should enable you to generate data in a test database (see Chapter 4) and test the various solutions you have thought of.

When you don't know exactly where the problem is, you must get as much information as you can from the database server cache. If monitoring facilities are available, use them. If there is no dedicated product, or if it doesn't provide the information you'd like, build your own. Read about *snapmon.sql* in Appendix A, under the "Chapter 1" heading. If you expect to be involved in performance analysis more than a few times, don't hesitate to create a tool based on this type of query. There is no need for a fancy user interface; it can be raw and ugly. And it doesn't really matter whether you output plain-text files, comma-separated files, HTML files (which is what I usually do), or sophisticated graphics. What you need is the list, by unit of time, of the SQL statements that used the most resources during the period you're investigating. Sort by (total) elapsed time in descending order, or if timing information is unavailable, by number of logical I/O operations. CPU time, if available, can be interesting to compare to the elapsed time. When I monitor a database, I usually take a snapshot of the database server cache every 10 minutes, and aggregate by the hour. MySQL requires more sustained polling. When monitoring tools show polling queries among the most resource-intensive queries, you know you have monitored too hard.

Don't forget to collect (and display) global statistics; by comparing what you have caught to global numbers, you will be able to assess the validity of your monitoring. If you miss more than 20% or 30% of logical I/O operations, you risk chasing the wrong target.

While monitoring is going on, you needn't stay idle: get better acquainted with the application. Check schema indexing, as explained in Chapter 2. Check statistics. Get information about locking and issues linked to concurrency. It may also be useful to collect statistical information regarding the relative weight, in terms of number of executions and resource consumption, of select statements versus statements that change the data.

Queries of Death

Sometimes "problem queries" have already been identified, or you discover that some very costly queries loom large among the top queries. In this case, Chapter 5 will be your chapter of choice.

Problem queries *are* complicated and ugly. This is often why they are problem queries in the first place. There is no need to panic.

- Check the true nature of the tables that appear in the query. If you have views, reinject them as subqueries into the statement (this may be a recursive process), and remove from these subqueries everything that isn't relevant to the current query (Chapter 3). Beware of distributed queries, too: nested loops between distant tables would kill any query.

- If you cannot modify the program, you can sometimes improve performance simply by rewriting views that reference other views so as to hit only base tables.

- For update, insert, and delete statements, check whether they are slow because of locks acquired by other statements that are much slower.

- For update, insert, and delete statements again, check whether triggers fire. That may be where the problem really is.

- Remove all optimizer directives, and reduce the query to its core. What is the input to the query? Where are the constants in the where clause? Which are the truly selective criteria that brutally cut down the number of rows to process? If you don't know, run a few group by statements (or check statistics if the tables are too big). Can there be data distribution problems? Does the optimizer have all the information required? Turn the optimizer into your ally.

- Among the columns that are returned, is the information stored in a single column among all tables, or is the column a join column that is common to several tables? Would it change anything then to return the information from another table?

- Identify tables that you need for data, tables that you need for conditions, and tables that you need for joins only. Move tables that are required only for conditions to subqueries. If they are very big and the expected result set is small, make these subqueries correlated subqueries. Otherwise, consider in ( ) or a join with the subquery in the from clause. Beware that in (*subquery*) adds an implicit distinct that must become explicit if the subquery is in the from clause.

- Beware, with subqueries, of null values that are neither equal to nor different from anything else, not even other null values. Be generous with is not null conditions for columns that are not mandatory.

- Beware that correlated and uncorrelated subqueries rest on different indexing assumptions.

- Which criterion should drive (be the starting point of) the query? If several criteria applied to different tables are possible candidates, would it be possible to isolate candidate rows from each query, and then combine them through joins or set operations such as intersect?

- Are there any user-defined functions? Are they called often? Are they called again and again with the same parameters? If they are likely to be called often, can their result be cached (Chapter 3)? What is the source code for these functions? Can their logic be coded into a single query (Chapter 6)? Can you use this single query in a join?

- Are there any functions that would prevent you from using an index? Beware also of implicit type conversions. Check that columns and values on both sides of conditions are of the same type.

- Are the columns of composite indexes suitably ordered (Chapter 2)? Get some warranties from people who know the application on the type of queries that may need an existing index that looks disordered. You don't want to break the quarterly report.

- Remember that accesses are more efficient when a composite index column to which inequality conditions are applied appears after columns to which equality conditions are applied.

- Be extremely careful with indexes, as they add much overhead to insert and delete operations. If a new index is required, try to identify another index that can be dispensed with because it is redundant or not selective enough. Try to keep the number of indexes constant.

- Are any patterns repeated throughout the query? Are certain tables visited several times? Can you visit tables only once?

- Do subqueries stamp a particular order on query execution through dependencies? For instance, does a correlated subquery depend on a column value that requires the execution of another subquery or join to be known? Is it possible to relax this order of execution and to give more freedom to the optimizer?

- If set operators appear in the query, is it possible to factorize?

- Could some self-joins be replaced with ranking functions?

All These Fast Queries

Big, ugly queries are still encountered on a routine basis, but more often high costs are associated with a high number of executions, and unitary costs are low. What matters is the overall cost (the unitary cost times number of executions), much more than just the unitary cost. When unitary costs are low, the question then isn't so much one of SQL query tuning than it is of algorithm, as you saw in Chapter 6.

- What is the ratio between the number of "business units" that are processed (whether they are the generation of invoices, trades, registrations, or whatever) and the number of queries? Is it reasonable? Can it be lowered?

- What is the reason behind loops?

- Can you replace any track of paranoid preventive checks with forensic analysis? Try to order SQL statements by number of executions; close numbers of executions often give very good clues about the logic without even seeing the code. In an SQL program, one must do, then check, why things have failed if they have. There is no need to check first if most cases pass the check.

- What is the ratio (the number of queries against the table times the number of active sessions, divided by the total number of rows in the table)? Is it justified? Do as much as you can in a single statement.

- Is there anything that looks like a query from a lookup function that is executed much too often?

- When input criteria are surrogate keys (system-generated sequential numbers), it is likely that the issue is in the algorithms more than the query itself, even if the query is slow. There must be a query somewhere that returns these surrogate keys from real, user-provided criteria. Try to join both queries; don't use a cursor loop.

- Among fast queries, you sometimes find recursive queries against the data dictionary. Try to find out what kind of internal operations they relate to, and whether these operations cannot be preemptively avoided by better table or index sizing, or anything of the kind. Work in tandem with a DBA if queries that refer to internal operations show up.

- Chase down count(*) queries. You can probably dispense with most of them.

- Chase down queries that merely execute simple operations or return values available through other means. A query that doesn't return data from a table is useless. For instance, if the application needs the time on the server, a single query should not be dedicated to that purpose; the time can be returned with "useful" data.

- Low unitary cost doesn't necessarily mean minimum unitary cost. If you can modify a frequently run query so that it performs the same work accessing three blocks instead of five, that will result in a 40% improvement that will noticeably lighten the burden of the server and free resources needed elsewhere. You can frequently obtain this type of improvement by avoiding indirections after an index search, through one of the following methods:

- Using a clustered index or index-organized table in which the index tree walk takes you to the row data, not to the index of the row

- Avoiding the need to visit the table by stuffing all necessary data inside the index

No Obvious Very Wrong Query

The case when you can concentrate on a few SQL "heavy hitters" is a simple one, whether they are costly queries executed a few times or low-cost queries executed millions of times. The situation is more challenging when no particular query weighs heavily, but you have many queries that each take some moderate amount of resources.

Sometimes such a situation just proves that there isn't much you can do (one cannot always win). But you may also encounter such a situation when statements are dynamically built by programs and are hardcoded.

- Check the commit rate, and its relation to the number of business transactions—that is, logically independent business units of work.

- Check whether making the DBMS substitute parameters for constants can help; this doesn't discharge you from the duty of pointing out bad practices to developers, though.

- One of the worst cases is the generation of in ( ) clauses by program. Is it possible to replace the list with the query that returns the various elements, if such a query exists? If not, is it possible to use one of the methods presented in Chapter 2 to bind lists of values?

- Does focusing on execution plans rather than statements tell a different story? Get, for each different plan, the costliest query as a sample.

- Could there be some contention issues that partitioning could help to solve?

- A system, especially a database system, is a series of queues that provide resources to concurrent clients. If clients don't require the same resources at the same time, increasing parallelism will increase throughput. When one queue lengthens somewhere in the system, performance takes the plunge.

- Don't fix the wrong problem. Alleviating contention at the wrong place will do nothing for performance.

- You can attempt to do only two things at the physical storage level: cluster rows or scatter them. Both can be useful, but for opposite classes of problem; you have to decide what the most important issue is.

- Physically reorganizing your tables may help make some queries run faster by minimizing the number of pages to inspect, but confirm that what improves a critical process will not make worse another process that is as critical—or even more critical—than the process you are improving.

> **NOTE**
> Performance improvement is an iterative process. Very often, another performance issue is hiding behind the issue you are fixing.

Time to Conclude

At times, I have a vague feeling that trying to improve SQL code is a Sisyphean challenge. There is much to do, and ever-expanding databases don't take long to reveal the weaknesses of code that has been in production for some time. As I have tried to show, there are many options and many routes that you can take. But reviewing and questioning the code will get you the best returns. Don't rely on "tuning," even if tuning has its place, and rely even less on "wizards" and "assistants" that are supposed to *automagically* make your queries faster. If it were that simple, there would never be any performance issues. This is not a dark art; it's through understanding the original business requirements, understanding the developers' intents, and applying some simple principles and some SQL skills that you can really transform applications to a level that will often impress. And you may even have fun doing it.

> **We could've been anything**
> **That we wanted to be**
> **And it's not too late to change**
> **I'd be delighted to give it some thought**
> **Maybe you'll agree that we really ought.**
>
> —*Paul Williams (b. 1940)*
>
> *Lyrics from "Bugsy Malone"*

Scripts and Sample Programs

THE BODY OF THIS BOOK CONTAINS MANY CODE SAMPLES AND SNIPPETS. I TOOK QUITE A NUMBER OF them (and slightly adapted them for confidentiality reasons) from code I have audited and modified; because these samples cannot run without a full array of tables and indexes filled with classified data, providing them makes little sense.

This book also includes many other programs and examples that I wrote specifically for it (which I sometimes merely allude to), as well as utility scripts that query the data dictionary and are of general use. These programs and scripts are available for download. You will find them on the O'Reilly website for this book, *http://www.oreilly.com/catalog/9780596514976*.

This appendix describes what you will find for download and provides a number of additional comments, which I hope you'll find interesting.

Because most people are interested in one particular DBMS, I have regrouped the code samples based on DBMS, with one archive file per DBMS. Within each archive file, I organized the code samples by chapter (one directory per chapter).

Note that some of the programs I wrote specifically for one DBMS and did not port them to the others (e.g., this is the case in all the Chapter 7 examples that were written for

MySQL exclusively). In several cases, you can adapt them to other products with some minor changes. Therefore, don't hesitate to look at the code for the other products if you are interested in a program that isn't provided for your favorite DBMS.

In the descriptions that follow, for programs that aren't available for MySQL, Oracle, and SQL Server, I have indicated in parentheses the DBMS product(s) for which they are provided. In other words, if nothing is specified, it means a version of the program or script is available for all three products. Note that in the case of scripts that query the data dictionary, a similar name doesn't mean all versions of the script return exactly the same information, but rather the same *type* of information.

Chapter 1

To begin, I used four scripts to create the tables in this chapter (these tables appear again in some examples in later chapters). If you want to run the programs on your own test database, you should start by generating the sample data.

These two scripts create the tables and the primary key indexes:

> *refactoring_big_tables.sql*
> *refactoring_small_tables.sql* (includes data)

These two scripts create additional indexes; the second script creates an index that replaces the index created by the first one (please refer to Chapter 1 for details):

> *additional_index.sql*
> *additional_index_alternate.sql*

The big transactions table is populated by *GenerateData.java*, which requires *database.properties*, which you must update to specify how to connect to your database.

Once the tables are created and populated, you can run the following programs:

> *FirstExample.java*
> *SecondExample.java*
> *ThirdExample.java* (Java 1.5 or later required)
> *FourthExample.java*
> *FifthExample.java*
> *SixthExample.java*

All of them use the same *database.properties* file as the data generation program.

The following scripts are product-specific:

- *dba_analysis.sql* (SQL Server) is the query the SQL Server DBA ran to diagnose problems (like all DBA scripts, it requires some system privileges).

- *profiler_analysis.sql* (SQL Server) is a query you can run if you save what the SQL Server profiler collects to a table. It includes a T-SQL function called Normalize to normalize statement text.

- *snapmon.sql* (Oracle, SQL Server) is my core monitoring tool. It collects statistical information regarding all the queries that are currently held in the cache, as well as global values, which are returned as though they were associated with a dummy query. In the course of my assignments, I have developed monitoring tools in various languages (shell script included), all based on this query or slight variants of it. Each query is identified by an identifier, and a particular value is assigned to the global statistics, which allow you to check whether you have collected meaningful information or whether you have missed a lot of statements. In the latter case, I suggest that you run a modified version of this query in which you identify queries by the identifier of their execution plan.

The values returned by *snapmon.sql* are cumulative. If you want values by time slice, you must compute each time you poll the difference with the previous results.

You can do this in several ways. You can dump the output of the query to files, merge and sort two successive files, or make creative use of awk or perl to get what you want. I advise you to use SQLite (*http://www.sqlite.org*), which has APIs for most languages and scripting languages, and proceed as follows:

1. Create two temporary tables, named snaptmp1 and snaptmp2. These tables must have a structure that matches the output of *snapmon.sql*. You must successively insert into snaptmp1 and snaptmp2. Note that you don't need to query the database very often. Within a few minutes, you can usually get a very detailed picture of what the database is doing.

2. After the second pass, begin to insert data into a permanent table with the same structure by executing a query on this pattern:

```
insert into ...
select <identifier>, abs(sum(<col1>)), ...., abs(sum(<coln>))
from (select <identifier>, <col1>, ... <coln>
      from snaptmp1
      union all
      select identifier, -1 * <col1>, ..., -1 * <coln>
      from snaptmp2) x
group by <identifier>
having sum(...) <> 0
```

   You can refine this further by selecting only the top queries (to which the dummy "global query" will necessarily belong). You should also have a table that holds the text of statements. Whenever new identifiers are encountered, you should get the associated statement text from the database. I don't want to stymie your creativity by suggesting too many things, but you can collect other information as well (e.g., waits) and generate graphics that will show you the load.

At the time of this writing, something similar wasn't available for MySQL, for which other monitoring means may be more adequate. Nevertheless, depending on the storage engine that is used, some useful data can be collected from information_schema.global_status (COM_*xxx* and INNODB_*xxx* parameters) as well as the falcon_*xxx* tables that will at least give you a global picture. This can be completed by select statements against information_schema.processlist, which must be sampled more frantically than the Oracle and SQL Server tables because it shows only current information.

Chapter 2

The following scripts are used to create the tables in Chapter 2:

- *IndexSelectivity.java* tests the impact of selectivity on index access performance.

- *stats.sql* (MySQL, Oracle) displays some statistical values regarding tables.

- *indexing.sql* lists all tables in the current schema and tells how many indexes they have, among other information.

- *checkparse.sql* is a script that tells you whether many statements are parsed on your database, which is always indicative of hardcoded statements (although the reverse isn't quite true, because the DBMS sometimes substitutes parameters with constants, as you saw in the chapter).

A few other *.java* programs come with the mandatory *database.properties* file. The following three programs test the performance loss of parsing:

> *HardCoded.java*
> *FirmCoded.java*
> *SoftCoded.java*

These programs show step by step how a list of values can be passed as a single parameter:

> *list0.sql*
> *list1.sql*
> *list2.sql*
> *list3.sql*

These three programs fetch rows from the transactions table; the first one uses the default fetch size, the second one takes the fetch size as a command-line argument, and the third one activates the MySQL streaming mode:

> *DumpTx_default.java*
> *DumpTx.java*
> *DumpTx_Stream.java* (MySQL only)

And finally, this program tests the impact of the commit rate on throughput:

> *UpdateTx.java*

Chapter 3

For Oracle, there are three different ways to write a function that counts patterns. There is also a script that creates a test table and successively applies the three functions to this table.

> *function1.sql* (Oracle)
> *function2.sql* (Oracle)
> *function3.sql* (Oracle)
> *test_search.sql* (Oracle)

Also for Oracle, there are three functions to check whether a date corresponds to a weekend day, first as a nondeterministic function and then as a deterministic function, and finally as a function that wraps a deterministic function after removing the time part from the date:

weekend_day1.sql (Oracle)
weekend_day2.sql (Oracle)
weekend_day3.sql (Oracle)

A naive function is available for computing the next business day (*NextBusinessDay.sql*). This function relies on a table created by *public_holidays.sql*.

Also, with Oracle (in particular) and with MySQL, there are various attempts at refactoring this function. For Oracle, *NextBusinessDay2.sql* and *NextBusinessDay3.sql* both require Oracle11g or later, which isn't the case for *NextBusinessDay4.sql*:

public_holidays.sql
NextBusinessDay.sql
NextBusinessDay2.sql (MySQL, Oracle)
NextBusinessDay3.sql (Oracle)
NextBusinessDay4.sql (Oracle)

Similarly, there is a naive currency conversion function called *fx_convert.sql* and, for Oracle and MySQL, alternative versions (the Oracle *fx_convert2.sql* file requires Oracle11g or later):

fx_convert.sql
fx_convert2.sql (MySQL, Oracle)
fx_convert3.sql (MySQL, Oracle)

Finally, one script replaces the function with a simple join:

fxjoin.sql

You'll find various views built on the tables created by the scripts and programs in Chapter 1:

v_amount_by_currency.sql
v_amount_main_currencies.sql
v_amount_other_currencies.sql
v_last_rate.sql

You'll also find a query that tries to identify complex views that might be a reason for poor query performance:

complex_views.sql

Chapter 4

For Chapter 4, there is the definition of the view, which returns 10 rows numbered 0 through 9:

ten_rows.sql

For SQL Server, there is the creation of the view that is required for further generation of random data, and the function that uses this view:

random_view.sql (SQL Server)
randuniform.sql (SQL Server)

Two functions to return random numbers that are not uniformly distributed in an interval are in these scripts:

randexp.sql
randgauss.sql

And if you want to see what the distribution looks like, a small script that draws a character-based histogram is available:

histogram.sql

To generate a string of random characters (which can be useful for password generation), you have this script:

randstring.sql

job_ref.sql shows how to generate job names that follow a predefined distribution.

To generate American names that are more realistic than those of all the people who email you to tout various drugs, anatomical enhancement devices, and fake watches, I suggest you go to *http://www.census.gov/genealogy/www/* and click the link that will bring you to a list of frequently occurring surnames. You should find there a spreadsheet that contains the top 1,000 names in the United States. Download it and save it as a *.csv* file; my scripts assume that a semicolon is used for a separator.

Once you have the data, create a table to load it:

name_ref.sql

The MySQL script creates the table, loads and normalizes the data, and creates an index, and so does the SQL Server script (which uses an ancillary *.xml* file).

For Oracle, *name_ref.sql* just creates the table. You must load the data using *name_ref.ctl*, which is a control file you can use with SQL*Loader as follows:

```
sqlldr <username>/<password> control=name_ref.ctl
```

Then, still with Oracle, run *name_ref2.sql* to normalize the data and index the table.

get_ten_names.sql generates 10 random American surnames.

For Oracle, there are three additional scripts: *dept_ref.sql* allows you to randomly pick a department number for the emp table; *gen_emp.sql* is a pure SQL generator of rows for the emp table that fails to get truly random data; and *gen_emp_pl.sql* is a PL/SQL version that works fine.

For the generation of random text, please see Appendix B.

check (MySQL and Oracle) is a bash script that runs the output of an arbitrary query through the md5sum program.

qrysum.sql is a function (Oracle) or procedure (MySQL and SQL Server) that checksums the output of an arbitrary query. The script *qrysum_complicated.sql* does the same for Oracle, but applies successful checksums to buffers. It is mostly interesting as a wild PL/SQL example of dynamic SQL.

> *qrysum.sql*
> *qrysum_complicated.sql* (Oracle)

Chapter 5

There is no script sample for this chapter. Examples in this chapter come from real cases.

Chapter 6

Most of the examples in this chapter also come from real cases, but I wrote some of them for this book.

The SQL Server directory contains the files for the example of unlocking accounts after payment. Two functions were written in Visual Basic—one that strictly follows specifications and another that performs the same task with a more clever use of SQL:

> *create_tables.sql* (SQL Server)
> *procs.vb* (SQL Server)
> *create_vb_procs.sql* (SQL Server)

There is also a rather complete PHP example written for MySQL, and a configuration file that must be updated with connection data. The first two examples show an incorrect and a correct use of found_rows( ) (very specific to MySQL):

> *config.php* (MySQL)
> *sample_bad.php* (MySQL)
> *sample_ok.php* (MySQL)

Another series of PHP programs shows how you can avoid counting before fetching data when there is an upper limit on the number of rows that will be displayed:

> *with_count.php* (MySQL)
> *with_count2.php* (MySQL)
> *without_count.php* (MySQL)

The most interesting query in the last program is a query that returns the total number of rows in the result set in the first row. It is provided (as a query on the transactions table that returns more than 500 rows) for all DBMS products (including MySQL).

top500GBP.sql

For Oracle users, a very simple example that uses emp and dept shows why I dislike cursor loops:

cursor.sql (Oracle)

Chapter 7 (MySQL)

For Chapter 7, there are code samples for MySQL only (however, SQL Server and Oracle users mustn't forget the Roughbench tool, which is described in Appendix B).

The table that is used in the examples is created by *fifo.sql*.

The various programs that simulate the processing of messages need the following sources and the accompanying *makefile*:

common.c
common.h
consumer_inno.c
consumer_lock.c
consumer_naive.c
consumer_not_so_naive.c
makefile

For the test of concurrent inserts, there are two subdirectories, one for each storage engine used. Scripts postfixed with *_ai* use an auto-increment key, and scripts postfixed with *_p* use a partitioned table. There are scripts to create the tables, and scripts to insert data, which you must run with Roughbench.

InnoDB

- *create_concurrent_insert.sql*

- *create_concurrent_insert_ai.sql*

- *create_concurrent_insert_p.sql*

- *insert_concurrent_insert.sql*

- *insert_concurrent_insert_ai.sql*

- *insert_concurrent_insert_p.sql*

MyISAM

- *create_concurrent_insert.sql*
- *create_concurrent_insert_ai.sql*
- *create_concurrent_insert_p.sql*
- *insert_concurrent_insert.sql*
- *insert_concurrent_insert_ai.sql*
- *insert_concurrent_insert_p.sql*

APPENDIX B

Tools

THIS APPENDIX DESCRIBES TWO TOOLS, THE SOURCE CODE FOR WHICH IS AVAILABLE FOR DOWNLOAD, and which I hope you'll find useful. The first one is actually a pair of programs, mklipsum and lipsum, which I briefly described in Chapter 4. The second one is a Java tool called Roughbench, which I have used often in my tests, in particular in Chapter 7.

These tools are released under the GPL license and come with the usual disclaimers.

mklipsum and lipsum

mklipsum and lipsum are tools for generating arbitrary random text. The source code is written in C, and I prepared it using GNU Autotools (as best as I could). Windows executables are also provided (they have been ported with Mingwin). Both programs require SQLite3, available from *http://www.sqlite.org*. For the record, mklipsum contains nontrivial SQL code.

How to Build mklipsum and lipsum

On a *nix machine, after having uncompressed and unarchived the files, you should be able to build the programs by typing `./configure`, then `make` and `make install` (read the *INSTALL* file for more information and to learn how to customize default settings).

How to Use mklipsum and lipsum

Using mklipsum and lipsum is fairly simple. mklipsum prepares an SQLite file for use by lipsum from text that it tokenizes and analyzes. The text is read from the standard input. The SQLite file stores the words using UTF8 encoding, and it should also be the character set used in the input. If, however, the library *libiconv*, which converts character sets, is available on your system, mklipsum will be able to perform character set conversion. The availability or nonavailability of the character set conversion feature is displayed when you run the program.

mklipsum can optionally take one parameter (two if character set conversion is available).

The first parameter is a file identifier that can be used to identify the language of the source file. By default, the SQLite file created is named *lipsum.db*.

If you run:

```
mklipsum xx < sample_text_file
```

the SQLite file will be named *lipsumxx.db*. This feature is intended for the generation of random text with words from different languages. You can use the ISO code of the language to identify the various files.

The second parameter, if character set conversion is available, is the character set used in the source file. Note that you cannot specify the character set alone, and that it must always follow a file identifier.

I have tested mklipsum and lipsum with different languages that use the Latin alphabet (with extensions); it is possible that languages that use the Cyrillic alphabet may require some adjustments to the programs, and very likely that a language such as Arabic or Hebrew, to say nothing of Chinese or Japanese, will require some rewrites (the programs try hard to retain the original capitalization, but follow Western rules and capitalize the first letter of words that follow a period, for instance).

Here is an example, using a few chapters from Thomas Hobbes' *Leviathan*:

```
$ ./mklipsum < leviathan_sample.txt
mklipsum $Revision$ with charset conversion
-- Reading input ...
-- Loading vocabulary ...
--- 770 words of length 1 analyzed
--- 761 words of length 2 analyzed
--- 800 words of length 3 analyzed
--- 614 words of length 4 analyzed
--- 474 words of length 5 analyzed
```

```
--- 312 words of length 6 analyzed
--- 237 words of length 7 analyzed
--- 152 words of length 8 analyzed
--- 119 words of length 9 analyzed
--- 72 words of length 10 analyzed
--- 43 words of length 11 analyzed
--- 22 words of length 12 analyzed
--- 21 words of length 13 analyzed
--- 5 words of length 14 analyzed
--- 1 words of length 15 analyzed
--- 1 words of length 16 analyzed
--- 1 words of length 19 analyzed
-- Vocabulary: 1029 distinct words loaded
-- Loading lengths relationships ...
--- ...........................................................................
...........................................................
-- Indexing
$
```

To generate random text, you must run the lipsum program that can take as a parameter a file identifier telling which SQLite file should be used.

```
$ ./lipsum
 Speech Thy Eye up with serves which no Businesse; can of is therefore
up can false a Joynts happen, he late Marcus, up any motion But Eyes
of hath Species; up my Cold which my How First Voyces my are up them
also exercise which a Death are any of parts if Circumstances; Image
whereas els waking is any must, Sees For office is am cease. Ever
say. Prognostiques many course, one cause I Speech mind of For removed
of though. Give not oncly Anger horse can them, well sight.
```

Here is an example using another file seeded by a German text written by Immanuel Kant:

```
$ ./lipsum de
 Sein daß Sitz Begriff Synthesis als, von priori Satz kann vorher
vielleicht. Lassen, in komme eine bewußt, des Kreis die ist. Um
allen selbst natürlicher a dieser die Prädikat hergibt Zufälligkeit
bewußt, priori Verstand a fassen leicht, er Begriffe. Hat wir wird
denn desjenigen der empfangen sollten. Seine in der einander ist
mithin man korrespondiert, als.
```

The lipsum program can take a number of flags:

```
$ ./lipsum -?
Usage : ./lipsum [flags] [suffix]
        This program looks in the current directory for an
        sqlite file named lipsum<suffix>.db that must have
        previously been generated by the mklipsum utility.
  Flags:
   -h, -?          : Display this and exit.
   -n <count>      : Number of paragraphs to generate (default 1)
   -w <len>[,<dev>] : Approximate number of words per paragraph.
                      The program generates paragraphs averaging <len>
                      words, with a standard deviation <dev>. By
                      default, <dev> is 20% of <len>.
                      Default for <len>: 500.
                      This flag is exclusive of -c.
```

```
-c <len>[,<dev>] : Same as -c, but based on character count instead of
                   word count.
-l <len>         : Insert a carriage return as soon as possible
                   after having output <len> characters. Default: 65.
```

Roughbench

Roughbench takes as a parameter the name of a simple SQL script, reads it, and executes it, for a number of times or for a certain duration of time, and can start several concurrent threads running the same script.

On completion, statistical information is displayed.

How to Build Roughbench

You need the J2SE Development Kit (JDK) version 1.5 or later to compile the program. The JDK is available from *http://java.sun.com/j2se*.

How to Use Roughbench

Using Roughbench is straightforward:

1. Specify the JDBC parameters in a file named *roughbench.properties*.

2. Check that your CLASSPATH environment variable is set properly.

3. Prepare a file containing the (single) statement you want to run. This statement can contain ? characters as placeholders for values generated by Roughbench.

4. Specify a number of options and how to generate values on the command line.

   The command line looks like this:

   ```
   java [options] roughbench <sqlfile> [generators ... ]
   ```

The roughbench.properties file

The *roughbench.properties* file must contain at least the following two values:

```
CONNECT=<JDBC URL>
DRIVER=<Driver package name>
```

Additionally, if there is no implicit authentication and if no authentication method is provided inside the JDBC URL, you must specify this:

```
USERNAME=<...>
```

and this:

```
PASSWORD=<...>
```

For example, assuming that we want to connect as user bench, password possward, to a database named *TEST* running on the same server, we can use the following:

roughbench.properties file with Oracle:
```
CONNECT=jdbc:oracle:thin:@localhost:1521:TEST
```

```
USERNAME=bench
PASSWORD=possward
DRIVER=oracle.jdbc.OracleDriver
```

Or, with MySQL, we can specify the username and password in the URL:

```
CONNECT=jdbc:mysql://localhost:3306/TEST?user=bench&password=possward
DRIVER=com.mysql.jdbc.Driver
```

Specifying options

Options, which are listed in Table B-1, are specified on the command line with the following syntax:

```
-D<option name>=<value>
```

TABLE B-1. Roughbench options

Option name	Comment	Default value
COMM	Number of executions between two successive commits (ignored for select statements).	1 (commit after every DML statement)
LOOPS	Number of times the SQL statement must be run. Exclusive of -DTIME=...	1
RATE	Number of executions per minute. The rate is an average; the interval between two successive executions is random.	
TAG	Identifier for the run.	Timestamp, format MonDD-hh:mn
THR	Number of concurrent threads to run. All threads execute the same SQL statement.	1
TIME	Number of minutes during which the SQL statement must be run. Exclusive of -DLOOPS=...	

Generating variables

You can generate random variables to bind to the statement by specifying as many generators on the command line as there are placeholders in the statement. Generators are specified as shown in Table B-2.

TABLE B-2. Generators

Generator	Meaning
C<constant>	Constant value; <constant> can be numeric or a string.
Ra,b,...,c	Uniform random value from the list (the same item can occur several times in the list to give it more weight). Values can be of any type.
Ra-b	Random value in the range a to b inclusive (numbers or chars).
N<avg>,<stddev>	Normal (Gaussian) distribution, with an average of <avg> and a standard deviation of <stddev>.
I[<start> [,<step>]]	Incremental value. <start> defaults to 1, <step> to 1.
S<min>[-<max>]	String of random letters of length between <min> and <max> inclusive; <max> defaults to the same value as <min>.

Generating integer or float values

The generation of integer or float values depends on the type of the first number given in the generator specification. For instance:

- R1-250000 will generate integer values between 1 and 250,000.
- R1.0-250000 will generate float values in the same range.

Generating dates

To generate dates, you must use the functions available with your DBMS and generate integer values to be used with date functions and date arithmetic.

For instance, you can use the following expressions in different SQL dialects associated to an incremental generator to generate dates in chronological order from the past 300 days. Because 300 days equal almost 26 million seconds, you can generate almost as many days as you want in the interval to the current date.

In MySQL:

```
date_add(date_sub(curdate( ), INTERVAL 300 DAY), INTERVAL ? SECOND)
```

In Oracle:

```
sysdate - 300 + ?/86400
```

In T-SQL (SQL Server/Sybase):

```
dateadd(ss, ?, dateadd(dd, -300, getdate( )))
```

and so on.

Output

Roughbench displays informational messages on the standard error and results on the standard output, which makes it easy to redirect clean results to a file.

The provided information consists of the following:

- Program name, version, and copyright/licensing information
- Reminder of the command-line parameters
- Text of the query being run

Results are displayed as follows:

```
tag<tab>filename<space>thread#<tab>tenth of second<tab>count
```

tag is the value of the tag specified by -DTAG=... on the command line. It defaults to a timestamp; for example, Jun11-15:42.

filename is the name of the file that contains the SQL statement.

thread# is the number (starting with 0) identifying a particular thread.

tenth of second and count tell how many statements were executed in what time. A value of 0 for *tenth of second* means less than 0.1 second, a value of 1 means between 0.1 and 0.2 seconds, and so forth.

For example, the following output means that for the run of October 23 at 4 p.m., thread 3 executed the script *insert.sql* 15,874 times, of which five times took between 0.1 and 0.2 seconds and the remainder took less than 0.1 second:

```
Oct23-16:00            insert.sql 3        0     15869
Oct23-16:00            insert.sql 3        1     5
```

Additional lines may also be displayed. For instance, when operating in loop mode, the total time to execute the required number of loops is displayed as follows:

```
tag<tab>filename<space>thread#<tab>elapsed (ms)<tab>time
```

If some of the executions end in failure, the number of successful executions and the number of failures will be output as shown here:

```
tag<tab>filename<space>thread#<tab>OK<tab>count
tag<tab>filename<space>thread#<tab>KO<tab>count
```

INDEX

Symbols

A

B

C

F

fetching
  everything needed at once, 192–193
  performance considerations, 70
fifo.sql script, 258
filtering
  activating early, 170–172
  core columns and, 154
  views, 104–105
first normal form, 239
fn_trace_gettable( ) function (SQL Server), 32
foreign keys
  core columns and, 154
  indexing, 44
found_rows( ) function, 195–197
Fowler, Martin, viii, ix
fragmentation in data blocks, 237
from clause
  cleaning up, 155–157
  outer joins and, 165
  refactoring considerations, 246
  repeated patterns and, 158
  rewriting queries and, 139
  subqueries and, 167
function-based indexes, 54
functions
  computation-only, 77–79
  deterministic, 80, 80–87
  improving, 102, 103
  refactoring considerations, 246
  user-defined, 76, 188, 246
  utility, 188
  (see also lookup functions)
FxConvert( ) conversion function, 95–102

G

Gaussian distribution, 118
gen_emp.sql script, 257
gen_emp_pl.sql script, 257
general_log variable (MySQL), 30
GenerateData.java script, 252
Gennick, Jonathan, vii
get_hash_value( ) function, 139
global counters, 28
GNU Autotools, 261
Gnu Statistical Library (GSL), 129
Goldwyn, Samuel, 22
greatest( ) function, 173
group by clause, 54, 245
GSL (Gnu Statistical Library), 129

H

hardcoded statements
  defined, 55
  parsing issues, 61–62
  replacing with softcoded, 61–63
  SQL engine treatment of, 21
hash joins, 176–177
hash( ) function, 139
hashbytes( ) function, 139
HashMap class, 11
having clause, 107

I

in clause, 66
indexes
  access considerations, 38
  bitmap, 53
  B-tree, 45, 52
  checking appropriateness, 37
  clustered, 53, 236, 248
  composite, 48–52, 246
  on computed columns, 54
  derived from database design, 44
  on expressions, 54
  function-based, 54
  null values and, 239
  performance considerations, 39, 45
  primary key, 236
  range scans, 10, 42–43
  refactoring considerations, 246
  reviewing, 44–54
  row order and, 234
indexes (*continued*)
  selectivity and, 39–40
  single-column, 48–52
  tables in schemas, 45–47
  types of, 44
IndexSelectivity.java script, 254
information_schema.global_status
    (MySQL), 56
information_schema.processlist (MySQL), 26
inner joins, 109
InnoDB storage engine, 219, 220, 227
insert statement
  functional comparisons and, 132
  grouping, 71
  refactoring considerations, 245
  splitting tables, 238
instr( ) function, 77
ISO standard, 218
isolation levels, 218–223

J

J2SE Development Kit (JDK), 264
JBoss application server, 31
JDBC
    p6spy tracer support, 31
    prepared statements, 4
JDK (J2SE Development Kit), 264
joins
    defined, 176
    inner, 109
    merge/hash, 176–177
    outer, 109
    query considerations, 155–157, 176–177
    refactoring considerations, 246, 247

K

Kyte, Tom, 138

L

large objects (LOBs), 237
least( ) function, 173
length( ) function, 77
lipsum tool, 261–263
lists
    batching, 69, 70
    passing as variables, 67–69
    temporary tables, 70
LOAD command (MySQL), 124
load data infile statement, 70
LOBs (large objects), 237
locators, 237
locks
    competing for resources, 209
    competing for resources and, 213
    isolation levels and, 218, 220
    multiple queues and, 225
logging
    client-side, 31
    in-between, 31
    server-side, 30–31
    statements to trace files, 29
logical reads
    defined, 26
    measuring work performance, 29
lookup functions
    calendar function example, 88–95
    conversion function example, 95–102
    defined, 76
    performance considerations, 88
    refactoring considerations, 247
    retrieving employee names, 85–87

loops
    analyzing, 206, 207
    challenging usage, 207–209
    getting rid of, 202–209
    nested, 176–177
    reasons behind, 204–206
    refactoring considerations, 247
lorem ipsum, 131

M

Markov chains, 131
Maslow, Abraham, 22
materialized views, 241–242
MD5 algorithm, 136, 139, 140, 144
md5( ) function, 139
mean (mu), 120
merge joins, 176–177
min( ) function, 159
minus operator (Oracle), 136
mklipsum tool, 261–263
mu (mean), 120
multiple queues, 225–230
MyISAM tables, 216, 227–230
MySQL
    baseline for example, 5
    brute force comparison, 134
    calendar function example, 90, 91, 94, 95
    checksum support, 139, 140, 143
    clustered indexes, 53
    conversion function example, 96
    count( ) function and, 195
    date values, 43
    detecting parsing issues, 56, 59
    deterministic functions, 80
    dynamic views, 26
    filtering views, 105, 107
    generating rows, 125
    InnoDB engine and, 219
    LOB support, 237
    materialized views, 241
    monitoring databases, 245
    random data generation, 120, 121
    refactoring views, 110
    repeatable read isolation level, 220
    session variables and, 101
    speed improvement comparison, 8–10, 13,
        14, 16–18
    traditional SQL tuning, 5–9
MySQL Proxy, 32
mysqldump tool, 134
mysqlsla tool, 32

procedures, 76
  (see also stored procedures)
processing
  client-side, 31, 71
  competing for resources, 209, 213–224
  isolating hot spots, 224–230
  parallelism and, 230–233
  refactoring considerations, 248
  server-side, 30–31, 55
profiler_analysis.sql script, 252

Q

qrysum.sql script, 257
queries
  analyzing, 152–157
  cleaning up from clause, 155–157
  merge/hash joins, 176–177
  nested loops, 176
  rebuilding, 176
  refactoring considerations, 245–248
query core
  activating filtering early, 170–172
  combining set operators, 175
  eliminating repeated patterns, 158–164
  identifying, 153–155
  simplifying aggregates, 174
  simplifying conditions, 172–174
  subqueries and, 165–170
  unitary analysis, 158
  with clause, 174
query optimizers (see optimizers)
question marks, 4
queues
  multiple, 225–230
  refactoring considerations, 248

R

rand( ) function, 119, 125, 126
random number generation, 40, 118–122
random text generation, 130, 131
random variable generation, 265
range scans
  defined, 10
  for indexes, 42–43
rank( ) function, 54
read committed isolation level, 219–220
read consistency, 219
read uncommitted isolation level, 218
READ_COMMITTED_SNAPSHOT database
      option, 219
recursive statements
  defined, 21
  refactoring considerations, 247

refactoring
  benefits, x
  database accesses, x, 10–15, 243, 245
  query considerations, 245–248
  rationale for, viii–ix
  single query approach, 18–19
  threshold values example, 10–15
  utility functions and, 188
  views, 110–113
referential integrity
  denormalization and, 240
  MyISAM tables and, 227
  random data and, 129
reorganizing processing
  benefits from, 234
  competing for resources, 213–224
  isolating hot spots, 224–230
  multiple queues, 225–230
  parallelism and, 230–233
  refactoring considerations, 248
repeatable read isolation level, 220
resources
  competing for, 209, 213–224
  refactoring considerations, 248
restructuring code (see code restructuring)
Roughbench tool, 264–267
row versioning, 219, 220
row_number( ) function, 54
rowid (Oracle), 223

S

scalability, 230
scalar subquery, 165
schemas, 45–47
select statement
  filtering and, 172
  functional comparisons and, 132
  splitting tables, 238
  subqueries and, 165–167
selectivity, indexes and, 39–40
serializable isolation level, 220
server-side processing
  logging, 30–31
  SQL statements, 55
Service Profile Identifier (SPID) (SQL
      Server), 31
service providers
  multiplying within applications, 216–223
  reorganizing processing, 213–215
service time, 213–215
session variables
  MySQL support, 101
  T-SQL limitations, 99

set operators
  combining, 175
  complex queries and, 158
  refactoring considerations, 246
  repeated patterns and, 158–164
  views and, 109
setDate( ) function, 4
setInt( ) function, 4
setLong( ) function, 4
SHA1 algorithm, 139
sigma (standard deviation), 120
single query approach, 18–19
single-column indexes, 48–52
skewness, data, 38–44
slow queries
  analyzing, 152–157
  refactoring considerations, 247
slow statements, 148
snapmon.sql script, 244, 253
snapshot too old error, 220
softcoded statements
  defined, 55
  replacing hardcoded, 61–63
sp_describe_cursor_columns stored procedure
      (SQL Server), 140
sp_executesql stored procedure (SQL
      Server), 140
sp_helpstats stored procedure (SQL
      Server), 42
sp_trace_filter stored procedure (SQL
      Server), 31
SPID (Service Profile Identifier) (SQL
      Server), 31
SQL injection, 61, 64
SQL mindset
  assuming success, 182–184
  writing statements, 180–182
SQL Profiler (SQL Server), 31
SQL Server
  baseline for example, 5
  brute force comparison, 135
  calendar function example, 89, 93
  checksum support, 139, 140, 143
  clustered indexes, 53
  conversion function example, 96
  count( ) function and, 195
  date values, 43
  detecting parsing issues, 57, 60
  deterministic functions, 80
  dynamic views, 26
  filtering views, 105, 107
  generating rows, 126
  global counters, 28

index searches, 40
LOB support, 237
materialized views, 241
parsing issues, 63
random functions and, 119, 120
refactoring views, 112
row versioning, 219
speed improvement comparison, 8–10, 13,
      14, 16–18
SQL Profiler, 31
SQL Server Integration Services, 70
SQL statements
  avoiding excesses, 202
  categories worth tuning, 27
  checking data, 136–139
  combining, 185
  comparing checksums, 139–144
  control structures and, 185–194
  dumping to trace files, 29
  execution plans, 29
  functional comparisons and, 133
  getting rid of loops, 202–209
  mindset for writing, 180–182
  refactoring considerations, 247
  rewriting, 102, 103
  server-side processing, 55
  stored procedures and, 28
  as telling stories, 148
  tuning, 179
sql_log_off session variable, 30
SqlCommand class, 62
SQLite, 32, 129, 262
SQL*Loader utility, 124
SqlPipe object, 71
SQL*Plus utility, 41
standard deviation (sigma), 120
statements
  hardcoded, 21, 55, 61–62
  prepared, 4, 66–70
  recursive, 21, 247
  slow, 148
  softcoded, 55, 61–63
  (see also SQL statements)
statistics
  checking, 37
  data skewness and, 38–44
  defined, 38
stats.sql script, 254
Stefanetti, Marco, 138
storage allocation
  performance and, 38
  serialization and, 225

stored procedures
  checking data, 136–139
  checksums and, 140
  statement execution and, 28
  views and, 75
strings
  counting patterns, 77–79
  splitting, 67–69
subpartitioning, 236
subqueries
  correlated, 168, 169, 246
  from clause, 167
  merging, 166
  minimizing, 172
  refactoring considerations, 245, 246
  repeated patterns and, 158
  scalar, 165
  select statement and, 165–167
  uncorrelated, 168, 169, 246
  where clause, 168–170
  writing, 156
substr( ) function, 77
surrogate keys, 224–225, 247
Sybase Open Server, 32
synchronization
  database calls and, 232
  materialized views and, 242
  parallelism and, 218
  serialization and, 225
sys.dm_exec_cached_plans (SQL Server), 29
sys.dm_exec_query_stats (SQL Server), 29
sys.dm_exec_requests (SQL Server), 26
sys.dm_os_performance_counters (SQL
        Server), 29

T

tables
  cleaning up from clause, 155–157
  comparing, 133–144
  contention in, 225
  nested loops, 176
  reasons behind loops, 205
  refactoring considerations, 246, 248
  schema indexing and, 45–47
  splitting, 237, 238
  strings looking like, 67–69
  temporary, 44, 70
  types of, 155
  unindexed, 47
  with multiple indexes, 47
  with single indexes, 47
  without unique indexes, 47
temporary tables
  lists and, 70
  volatility, 44

testing framework
  comparing crudely, 132
  comparing tables and results, 133–144
  generating random text, 130, 131
  generating rows, 125–129
  generating test data, 116, 117
  limits of comparison, 144
  matching distributions, 122–125
  multiplying rows, 117, 118
  random functions, 118–122
  referential integrity, 129
  unit testing, 132
threshold values, checking transactions
  code to generate transactions, 2–5, 8–9
  refactoring, 10–15
  traditional SQL tuning, 5–9
  tuning comparisons, 16–18
@@TIMETICKS variable (SQL Server), 28
tkprof tool (Oracle), 32
tools
  lipsum, 261–263
  mklipsum, 261–263
  Roughbench, 264–267
@@TOTAL_READ variable (SQL Server), 28
@@TOTAL_WRITE variable (SQL Server), 28
trace files
  dumping statements into, 29
  exploiting, 32, 33
transactions
  checking threshold values, 2–18
  loops and, 208, 209
  performance considerations, 73–74
tree structures, indexes as, 44
trunc( ) function, 83
T-SQL, 99, 100
Twain, Mark, 20

U

uncorrelated subqueries, 168, 169, 246
undo operation, 208
uniform number distribution, 40, 42, 118
unions
  combining, 175
  complex queries and, 158
  repeated patterns and, 158–164
  views built as, 109
unit testing, 132
unitary analysis, 158, 247
update statement
  functional comparisons and, 132
  refactoring considerations, 245
  splitting tables, 238
user-defined functions
  categories of, 76
  refactoring considerations, 246
  restructuring code with, 188

UTF8 encoding, 262
utility functions, 188

V

variables
    array, 101
    generating random, 265
    passing lists as, 67–69
    session, 99, 101
version control software, 219
views
    dynamic, 26–29
    filtering, 104–105
    functionality, 103
    materializing, 241–242
    performance considerations, 103–110
    refactoring, 110–113
    stored procedures and, 75
v$session (Oracle), 26
v$sql_plan_statistics (Oracle), 29
v$sqlstats (Oracle), 26, 29
v$ssystat (Oracle), 55–57

W

wait times, 22
WebLogic application server, 31
WebSphere application server, 31
where clause
    refactoring considerations, 245
    repeated patterns and, 158
    slow statements and, 148
    subqueries and, 168–170
    views and, 107
with clause, 174

X

XML data, 130

Stéphane Faroult first discovered relational databases and the SQL language back in 1983. He joined Oracle France in its early days (after a brief spell with IBM and a bout of teaching at the University of Ottawa) and soon developed an interest in performance and tuning topics. After leaving Oracle in 1988, he briefly tried to reform and did a bit of operational research, but after one year, he succumbed again to relational databases. He has been continuously performing database consultancy since then, and founded RoughSea Ltd in 1998.

Pascal L'Hermite has been working with relational databases in OLTP, production, and development environments on Oracle databases for the past 12 years and on Microsoft SQL Server for the past 5 years.